D1137897

Motor-racing's Strangest Races

Motor-racing's Strangest Races

GEOFF TIBBALLS

ROBSON BOOKS

This edition first published in Great Britain in 2004 by Robson Books, The Chrysalis Building, Bramley Road, London W10 6SP

An imprint of **Chrysalis** Books Group plc

British Library Cataloguing in Publication Data
A catalogue record for this title is available from the British Library.

ISBN 1 86105 411 4

Typeset by FiSH Books, London WC1
Printed by Creative Print & Design (Wales), Ebbw Vale

CONTENTS

ACKNOWLEDGEMENTS

A big thank you to the following for making hours of research so rewarding: The British Newspaper Library, Nottinghamshire Library Services, Westminster Library, Marylebone Library, Derby City Library, Sheffield Library, Southport Local Studies Library, Donington Park race track and the *Derby Evening Telegraph*. Thanks also to Lorna Russell and Joanne Brooks at Robson Books, and to Jeremy Robson for giving the project the green light.

Introduction

When the motley assortment of steam and petrol-powered vehicles lined up in Paris in 1894 at the start of the trial to Rouen, they launched the colourful history of motor racing. Many of the pioneering events were death-defying, trans-continental marathons, occasionally visiting remote settlements that had never before seen a motor car, in which the competitors were obliged to negotiate basic dirt tracks, muddy bogs, fast-flowing rivers, over-zealous policemen and a seemingly endless supply of stray dogs.

France led the way, not only in *chiens perdus*, but also in promoting the sport of motor racing. One of many ingenious events was an 1899 handicap race between walkers, horsemen, cycles, motorcycles and cars over the 104 miles between Paris and Trouville. The horses were allotted 14 hours and finished first and second; the cars, allowed three hours, were third and fourth. The walkers are probably still out there somewhere.

Meanwhile the United States specialised in endurance contests, some of which were highly charged affairs. In 1902 one John Grant Lyman was suspended for six months by the Automobile Club of America for the heinous crime of exceeding 20mph during the Long Island Endurance Run.

The first regular circuit race, the Circuit des Ardennes, took place in 1902 but it was several years before this type of event became popular. And in those days a lap could be anything up to 75 miles – as in Germany's Kaiserpreis – and take the best part of an hour and a half. Spectator satisfaction was not exactly high on the list of priorities.

Since these humble beginnings, the human race has done many strange things to motor cars in the name of sport – some barely legal. Cars have been bullied and coerced in a manner which would make even Basil Fawlty blush and have taken part in events best classified as innovative. How else would you describe a race where a four-poster bed chases a garden shed around a Grand Prix circuit?

Gathered here are races with strange beginnings, strange middle bits and strange finishes, as well as races which were just . . . strange. They include the Frenchman who drove 25 miles in reverse; the Grand Prix where the leading drivers were so far ahead that they stopped for a meal in the pits; the Le Mans 24-Hour Race won by a car patched up with chewing gum; and the driver who drank six bottles of champagne – virtually one per pit stop – on the way to winning the Indianapolis 500. Most of the great names are featured as sometimes willing, sometimes baffled, participants – Boillot, Nuvolari, Varzi, Farina, Fangio, Moss, Brabham, Stewart, Hunt, Mansell, Senna and Schumacher.

For the purposes of this book, I have included a few memorable rallies, too, partly because rallies are races in all but name and also because their catalogues of incomprehensible rules and regulations lend themselves to the bizarre. A race against time which ends with a stage to see who can go the slowest really does defy description! Yet that was precisely what the organisers of the Monte Carlo Rally came up with in 1932.

Dick Dastardly and Muttley would have loved every minute!

Geoff Tibballs, March 2001

WORKING UP A HEAD OF STEAM

PARIS TO ROUEN TRIAL, 22 JULY 1894

Motoring was still very much in its infancy when Pierre Giffard, editor and owner of the Parisian newspaper *Le Petit Journal*, hit upon the idea of staging the world's first motor event. It was not a race as such but an 80-mile trial along the bumpy roads between Paris and Rouen, the winner to be the vehicle which, in the opinion of the judges (all of whom were on the staff of *Le Petit Journal*) most closely adhered to their ideal of '*d'être sans danger, aisément maniable pour les voyagers, et de ne pas coûter trop cher sur la route*', in other words safe, easy to handle and cheap to run. Hoping for a large turn-out to ensure maximum publicity for his newspaper, M. Giffard was no doubt heartened to receive entries from 102 drivers putting their names forward to compete for the handsome first prize of 5,000 francs. The entry list contained a vast array of vehicles, hardly any two alike, and featuring no fewer than 20 different methods of propulsion. These ranged from the more conventional steam-powered designs or the new-fangled petrol-powered cars to contraptions driven by compressed air, clockwork, gravity, a system of pendulums, 'a combination of animate and mechanical motor' and even the rocket-like Baricycle, a device which was propelled solely by the weight of its passengers!

The organisers laid down strict regulations governing which vehicles would actually be allowed to compete. First there was an inspection test which eliminated all but 25 of the original

102, principally the more bizarre entries. The event itself was scheduled for 7 June but with a number of vehicles still not ready by the start of that month, it was postponed until 22 July. This allowed more opportunity to arrange a 32-mile qualifying trial, which every competitor had to pass. The time limit set was three hours, thus necessitating an average speed of just over 10mph, but this was deemed too harsh and so the time was extended to four hours, thereby reducing the required speed to a more attainable 8mph. Seventeen vehicles took part in the first qualifying run on 19 July, but only 13 passed. A second run on the 20th saw all six starters pass and two more qualified the following day, to leave a starting line-up of 21 (all powered by either petrol or steam engines) for the 80-mile journey to Rouen.

The festivities began at 8 a.m. in the Paris suburb of Neuilly and the route ran via Nanterre, St Germain, Mantes (where drivers would stop for lunch) and Vernon to Rouen. Along the way entire villages turned out to cheer and to shower the vehicles with flowers and fruit. Families set up picnic tables at the side of the road so that they could gawp at the great monsters as they trundled by. For some, it would be the first time they had ever seen a motor car. On board each car, in addition to the driver and passenger, was an official observer to determine whether the criteria for the first prize were met. The vehicles were flagged off at 30-second intervals, but it soon became apparent that the most powerful vehicle by far was a giant De Dion articulated steam tractor driven by wealthy playboy and renowned duellist Count Jules de Dion. The leaders covered the 30 miles to Mantes by 11 a.m., de Dion showing the way to Georges Lemaître in a Peugeot and Emile Levassor in a Panhard. The attempts at official timekeeping at Mantes were singularly chaotic, but after a leisurely lunch, the drivers began the second leg of their journey at 1.30 p.m.

It came as no surprise that Count de Dion maintained his lead all the way to Rouen. He had the odd hair-raising moment along the way, once having to be hauled free by spectators after his vehicle became stuck on the road's loose stone surface, and on another occasion taking a wrong turning and ending up in a potato field. He finished in 6hr 48min at a commendable average speed of 11.66mph, three and a half minutes ahead of Lemaître. However, the Count did not win the coveted first prize, the judges ruling that because it needed two people to handle it – a driver to steer and a stoker to tend the engine – the De Dion tractor did not comply with the event's aims. Therefore he was demoted to second although he was praised for his 'interesting steam tractor which... develops a speed absolutely beyond comparison, especially when going uphill'. Instead the prize was awarded jointly to Lemaître and Levassor for their petrol cars. Indeed the day was a triumph for the brash new petrol machines. For while all 13 petrol-powered cars completed the course, four of the eight steam-powered vehicles broke down. For reliability, it was clear that the future of motoring lay with petrol.

A MODEST BEGINNING

CHICAGO EXHIBITION RUN,
28 NOVEMBER 1895

Judging from the widespread apathy on display at America's first organised race, it must have been hard to believe that motoring would ever catch on in that country. Competitors and spectators alike seemed distinctly underwhelmed by the prospect of a 94-mile round trip from Chicago to Waukegan, with the result that the victorious vehicle in this trailblazing event returned home to little more than polite applause from a handful of hardy souls.

The competition was modelled on the Paris-Rouen Trial, coverage of which had been relayed to the United States by an enthusiastic young *New York Herald* reporter who followed the drivers part of the way through France on a bicycle. His reports of the adventurers across the Atlantic and of the thousands of people who had turned out to watch spurred American newspapers to attempt something similar. The American counterpart was sponsored by the *Chicago Times-Herald,* and 2 November was set aside for what promised to be one of the most exciting spectacles to grace the city all year. The omens appeared good when over 100 entries were received, but come the day of the 'exhibition run', as it was called, only two turned up – a Duryea Motor Wagon, driven by Frank Duryea, and a Mueller-Benz, driven by the designer's son, Oscar Mueller. This was not exactly the grand pageant that the organisers had in mind. In a decidedly low-key affair, the pair set off from 55th Street on their journey to Waukegan, but, if possible, the finish was even less impressive than the start. For the Duryea broke down, allowing Mueller to come home in splendid isolation and win the reduced prize of $500 which was awarded just for finishing.

The event was such a disappointment that the organisers decided to try again and rescheduled it for 28 November. This time six cars – four petrol and two electric – were set to start before once again fate took a hand, this time in the shape of the weather. Blizzard conditions had deposited two feet of snow on parts of the city, forcing the route to be shortened to 54 miles – to Evanston and back. Worse still, one of the entries, a de la Vergne-Benz, became stuck in the slush on the way to the start at Jackson Park and had to withdraw. So just five started – Duryea and Mueller again, a Morris and Slalom electric car, a Sturges electric motorcycle, and a Macy-Benz. It was Jerry O'Connor in the Macy-Benz who set the pace, despite an unfortunate incident when he hit a horse-drawn bus, slid over a railroad track and collided with a sleigh carrying journalists. Happily nobody was injured but the Benz's steering was never quite the same after that. Nevertheless, O'Connor still led Duryea by two minutes at the Evanston turning point. However, on the homeward journey the steering deteriorated to such an extent that he had to retire. This left the way – if not the road — clear for Duryea, profiting from the ingenuity of his brother Charles who used a horse-drawn sleigh to service the car.

Back in Jackson Park, Chicago, the crowd were growing restless. They'd had enough after nearly eight hours of standing in the bitter cold and when dusk arrived with still no sign of the cars, they began to drift home. By the time Duryea eventually arrived, there were barely 50 people to see him cross the finish line. He covered the distance in 8hr 23min at an average speed of just over 6mph, his efforts earning him the full first prize of $2,000. Nearly half an hour later, the only other finisher, the Mueller-Benz, rumbled into the park, with the race umpire, Charles King, doing the steering. He was using one hand to steer the car and the other to prop up the miserable Mueller, who had collapsed from exposure. All in all, it was an inauspicious climax to a somewhat unsatisfactory event. For American motor sport things could only get better – and fortunately they did.

POLICE BRUTALITY

PARIS-AMSTERDAM-PARIS, 7 JULY 1898

While the Americans were still fighting shy of motoring, the French had embraced it with open arms. France was the only country with a network of half-decent roads, the rest of the world having to make do with dusty tracks which deteriorated into mud pools when it rained. Encouraged by the wave of enthusiasm from the French public, the Automobile Club de France announced the first international race, to go from France through Belgium, on to Holland and back. The Paris-Amsterdam-Paris event was eagerly anticipated by almost everyone... except for a Monsieur Bochet, the chief engineer of the Paris police.

Bochet was concerned about the safety aspect following two deaths in the Course de Périgueux which had been staged two months earlier in the south-west of the country. So as the start for the Paris-Amsterdam-Paris race drew near, he informed the ACF that under an obscure local by-law which he had unearthed, all of the competing cars would first have to be issued with a certificate stating that they were safe to be driven on public roads. To obtain the necessary certificate, they would have to submit to a personal inspection from him. When the drivers duly presented their cars for inspection, he took great delight in rejecting the vast majority. Outraged by this interference, the drivers declared their intention to race anyway, regardless of M. Bochet's orders, whereupon he warned them that half a squadron of the 23rd Hussars and two cannon would be placed in the middle of the road at the start, with instructions to shoot anyone who tried to defy his ban. Determined to race, the ACF neatly circumnavigated the officious Bochet by switching the start from Paris to Villiers, which was outside his jurisdiction. The drivers proceeded to tow their cars to Villiers behind horses or transport them there by train, leaving the frustrated Bochet (and his army) to retreat to his office with his tail firmly between his legs.

At 8.30 the following morning Fernand Charron in a Panhard et Levassor was first away, followed by the rest of the 48-strong field at 30-second intervals. Charron's vehicle, one of the first racing cars to be fitted with a steering wheel instead of a tiller, maintained a strong pace to lead from Gilles Hourgières until a seized engine delayed Hourgières by as long as 15 hours and allowed Léonce Girardot's Panhard to move up to second. At the end of the first day 183 miles had been covered and Charron led Girardot by 12min 44sec. The 30 vehicles still remaining set off the following morning for Nijmegen but although Hourgières was the fastest on the road, he was unable to make up all the time he had lost back in France. On the third day, the competitors reached Amsterdam, by which time Charron's place at the head of affairs had been usurped by François Giraud in a Bollée, who led by three and a half minutes at the Dutch capital.

Following a day's rest in Amsterdam, the cars began the homeward journey, which soon developed into a battle between Charron and Girardot with Giraud close behind in third. After day five Charron was in the lead but he dropped back the following day, at the end of which Girardot led by an impressive nine minutes. Meanwhile Giraud had lost ground by overturning, although he managed to right the Bollée and reach Verdun in second place. Just when everything was set for a thrilling finish, M. Bochet reared his ugly head again, declaring that any driver whose car had not passed his original inspection would be arrested on arrival in Paris. Since this would have meant most of the entrants ending up in prison, the ACF outfoxed Bochet once more by moving the finish to

Montgeron, just outside Paris, and therefore tantalisingly out of the policeman's clutches.

On the seventh and final day, Charron overtook both Giraud and Girardot by dint of suffering fewer punctures and arrived at Montgeron the winner, having covered the 889 miles in 33hr 4min 34sec at an average speed of 26.9mph. Girardot finished second, just ahead of Giraud to complete the anticipated French one-two-three.

In the meantime vast crowds had gathered at Versailles, where it had originally been intended that the race would finish. Cheated of their entertainment, they begged the organisers to send the winning cars forward from Montgeron. So Charron and Girardot drove on to Versailles, where they were mobbed by well-wishers. M. Bochet was poised to pounce but concluded that to arrest France's newest national heroes might provoke a riot. For once in his career, he reasoned that discretion was the better part of valour.

CHARRON IN REVERSE

TOUR DE FRANCE, 16 JULY 1899

Buoyed by the success of its enterprising racing calendar, the Automobile Club de France began preparations for the longest motor race in the world to date – a 1,423-mile circuit of France to be spread over nine days. The schedule was as follows:

Day 1 – Paris to Nancy (180 miles)
Day 2 – Nancy to Aix-les-Bains (274 miles)
Day 3 – Rest day
Day 4 – Aix-les-Bains to Vichy (238 miles)
Day 5 – Rest day
Day 6 – Vichy to Périgueux (186 miles)
Day 7 – Périgueux to Nantes (210 miles)
Day 8 – Nantes to Cabourg (216 miles)
Day 9 – Cabourg to Paris (119 miles)

Sponsorship by *Le Matin* had attracted 48 starters – 19 cars, 25 motorcycles, and four lighter vehicles or voiturettes. The favourites were the French trio of Fernand Charron, René de Knyff and Léonce Girardot, whose Panhards had finished first, second and third in the Paris to Bordeaux race two months earlier. The start took place on a Sunday morning at the foot of a long hill just outside the Parisian suburban town of Champigny. One absentee was the Panhard driven by Comte Berthier de Savigny who, on his way to the start, tried to avoid a pedestrian in the centre of Paris, but went up on the pavement and knocked down a lamp-post. While the Comte was unharmed, the car was wrecked. Charron was first away at 8 a.m., followed by Girardot 30 seconds later, the remainder of the field following at similar intervals. Last away was the Vallée car driven by Flash, a pseudonym for Dr E. Lewhess. It was expected to create an impression and it certainly did, although not quite in the way its driver had envisaged. For it was unable even to climb the first hill. It eventually reached the summit after ten long minutes but only because the mechanic got out and pushed. As if this ignominious start was not enough to have the good doctor reaching for his pills, a tyre then burst. With no spare on board, Lewhess had to catch a cab back to Paris to fetch a new one. Not surprisingly, he decided to retire shortly afterwards.

There were numerous hazards en route. Several drivers ended up in ditches trying to avoid spectators or wagons, while dogs were a constant menace, packs of them chasing the drivers through every village. The route was also littered with level crossings which damaged the wheels and suspensions, leading to further retirements. An added obstacle was that, on approaching Nancy at the end of the first day, the drivers discovered that a steep hill was not fit for vehicles, requiring them to seek an alternative way into the town. De Knyff led the field after that first stage, but Charron had forged ahead by Aix-les-Bains. The much-fancied Girardot suffered a setback when he broke a wheel but, resourceful as ever, he managed to borrow a replacement from a farmer's cart. It is not known whether he ever actually returned the wheel to the farmer. And Camille Jenatzy ended up in a ditch after smashing a wheel. He was able to continue after repairing the damage but had lost precious time.

At the outset of day four, de Knyff lost 30 minutes repairing the springs on his car and more time ebbed away when he stopped to help one of the motorcyclists, Williams, who had come off his machine. Nobly, de Knyff drove the injured rider to St Etienne, where Williams suddenly came to his senses and refused to let de Knyff help him further in case the delay cost him the race. Remarkably, de Knyff was able to make up the ground and finished the day five minutes ahead of Charron. Less fortunate was a M. Degrais, whose motorised tricycle skidded out of control after a chicken had got caught between the front wheel and the mudguard . . .

Following the second rest day, there were 30 competitors still going at the start of day six. A minor – but time-consuming – accident to Charron put de Knyff 35 minutes ahead at Périgueux, by which time the field had been thinned to 23. De Knyff was still ahead at Nantes, and his victory was sealed on the next stage to Cabourg when Charron's forward transmission gear broke near Le Mans. Unable to go forward, Charron refused to admit defeat, turned the car round and drove the 25 miles to Alençon in reverse! Alas, the prospect of reversing all the way to Paris proved too daunting and he was forced to retire.

De Knyff was never troubled after that and went on to win the first prize of £240 by five hours from Girardot, with Comte Gaston de Chasseloup-Laubat third in another Panhard. De Knyff's average speed was 30.2mph, and there were 20 finishers – ten cars, eight motorcycles and two voiturettes.

THE TOUR OF BRITAIN

THE THOUSAND MILES TRIAL, 23 APRIL 1900

At the turn of the century it was estimated that fewer than one Briton in a hundred had seen a motor car. That is, until the Thousand Miles Trial of 1900 – an event designed to test vehicles to the limit and one which took the motor car the length and breadth of the land.

The other aim of the trial was to raise funds for the Automobile Club of Great Britain and Ireland (the forerunner of the RAC), which had been founded in 1897 but which had lost £1,600 on an exhibition in London's Richmond Park during the summer of 1899. This left the club in dire straits financially, prompting secretary Claude Johnson to seek new sources of income. To this end, he obtained the backing of newspaper baron Alfred Harmsworth who put up £452 in prize money and provided breakfast for every competitor at his country estate, Calcot Park, near Reading.

Sixty-five cars and tricycles lined up at Hyde Park Corner for a 7 a.m. start. Thirty-three were of British manufacture – including Daimler, MMC, Napier, Marshall and Star – while the overseas challenge was headed by Peugeot, De Dion, Panhard and Benz. There were also two interesting steam cars from the United States – a Locomobile and a Brown-Whitney. From London the cars travelled west to Bristol where, as at the other main stops on the route, they were exhibited to the public for a day. As many as 4,000 people crammed into Bristol Drill Hall to catch a glimpse of these new machines that everyone was talking about.

On the following day, the competitors moved north up to Birmingham, Manchester and eventually Edinburgh, the halfway point on their journey. The stiffest obstacle to be overcome was the gradient of Shap Fell in the Lake District – a climb so steep that it was optional for the cars. Nevertheless 26 competitors tackled it, the fastest being C.S. Rolls in a Panhard at 27.5mph, the slowest the Locomobile at just 6mph. Another climb, Dunmail Ralse, was compulsory, however, and, in order to get up, several cars had to shed their passengers.

Mishaps were numerous. Few of the cars had brakes that were efficient enough to hold the vehicle if it ran backwards – a situation which led to J.R. Hargreaves stopping his retreating Daimler by deliberately steering it into a wall! When Montagu Grahame-White's Daimler ran into a ditch, the bracket supporting the starting gear was broken. Using his initiative, Grahame-White found that by standing on the step he could reach the nave of one of the front wheels with his boot. So he steered the car for 52 miles to Newcastle by this method, discovering on his arrival on Tyneside that the sole of his boot had worn through completely.

At the end of the nine-day event, only 35 of the starters made it back to London, the gold medal for the most meritorious drive being awarded to C.S. Rolls. More significantly, the absence of any serious accidents greatly furthered the cause of the motor car in Britain.

THE HOUND FROM HELL

GORDON BENNETT TROPHY, 14 JUNE 1900

Motor racing in France had received a temporary setback when Mme Bos, wife of a prominent French politician, suffered a broken leg after being hit by a car while watching a race from Paris to Roubaix. Every competitor in that race was immediately arrested on criminal charges and the future of the sport appeared in jeopardy. But any mutterings of discontent were quickly forgotten as Mme Bos regained the use of her leg and the French motor industry exercised its considerable influence. The French became the envy of the world, their escapades on the road reaching the ears of American newspaper magnate Gordon Bennett, publisher of the *New York Herald*, and the man hitherto best known for having sent Stanley off to find Livingstone. Bennett heard about a challenge issued by Fernand Charron to American motoring pioneer Alexander Winton and, in 1899, eager to end the French monopoly of motor racing and to encourage manufacturers in other countries – especially the United States – he proposed an international event bearing his own name. Ironically, the first Gordon Bennett Trophy race in 1900 was won by a Frenchman!

The race became a mainstay of the European motor racing scene at the turn of the century. It was a competition between teams of no more than three cars from each participating country, the winning nation having to organise the following year's event, rather like the Eurovision Song Contest, although it has to be said that was where the similarity ended. When Englishman Selwyn Edge won the 1902 event in a Napier – largely by being the only finisher – this caused some embarrassment since motor racing was illegal on English roads. The difficulty was resolved by staging the 1903 Gordon Bennett race at the Athy circuit in Ireland. The Gordon Bennett races were also significant in being the first in which national racing colours were used. For 1900, France carried blue, Germany white, Belgium yellow, and the United States red.

That inaugural competition was held on French soil between Paris and Lyons, a journey of 353 miles. The French selected Panhard as their official team, much to the disgust of Mors who decided to put forward its own entrant to prove that it was the equal of the powerful Panhards. So in addition to Fernand Charron, René de Knyff and Léonce Girardot in Panhards, 'Levegh' (the pseudonym of Pierre Velghe) drove a supposedly non-competing Mors. The overseas challenge was to be represented by Camille Jenatzy in a Bolide for Belgium; Eugen Benz in a Benz for Germany; and Alexander Winton and Anthony Riker in Wintons for the United States, the first American cars to compete in Europe. The Benz, however, withdrew because of tyre problems and Riker's Winton was not ready in time, leaving just five cars plus the rogue Mors.

To the embarrassment of the French, it was Levegh who set the early pace, soon building up a lead of half an hour over the three Panhards, followed by Jenatzy, with Winton a distant last. Then each car began to fall victim to problems of varying severity. De Knyff, Jenatzy and Winton all retired, Levegh was beset with mechanical difficulties, and Girardot got lost near Orléans! This left Charron in the lead even though he had bent the Panhard's rear axle driving over a gutter, as a result of which his faithful mechanic, Henri Fournier, had to trickle oil continuously on to the chains to keep the car going.

The saying about it never being over until the fat lady sings was never more true than in those early days of motor racing. Nobody could take victory for granted. However, the fat lady was definitely clearing her throat when, just ten miles from the finish in Lyons, Charron's Panhard, powering downhill at 60mph, was suddenly charged by a large dog. The animal went under the front wheels and finished up jammed in the steering, sending the car veering across a field before skidding back on to the road. There, Fournier calmly removed the dead dog before restarting the engine. But the collision had broken the water pump from its mounting, so as well as keeping a steady supply of oil on the chains, Fournier also had to hold the drive against the flywheel in order to keep the water circulating. He certainly had his hands full over those last ten miles.

Eventually Charron struggled through to Lyons, winning from the unclassified Levegh and the geographically challenged Girardot. Panhard's blushes were spared, but only temporarily. For the following month Mors and Levegh gained their revenge by emphatically defeating their great rivals in the Paris-Toulouse race.

The Gordon Bennett Trophy remained a fixture until 1905 before being superseded by the French Grand Prix.

FUELLED BY ALCOHOL

CIRCUIT DU NORD, 15 MAY 1902

Around the turn of the century a series of rallies and races took place in France which were designed to promote alcohol as a fuel. The idea, by no means a new one, was born out of economic necessity. With few domestic oil reserves, France was eager to encourage the development of a fuel which could be readily distilled from domestic farm products. The French Ministry of Agriculture was certain that, when tested, alcohol would prove to be a viable – as well as cheaper — alternative to petrol.

Accordingly, in 1899 four alcohol-fuelled cars raced from Paris to Chantilly. The fact that only one completed the distance – and slowly — might have deterred some politicians from persevering with the experiment but within two years an assortment of 50 vehicles, ranging from lightweight quadricycles to heavy trucks, took part in a 167-mile run from Paris to Roubaix, an event sponsored by the Automobile Club of Paris. Fuels varied from pure alcohol to a mix of 50 per cent alcohol and 50 per cent petrol. Most drivers stated categorically that they preferred the 50-50 blend. Given the choice, they would undoubtedly have chosen pure petrol.

Undaunted, Minister of Agriculture Jean Dupuy organised his most ambitious project to date, the 537-mile Circuit du Nord, or the 'Alcohol Race' as it became known. The race was run in two heats – the first from Champigny to Arras on day one; the second from Arras to St Germain (via Boulogne and

Dieppe) on day two. A strict condition of the race was that all competitors used only fuel of pure alcohol – no mixers. However, enforcing this regulation proved well nigh impossible once the cars were out in the country and many drivers are believed to have used as little alcohol fuel as possible because it gave their vehicles reduced power. Instead they would sneak in supplies of petrol and hope to fool the scrutineers. Reports were rife of strange odours coming from behind certain cars . . .

A total of 85 had put their names down for the race but at the roll-call there were 20 absentees, among them Henri Fournier, winner of the Paris-Bordeaux and Paris-Berlin events of 1901. The competitors were split into three categories – heavy cars, light cars and voiturettes. The first man was away at 4 a.m. sharp, the remainder following at respectful three-minute intervals. The first to reach Arras – and in the fastest time of 4hr 48min 5sec – was Frenchman Maurice Farman in a Panhard. The second arrival was fellow countryman Marcellin Javott in a Darracq. They were met by the enthusiastic M. Dupuy, who had travelled by special train to greet the victors and proceeded to deliver an optimistic speech on the virtues of alcohol which, he claimed, had proved its capacity to rival petrol. Little did he know of the skulduggery that was afoot.

The next day Farman left Arras at 4 a.m. and reached St Germain at 1 p.m., thereby winning the second heat as well. He was followed 58 minutes later by Englishman Charles Jarrott in another Panhard. When the results of the two heats were added together, Farman was declared the winner of the heavy car section at an average speed of 44.8mph, with Jarrott second. Javott's Darracq won the light car group at a speed of 41.2mph and M. Grus's Renault was the quickest voiturette at 33.6mph.

The speeds – albeit enhanced by petrol – stood up reasonably well, and M. Dupuy remained convinced that alcohol fuel was the way forward. History would prove him wrong.

JARROTT'S RUNNING REPAIRS

PARIS TO VIENNA, 26 JUNE 1902

At the height of Europe's inter-city races, 148 competitors set off from Paris to Vienna in an event run concurrently with the annual Gordon Bennett race. The duality not only contributed to the excessive number of starters but also created a line-up of all shapes and sizes, from tiny Renaults to the more powerful but occasionally sluggish Panhards, Mors and Mercedes. The field included a number of wealthy amateurs, among them the colourful Count Eliot Zborowski in a Mercedes, the American driver William K. Vanderbilt in a Mors and another American, George Heath, in a Panhard.

Once the cars were away from Paris, hundreds of spectators rushed to board a special train for Belfort to witness the end of the first stage. Near Nangis the railway ran alongside the road and startled passengers watched as Henri Fournier's car sped past them at a speed approaching 80mph. Fournier paid the price shortly afterwards when his car suffered a broken gear shaft. Well down the field in 18th at the conclusion of that first section was Frenchman Marcel Renault in a little 16hp car made by Renault Frères, the company he had founded with his brother Louis. Although he couldn't hope to match the bigger cars on the fast stretches, Renault came into his own on the twisty mountainous sections, notably on the third day when the field tackled the 5,912 foot Arlberg peak in western Austria. The descent from the mountain was extremely dangerous because car brakes had never previously been subjected to such a rigorous test, but Renault coped admirably and made up so much ground through Switzerland and Austria that he held a clear lead by the time he reached Vienna on 29 June after four days of hard driving. Then right at the death he nearly threw it away. The finish was in a trotting track on the outskirts of the city, but on entering the stadium, Renault drove round the track the wrong way. The race organisers insisted that he leave the stadium and re-enter in the proper manner – a detour which cost him 15 minutes and meant that his margin of victory over Count Zborowski was much smaller than it would otherwise have been. Six other Renaults made it to the finish, including brother Louis despite his car being hit by the Mercedes of Baron de Caters while waiting to check in at the Salzburg control. The collision left the Renault with several broken spokes in one of the front wheels. With no spare wheel, Louis' intrepid mechanic found some wood and used a sharp knife to create makeshift spokes strong enough to take the car through Austria to the finish.

However, the misfortunes of the Renault brothers were nothing compared to the adventures experienced by Charles Jarrott at the wheel of a 13.72 litre Panhard. On the second day of the race the car's wooden chassis collapsed just short of the overnight stop at Bregenz in Austria. Jarrott and his mechanic, George Du Cros, felt that if they could somehow strengthen the frame, it might carry them through the next stage to Salzburg at the very least. They managed to acquire a drill and some bolts but attempts to find four long pieces of wood proved fruitless, until inspiration came just as Jarrott was preparing to settle down for the night at their hotel. He later wrote: 'I was just getting into bed and had turned to put out the light, when my eye fell upon a stand used for carrying a tray, and in a second I perceived that the four legs of that stand were exactly what I wanted.' Conveniently reasoning that it was too late at night to ask the hotel manager whether he would be interested in selling them the stand, they set about dismantling it anyway and drilled four holes in each length of wood so that in the morning they could bolt the pieces on each side of the broken chassis frame. The wood being extremely resilient, Du Cros had the bright idea of drilling against the wall. 'He was delightfully successful,' recorded Jarrott, 'but the trouble was that he drove it through too far, and brought down half the plaster. And then, in endeavouring to show how easy it was on another portion of the wall, he succeeded in bringing that down also.' At that juncture Jarrott managed to drill a hole through his arm instead of the wood and for the next half-hour the pair had to rip up bed linen for bandages. 'There was nothing in the room we did not utilise for something or other,' said Jarrott. 'I hate to think what must have been the expression on the proprietor's face when he discovered what had taken place.'

The following morning they evaded detection by creeping out of the hotel at first light and were on the road by seven o'clock, reaching Salzburg just in time to scotch a rumour (which *The Times* correspondent was in the act of cabling to London) that they had been killed in a crash. The makeshift chassis did its job, although at one point on the final stage Du Cros had to lie full length along the bonnet with a towel wrapped around the pipe to prevent water from leaking from the radiator. But then, no more than three miles from Vienna, the distorted chassis frame caused the gearbox to break and lumps of machinery fell into the road. The indefatigable Jarrott commandeered a bicycle and pedalled off to get help. He returned to find Du Cros being towed towards the finish behind a horse-drawn cab. This ignominy was too much for Jarrott to take and he promptly slashed the tow rope and jumped behind the wheel. As the car rumbled away, belching smoke and flame, the exhaust box fell off. The gearless monster lurched uncontrollably across the finish line, at which point it finally expired. It wouldn't move another yard, but Jarrott and Du Cros were unconcerned. Against all the odds, they had completed the Paris to Vienna motor race.

THE RACE TO DEATH

PARIS TO MADRID, 24 MAY 1903

When road racing was first introduced to Europe less than a decade earlier, the sedate speeds posed relatively little threat to spectators or participants. But the technological advances which had been made in the motor industry in the intervening years had enabled cars to achieve speeds in excess of 90mph. Clearly this represented a considerable hazard on public roads, especially to a public which was still not fully accustomed to the motor car. The death of a boy spectator during the 1901 Paris-Berlin race had resulted in the French government banning all road racing in France, but when the 1902 Paris-Vienna marathon passed off without any fatalities, the authorities bowed to pressure to allow racing to resume on public thoroughfares. In doing so, they gave the green light to a contest which would be known thereafter as the 'race to death'.

The Auto Club de France came up with the idea of a three-day race from Paris to Madrid – a distance of 872 miles, much of it over roads which had barely seen a motor car. The first day was to take the drivers 342 miles through Chartres, Tours, Poitiers and Angoulême to Bordeaux. The second and third days were to be spent negotiating the treacherous tracks across the Guadarrama mountains near Madrid. This was reckoned to be the most difficult section of the route, but in the event, none of the drivers got that far.

King Alfonso of Spain raised no objections to the proposed race and when the French government also consented, planning

25

began in earnest for what was expected to be a major spectacle for both countries. Indeed no fewer than three million spectators lined the route between Paris and Bordeaux. The starters – 275 in all – were divided into four groups. There were 112 in the heavy car group (including 1.5-litre Panhards and 12.5-litre Mercedes); 64 light cars; 40 voiturettes (the section for vehicles under 1.5-litres); and 59 motorcycles. To reduce weight, most of the cars were stripped down to the bare minimum with the result that the drivers sat on nothing more comfortable than a wooden plank. The entrants gathered at Versailles on Sunday 24 May for a 3.45 a.m. start, which, even by the standards of those days, was unreasonably early. First to go was Charles Jarrott in a De Dietrich, the remainder following at one-minute intervals. So by the time the final car was away, the leaders were 135 miles off down the road.

The Renault brothers were again to the fore, Marcel having a starting number of 39 and Louis being third away. When the two cars in front of Louis fell back, he had the benefit of a clear road ahead from Rambouillet to Bordeaux while those behind had to battle through clouds of dust. Louis Renault duly reached Bordeaux at 12.15 p.m. after some eight and a half hours on the road, having averaged over 62mph. He was followed 16 minutes later by Jarrott, but behind him there was carnage. Marcel Renault had worked his way up to third when, travelling at speed between Poitiers and Angoulême, he put two wheels in a ditch while trying to overtake a slower car. Marcel's car overturned and he was killed. On the outskirts of Bordeaux, Lorraine Barrow's De Dietrich swerved off the road in trying to avoid a dog. The car smashed into a tree, killing Barrow's companion Pierre Rodez. Stray spectators were as great a danger as dogs. At one point a child ran into the road in front of a Brouhot driven by M. Touran. In taking evasive action, the unfortunate Touran careered into a crowd of onlookers. His own passenger, one spectator and the errant child were all killed. In another horrific smash, Leslie Porter's Wolseley veered out of control on the approach to a level crossing, ploughed into a house and caught fire. His riding mechanic, Nixon, was thrown to his death.

With ten deaths and countless injuries, the French Prime Minister, Emile Combes, ordered the race to be stopped at Bordeaux. It was all too apparent that spectators had no regard for their own safety and that today's motor cars were simply too fast for racing on public highways. The authorities suddenly became so jumpy that, having called a halt to proceedings, they would not even permit the cars to be driven under their own power to Bordeaux railway station in readiness for the return trip to Paris. Instead each car had to be towed to the station by horse. The inevitable backlash to the tragedy followed, both French and Spanish governments issuing edicts banning all further racing. Paris to Madrid would go down in history as the last of the great city-to-city races.

Amidst the rows and recriminations, the outcome of the curtailed race was almost incidental. Yet there were some heroic performances, including that of Madame Camille du Gast in a 5.7-litre De Dietrich. An accomplished and versatile sportswoman, she had attained the lofty heights of fifth place by the town of Châtellerault, north of Poitiers, before dropping back to 45th after stopping to help a fellow competitor who had been involved in an accident. In the end, first place was awarded to Fernand Gabriel who, having started a lowly 82nd, reached Bordeaux in his 12-litre Mors in third place, just 40 minutes behind Charles Jarrott. His average speed of 65.3mph put him ahead of Louis Renault, Joseph Salleron in a Mors and Jarrott. But few people, least of all Louis Renault who had just lost his brother, felt much like celebrating.

JOURNEY INTO THE UNKNOWN

PEKING TO PARIS, 10 JUNE 1907

In the aftermath of the Paris-Madrid débâcle, motor racing in France kept a low profile for a couple of years. But the staging of the first French Grand Prix in 1906 once again whetted the appetite of the pioneer motorists, and thoughts turned to an epic test of endurance rather than one of pure speed. On 31 January 1907 the celebrated French newspaper *Le Matin* carried the following headline on its front page: 'PARIS-PEKING AUTOMOBILE: A Stupendous Challenge.' The article dismissed circuit races such as the Grand Prix and accused organisers of motor races of failing to realise the car's full potential. 'The whole *raison d'être* of cars is that they make possible the most ambitious and unpremeditated trips to far horizons. For this reason the general public fails to see the logic of making motor cars chase their tails in tight circles... What needs to be proved today is that as a man has a car he can do anything and go anywhere.' Then came the killer question: 'Is there anyone who will undertake to travel this summer from Paris to Peking by automobile?'

The first to respond was the Count de Dion, doyen of the French motor industry, who replied in heroic terms: 'It is my belief that if a motor car can get through, the De Dion-Bouton will get through. I take up this challenge here and now.' The challenge also captured the imagination of Prince Scipione Borghese, an Italian nobleman, who wasted no time in ordering a car from the Itala factory in Turin. By the end of the first week in February as many as ten works teams were believed to have expressed serious interest in the great adventure. The organisers then decided to reverse the route so that the race started in Peking and finished in Paris. This would not only avoid the beginning of the rainy season in China, where the 'roads' were nothing more than dirt tracks, but would also provide *Le Matin* with the glorious spectacle of a Parisian climax.

Although 25 teams would eventually consider taking part, many were scared away by the entry fee of 2,200 francs and, as the day drew nearer, by the sheer enormity of the task. In the end the starting line-up was just five. Prince Borghese, who appeared singularly undaunted by the trans-continental trek, was very much the race favourite in his four-cylinder, 7.4-litre Itala in which he was joined by mechanic Ettore Guizzardi and Milan journalist Luigi Barzini, whose account of the race would grace the pages of, among other publications, the *Daily Telegraph*. Borghese's rivals were former jockey and stunt motorcyclist Charles Godard, driving a four-cylinder Dutch Spyker with Jean du Taillis as his passenger; Georges Cormier and passenger Edgardo Longini in a two-cylinder De Dion-Bouton; Victor Collignon with mechanic Jean Bizac in an identical De Dion-Bouton; and last, and certainly least, Auguste Pons and mechanic Octave Foucault in an alarmingly lightweight one-cylinder Contal tri-car, a vehicle so small that it had no room for serious rations or bedding – something of a handicap when planning to spend the next three months travelling across the wilds of Mongolia and Siberia. From Peking, the route was to take them north-west to Mongolia, across the barren Gobi desert, over the uncharted plains of Siberia and eastern Russia to Moscow, and then, via more recognisable roads, to Warsaw, Berlin and Paris. The total race distance was some 10,000 miles. Even getting to Peking in the first place was an ordeal, Borghese being obliged to cross Asia on horse, camel and foot. It was scarcely the ideal preparation, but seemed to have no adverse effect on the redoubtable Italian.

It was with a degree of unease that the Chinese authorities observed the start in their capital at 8 a.m. on 10 June. The State Council of the Celestial Chinese Empire feared that these 'fuel chariots' were using the race as a cover for surveying routes by which the West could invade China at some future date. The Council were also concerned that these strange machines might exert a disturbing influence on the Chinese people and declared that they wanted the cars out of Peking as quickly as possible in the belief that 'they would cause an upheaval in the popular mind and spread everywhere the fatal germs of western corruption'. Given the unpredictable nature of the route through China, the quintet of drivers agreed to stay in convoy until they reached Irkutsk in Russia, after which the race could begin in earnest. It was an admirable notion, but one which foundered almost immediately when, barely a quarter of a mile out of Peking, Collignon and Pons both succeeded in getting lost. Godard fared little better. Unable to read a map, he had only the vaguest idea of geography. His Spyker was decorated in vertical stripes of red, white and blue and along the body were painted the words SIBERIA, RUSSIA, GERMANY. This was supposedly to inform passers-by of the route, but there was also the suggestion that it served to remind Godard which way to go. The hopelessly inadequate Contal was struggling so badly on the uneven Chinese roads that Pons decided to retrace his steps and complete the first leg to Nankow by train. The other four pressed on, but took seven days to cover the initial 200 miles, constantly being delayed by having to be manhandled over ancient bridges on the Peking plain. Teams of coolies with mules had to drag the cars through the Nankow Gorge and over the mountains towards the Great Wall after first stripping the bodywork to a bare minimum and removing all provisions on board. The Chinese routes – constructed from broken stones and huge boulders – were frequently impassable, necessitating the use of a pick-axe to smash a path for the cars. As a result of the appalling Chinese road surfaces, the cars could not run unaided until the Mongolian plateau had been reached.

It was in the Gobi desert that the Contal finally gave up the ghost. Once again Pons had become lost and had fallen way behind the others. Tired of having to carry his supplies and of repeatedly having to go back and search for him, the remaining four decided not to bother this time. The Contal ran out of fuel and was eliminated from the race.

The abysmal lack of preparation by the Contal team was in stark contrast to Borghese's crew. In advance they had sent camel caravans out into the desert to lay down supplies of fuel, tyres and provisions at strategic points. For the best part of 800 miles across the Gobi the cars doggedly followed telegraph wires until, in the words of Barzini, 'they seemed to be taking a wrong direction for our purpose'. Then the Itala would veer off into the wilderness 'for hours and hours, with no guide except our common sense'. The extra power of the Itala gave it a considerable advantage in terms of speed but its weight proved a handicap when crossing Mongolian marshland. Between Urga and Kiakhta the car suddenly sank in a bog. Passing tribesmen took one look at the sinking car and continued on their way but, by a stroke of good fortune, a team of Mongolian horsemen appeared on the scene. They wedged planks under the wheels and got their oxen to pull but this had no effect until someone had the bright idea of starting the engine. Barzini recalled: 'At the sudden noise, the four terrified beasts pulled desperately, and suddenly the car came out of its furrow with one bound.' Following this close shave, Borghese and his crew carefully reconnoitred any suspect ground before driving over it. Eventually they reached the River Iro, where they again required the services of local oxen to haul the car through waist-high water. They were a day ahead of the rest of the field by the time they reached the Russian border, 'our faces literally black with dust, and over our clothes a thick crust of the different kinds of mud with which we had come in intimate contact all along our way'.

The 6,000 mile journey across Siberia and Russia was distinctly uncomfortable for Borghese and his men, travelling in an open car in what was often torrential rain. Borghese's only protection was the pith helmet which he wore for much of the race. To make matters worse, following the construction of the Trans-Siberian Railway, much of the Siberian highway system was in a state of chronic disrepair, deteriorating into a series of bumpy tracks and treacherous bogs. At Lake Baikal, the road and bridges were impassable, so Borghese obtained permission to drive on the railway track! When forced to make a hasty detour by road because of an approaching train, the Itala fell foul of a rickety wooden bridge which collapsed under the car's weight, almost crushing Borghese, Barzini and Ettore. The car was eventually winched to safety from the ravine by a gang of Siberian railway workers and returned to the relative security of the railway track, only to endure another near miss seconds later when surprised by a freight train. Later in the Ural mountains a rear wheel collapsed on the Itala, its wooden spokes weakened by the muddy roads. A local wagon-builder – the only one for hundreds of miles – made an effective replacement. Behind, the other crews hitched their cars to half-wild horses in order to ford Siberian rivers and carried out emergency repairs with rashers of raw bacon. The unscrupulous Godard reportedly resorted to theft so as to stay in the race.

Prince Borghese reached Moscow while the other competitors were still battling through Siberia. With a lead of 18 days, he could even afford to take a lengthy detour up to St Petersburg before heading down triumphantly through Germany, Belgium and northern France. Despite losing additional time on social engagements, the prince increased his lead through Europe, entering the French capital on 10 August flanked by well-wishers as well as three brand new Italas which had been sent out to greet him by the firm's Paris agent. Covering 10,000 miles in 60 days across some of the world's most inhospitable terrain was, after all, a pretty good advertisement for the car's sturdiness and reliability. Pulling up in front of the offices of *Le Matin*, Borghese explained the secret of his success to reporters: 'We never thought of the final goal, never admitted that our end was Paris. Every day when we awoke we concentrated on nothing but getting the day's stage done well.' He added: 'Such a journey requires more patience than daring.'

It was a further 20 days before the Spyker and the two De Dions arrived together in Paris. Godard had been arrested in Germany on the orders of *Le Matin*, who wanted the two French cars to beat him, but had managed to talk his way out of trouble and resume his place behind the wheel.

Following its remarkable victory, the Itala was in great demand and, along with the two De Dions, was shown in London at the 1908 Olympia Motor Show. However, the car met an untimely end when, en route to being shipped to New York for another exhibition, it rolled into the dockside water at Genoa. The car was eventually salvaged but was badly damaged. The Itala thus went down in history as being the only car to survive a 10,000-mile race but not the subsequent exhibition.

THE RACE AROUND THE WORLD

NEW YORK TO PARIS, 12 FEBRUARY 1908

A matter of weeks after the finish of the Peking to Paris race, *Le Matin* joined forces with the *New York Times* to announce another motoring marathon, one which would encircle the globe from New York to Paris. To put it mildly, the planned route was ambitious, incorporating a winter overland journey through western Canada and Alaska, followed by a trip across the ice of the Bering Straits to Russia! *The Motor* dismissed the whole idea as 'mad-brained'. Not surprisingly, one or two revisions had to be made once the event was under way.

Seven cars were due to start, but an Itala was withdrawn at the last minute when it emerged that the race organisers were going to handicap its time by the small matter of a week, presumably on account of the company's success in the Peking-Paris jaunt. As it was, six vehicles lined up outside the *New York Times* offices in Times Square. There were French cars – a Motobloc (driven by Peking-Paris survivor Charles Godard), a De Dion-Bouton and a Sizaire-Naudin; an Italian Züst, driven by Antonio Scarfoglio, poet, writer and son of a Naples newspaper publisher; the American Thomas Flyer, piloted by George Schuster; and a German Protos, entered in the name of the Kaiser and driven by Lt. Hans Koeppen of the 15th Prussian infantry. The Kaiser had sent a special greeting to the German team. A crowd of over 250,000 New Yorkers watched the cars set off amid flying champagne corks and much waving of national flags. In readiness for the gruelling journey which lay ahead, each vehicle carried spare parts, shovels, sails, skis, food and, just in case, firearms.

If the competitors were expecting a comparatively trouble-free ride until they hit Alaska, they were sorely mistaken. For the worst weather in the whole race was reserved for New York State. Thick snow and mud rendered roads impassable, prompting the unscrupulous Godard to put the Motobloc on a train, a deed which resulted in his instant disqualification. The Sizaire-Naudin also dropped out shortly afterwards with a broken back axle. The remaining four ploughed west but, after three weeks of motoring, they had only got as far as Chicago. The intention had been to ship the cars to Alaska from Seattle on 10 March but the snow had completely disrupted the timetable. With its American factory able to provide the best service for this section of the race, the Thomas Flyer led the way across the Midwest. When the car became stuck in deep mud in Nebraska, local farmers dug it out. Worse was to follow in Wyoming, when the three-man crew found the route blocked by snow and were obliged to drive along 45 miles of railroad track from Carter to Evanston. This would subsequently be used in evidence against them.

The Thomas arrived in San Francisco on 24 March and four days later Schuster set sail for Alaska. Once there, it quickly became apparent that the Arctic crossing was a non-starter and so he began to retrace his steps, only to discover that the Protos, having been bogged down in the Wyoming mud, had travelled from Ogden, Utah, by train to Seattle and caught a ship to Russia. Meanwhile the De Dion and the Züst had boarded a boat to Japan. In a panic, *Le Matin* suddenly announced that the great slog across America had been to no avail since the race was now going to be restarted from Vladivostok! As a concession to the efforts of the Thomas crew in actually reaching Alaska, it was granted a 22-day bonus which allowed it to catch up with the others. Conversely, the Protos was penalised 30 days for travelling by train. The entire event was degenerating into a shambles, attracting scorn from motoring publications. *The Autocar* – as the magazine was known in those days —commented: 'Seeing that the organisers are endeavouring to simplify the race as much as possible, it may be suggested whether, after all, it would not have been more satisfactory to ship the cars from New York to Le Havre, and then proceed by road to Paris.'

The crossing to Japan passed without incident and when Schuster arrived at the Maibara Inn in a rural region of the country, it was recorded as being the first time that a motor car had ever been seen there. After negotiating the dirt tracks of Japan, the three cars were loaded on to another ship bound for Vladivostok where they met up with the Protos. However, in protest at the rail journeys made by both the Thomas and the Protos, the De Dion was withdrawn on the orders of the Count himself, leaving just three cars to set off from Vladivostok at the restart on 22 May.

The Thomas again set the pace, albeit at a sloth-like ten miles per day as it struggled through the boggy conditions. Following the tracks of the Peking-Paris pioneers, it then took to the line of the Trans-Siberian Railway until the gearbox broke, allowing the Protos to seize the initiative. In the meantime the Züst crew were nearly drowned on what they thought was dry land, and on another occasion they improvised a new crankshaft bearing from a cough sweet tin, some mud, some pieces of wood, and a quantity of bullets. As the race entered Europe, *Le Matin* panicked again, this time at the prospect of a German car, the Protos, being the first to reach Paris. So the newspaper changed the rules, altering the Protos's finishing point to Berlin. The Züst was to proceed to Paris, as planned, while the Thomas Flyer was ordered to make its way back to New York via transatlantic shipping. Fortunately nobody paid any attention to *Le Matin*'s instructions and the Protos drove on to Paris, arriving there on the night of 30 July to what one observer described as an 'embarrassed silence'. Four days later, having covered 13,341 miles in 169 days, the Thomas car reached Paris to a triumphant welcome and an immediate declaration of victory. It was now that the fun really started, with all three cars claiming victory.

Schuster was certain that he was the winner because, despite finishing four days behind the Protos, he thought the German car had incurred a 30-day penalty. There was also the small matter of the Protos missing out Japan completely. The Germans responded by accusing the Americans of having themselves travelled by rail across Wyoming. Then there was the Züst team. They didn't arrive in Paris for another two months, having been delayed at Omsk where the crew were seized as spies when they tried to send a cable in Italian. On eventually reaching France, they immediately claimed victory as theirs, insisting that the other two had cheated.

When all the fuss had died down, the organisers confirmed the Thomas Flyer as the winner. The race provided a massive boost to the US motor industry with sales of the Thomas jumping by 27 per cent. George Schuster became a national celebrity. Fate was less kind to the Züst. With eerie echoes of the fate of the victorious Itala from the Peking-Paris event, this latest Italian model was taken to England after the race, only to be destroyed by fire at a railway station.

THE FIRING SQUAD

US GRAND PRIZE, 26 NOVEMBER 1908

Although the home of motor racing was Europe, the sport had
started to take off in the United States. However, the hopes of
attracting the leading European drivers had been dealt a severe
blow by the 1906 Vanderbilt Cup race at Long Island, New
York – an event marred by poor crowd control. Many drivers
had felt intimidated by spectators who had broken through the
wire netting barriers and swamped the circuit. So the
authorities decided to take no chances for the Grand Prize of
the Automobile Club of America, to be run on Thanksgiving
Day, 1908, at Savannah, Georgia, and arranged for the track to
be patrolled by armed soldiers and policemen. These officers
didn't quite operate a 'shoot to kill' policy, but they were
decidedly trigger-happy.

The 25-mile Savannah circuit wound its way along roads
lined with palm trees, and the race distance of 402 miles was
relatively short for that time. There were 20 entrants, including
a strong European contingent with three Fiats and three Italas
from Italy, three Benz cars from Germany and two Renaults
from France. The Fiat team consisted of Felice Nazzaro, Louis
Wagner and Ralph de Palma, a young Italian-born American
driving in his first big race. His riding mechanic was Pietro
Bordino, who went on to become the leading Italian driver of
the early 1920s. In addition there were six American drivers –
Ralph Mulford, Joe Seymour, Bob Burman, Willie Haupt, Len
Zengle and Hugh Harding – each at the wheel of an American

car. The Fiats and Renaults appeared to have a major advantage when it came to tyre stops thanks to the introduction of detachable rims. When a car sustained a puncture, the old tyre usually had to be slashed off with a knife, then a new inner tube and outer casing had to be fitted using levers before finally being inflated. It was a laborious process which resulted in lengthy pit stops. But Fiat and Renault were now using detachable rims which could be unbolted and bolted back on complete, thereby reducing the time taken by around ten minutes.

Following an extensive ten days of practice, the race was due to start at 9 a.m. but was postponed 45 minutes because of fog. As was the norm in those days, the cars were started at intervals (massed starts not being widely introduced until 1922) with the result calculated on time rather than finishing position on the track. When the cars got away, it was de Palma who took the lead, followed by Wagner, René Hanriot in a Benz and with the fancied Nazzaro back in sixth. De Palma retained his lead until the third lap when tyre trouble dropped him back to last place. This allowed Hanriot to take over at the head of the field, pursued by Hungarian driver Ferenc Szisz in a Renault, Wagner, Victor Hémery (Benz) and Nazzaro. All the while the militia men, rifles poised, were keeping a close watch on the spectators. Then suddenly for some inexplicable reason, one of the locals tried to drive a horse and buggy across the track at the height of the race. The soldiers fired on the driver in an instant. He got the message.

Hanriot maintained his advantage until lap eight, by which time Hémery had moved up to second. As Hanriot fell away, Hémery began to dispute the lead with Nazzaro and Wagner. On lap 11 Erle, who was in fourth place, was knocked unconscious when a tyre burst and his Benz careered along the course for a further quarter of a mile before overturning. Luckily he received only minor injuries and his mechanic escaped unhurt. Then came more drama when the police captain shot at Hanriot for what was described as an infringement of the regulations. Somehow the black flag seems a more civilised method of dealing with transgressions. Remarkably, Hanriot bore no ill feelings and later presented his gloves and goggles to the officer.

Starting the final lap, Nazzaro had a lead of nearly two minutes over Hémery who, in turn, was just two seconds ahead of Wagner. Hanriot, still running despite his scare, was 12 minutes back in fourth. But 15 miles from the finish Nazzaro lost a tyre and was relegated to third. Hémery crossed the line first but it was Wagner who, by virtue of a storming last lap, was declared the winner on corrected time – by 57 seconds after more than six hours of racing. Wagner and Hémery made it a French one-two with the Italian Nazzaro back in third.

Despite the over-zealous policing, the event was declared a resounding success. The drivers much preferred Savannah to Long Island and were delighted when the 1910 Grand Prize was switched from New York to Georgia. For that occasion, a new course was laid out using convict labour, the prisoners being rewarded with a special enclosure on race day. 'It will be grand,' enthused Hémery. 'Not even Europe has ever furnished a more perfectly patrolled course.' Then again, he hadn't been shot at in 1908.

DOGGED BY MISFORTUNE

FRENCH GRAND PRIX, 25 JUNE 1912

Following a three-year break, the world's oldest Grand Prix reappeared on the calendar with a two-day race at Dieppe over a distance of 956 miles, making it the longest event of the century at that point. It was also the last race of the giant cars, many of which were almost as high as a man. Since the only entry specification was a minimum cockpit width of 175mm, an army of these monster machines was unleashed on the Dieppe circuit – 17-litre Lorraine-Dietrichs and 14-litre Fiats dwarfing the 7.6-litre Peugeots and especially the little Sunbeams which were competing in the 3-litre voiturette class for the Coupe de l'Auto. The latter was run in conjunction with the Grand Prix and attracted an entry of 33 cars. Despite a partial German boycott, there were 14 vehicles taking part in the Grand Prix (an Excelsior, three Fiats, four Lorraines, one Mathis, two Rolland-Pilains and three Peugeots), making a total of 47.

With size considered to be everything, the clear favourites were the Fiats and the Lorraines. Among the Fiat drivers were the American amateur David Bruce-Brown and fellow countryman Ralph de Palma, who was due a change of luck. The previous month he had looked a certain winner of the Indianapolis 500 until his engine failed with two laps remaining. De Palma and his mechanic, Rupert Jeffkins, bravely pushed the car towards the finish, only to be overtaken.

During the week prior to the race Dieppe was invaded by motor racing fans of all nationalities. The casino did excellent

41

business and the authorities organised a series of boxing contests to entertain the visitors. Hotel accommodation was at a premium, rooms being let for four days only – two days preceding the Grand Prix and the two days of the race itself. So anyone wishing to stay for just two days had to pay for four. As a result of this blatant exploitation, many followers preferred to camp out around the circuit.

The cars were flagged away from 5.30 a.m. at 30-second intervals in front of a packed grandstand even at such an early hour. Victor Rigal's Sunbeam was first away for the voiturettes and Victor Hémery in his huge Lorraine was the first Grand Prix car to start, at 5.33. Hémery was also the first to reappear at the end of the opening 47-mile lap at 6.12 a.m., but the race leader was Bruce-Brown in the Fiat S74, who came round ten minutes later having taken 37min 18sec for the lap. Georges Boillot was second in a Peugeot with Hémery third and Jules Goux fourth in another Peugeot. Hémery suffered engine failure on the second lap and a lap later Goux dropped from third to 40th so that after five laps (quarter-distance for the race), Bruce-Brown led from Boillot and Louis Wagner's Fiat. The leading positions remained unaltered for the rest of the day and at the end of that ten-lap session, Bruce-Brown led Boillot by 2min 1sec with Wagner nearly half an hour back in third. A highly creditable fourth was Dario Resta in a little Sunbeam. A total of 19 cars were still going. Bruce-Brown's driving had been a revelation, particularly his smooth, fast cornering. Nowhere was this more evident than at the S bend near the railway bridge at Ancourt, where a bugler was stationed to give audible warning of each car as it approached. The Fiat cars had on the whole been very impressive, too, being described as 'running with gyroscopic steadiness as solidly as the proverbial rock'. Their Achilles' heel, however, was pit stops. Although the new tarred road surfaces represented a vast improvement on the old dirt tracks, the Fiats were extremely hard on tyres and had to stop for regular wheel changes. The Italian company had made the mistake of persisting with fixed wooden wheels with detachable rims instead of the newly invented detachable wire wheels with knock-off hubs that were favoured by Peugeot. As a result Fiat pit stops were considerably longer than those of Peugeot. Fiat also lost valuable time refuelling by churn and funnel, whereas Peugeot used a more advanced pressure system. So despite the fact that the Fiats were markedly quicker on the road – as would be expected from their superior power – the delays caused by pit stops kept them within reach of their French rivals. Nevertheless Bruce-Brown, in his familiar woollen windsock hat, was in pole position and was confident of cementing a famous victory on the second day.

The cars started the second day at the intervals and in the order in which they had finished the first...minus René Hanriot's Lorraine which had mysteriously caught fire overnight. The race conditions had also changed during the hours of darkness, persistent rain having created a slippery surface which suited Boillot better than Bruce-Brown. Consequently the Frenchman steadily whittled away at the lead until after two laps on the second day (12 overall), Bruce-Brown's advantage was down to a mere 11 seconds. Bruce-Brown was still ahead when, out in the country, his car had the misfortune to collide with a stray dog, an impact which ruptured the fuel tank, causing it to leak. As he struggled to carry on, he was promptly disqualified for refuelling away from the pits. De Palma and Goux fell foul of the same rule.

Profiting from the hound's intervention, Boillot moved into first place and stayed there. His only worrying moment occurred on the penultimate lap when the Peugeot suffered a jammed gearbox. It took Boillot and riding mechanic Charles Prévost 20 minutes to fix it and they set off again, but with only second and fourth gears. Fortunately Boillot's lead was such that he was able to coast home by 13 minutes from Wagner with Rigal third and Resta fourth. By finishing third, fourth and fifth overall, the Sunbeams easily won the Coupe de l'Auto. As for Bruce-Brown, he kept going to the finish despite his disqualification, but never again would a car of over 10-litres come so close to winning a classic road race. And later that year he was killed during practice for the US Grand Prize at Milwaukee.

CHAMPAGNE JULES

INDIANAPOLIS 500, 30 MAY 1913

The 2.5 mile oval circuit at Indianapolis was laid down in 1909 at a cost of $250,000. The original surface was natural rock which had been steamrollered flat, but this proved too dangerous and so the circuit was paved with three million bricks, earning it the nickname of 'The Brickyard'. This surface remained until 1935 when, with the exception of the start/finish straight, the track was asphalted. The last of the brick paving disappeared in 1961 when the entire circuit, apart from a symbolic brick strip at the finish line, was asphalted. Until 1971, the 200-lap, 500-mile spectacular was raced on Memorial Day, the day each year on which the United States remembers its war dead, but that year it was moved to the last Sunday in May. The first '500' took place in 1911 and the following year Ralph Mulford completed the race down the field at a leisurely 56mph solely to qualify for starting money, even stopping for lunch on the way! In 1913 it was drink rather than food which would make the headlines.

The first two years of the '500' had been essentially an American preserve, but in 1913 there was a significant European challenge. Five foreign drivers ('swarthy skinned aliens' as the American press called them) took part and the line-up included eight foreign cars – two Peugeots, two Mercedes and three Isotta-Fraschinis and a Sunbeam. As the American cars were much smaller than their European counterparts, none of the monster machines were entered. Of the European contingent only Frenchman Jules Goux had any experience of a banked circuit like Indianapolis, having raced in the spring of that year at Brooklands where he had lapped at a highly impressive 109.22mph. For Indianapolis Goux was at the wheel of the same 7.4-litre Peugeot in which Georges Boillot had won the eventful 1912 French Grand Prix. It was to prove a good omen.

America's Robert Evans led for the first few laps in a Mason but the race soon settled down into a battle between the Peugeots of Goux and Paul Zuccarelli, American Bob Burman in a 7.2-litre Keeton, and Albert Guyot in the strongly fancied Sunbeam. Alas, Guyot did not enjoy one of his more auspicious drives. R.F. Crossman accompanied him as riding mechanic and some observers thought the Sunbeam might have fared better had the situations been reversed. For despite having to change just one tyre throughout the 500 miles, Guyot could only finish a disappointing fourth, never really threatening the leaders. Up front, Goux made numerous tyre stops and during each one he guzzled a quantity of the Frenchman's favourite tipple, champagne. In the course of the race, he downed no fewer than six bottles! Far from having an adverse effect on his driving, the alcohol intake spurred him on to greater heights and when Burman dropped out in the second 100 miles, then Zuccarelli retired with carburettor trouble while lying second, Goux was left unchallenged in the lead. He went on to become the first European to win at Indianapolis (pocketing the prize money of £8,750), finishing well ahead of Spencer Wishart's 4.9-litre Mercer, which crossed the line on fire, and Charlie Merz's Stutz.

Goux's triumph saw him acclaimed as a national hero on his return to Paris. Over the ensuing years there was much debate as to whether or not the champagne story was apocryphal, but Goux himself subsequently confirmed that it was definitely champagne and not water that he had consumed during those pit stops. He added that it was the finest vintage, procured before the race with great difficulty by a Mr Kaufman of New York, Peugeot's representative in the United States.

THE DISTRESSED MECHANIC

FRENCH GRAND PRIX, 12 JULY 1913

Barely had the celebrations subsided following the historic win at Indianapolis when the Peugeot team was plunged into gloom by the death of Paul Zuccarelli, killed while testing on a long straight road in Normandy when a local farmer pulled his hay cart out of a side lane without looking. Three weeks later the action moved to Amiens in Picardy for the highlight of the European season, the French Grand Prix. In an effort to reverse the trend towards bigger engines and heavier cars, the rules for this year's race stipulated that the cars had to weigh between 800 and 1,100kg and use a maximum 20 litres of fuel per 60 miles. As a result there were fewer entries than usual but Peugeot still paraded a formidable duo in Georges Boillot and Jules Goux. Designed by Swiss engineer Ernest Henry, the Peugeots were the most technically advanced cars of their time and were firm favourites to repeat their win of the previous year. However, they faced stiff opposition from the first Grand Prix appearance of two French Delages driven by Paul Bablot and Albert Guyot, three Italas (the largest cars in the race) and, at the other end of the scale, four Sunbeams stepping up from the voiturette class. Among the Sunbeam drivers was Jean Chassagne, Victor Rigal's mechanic, who took over from Rigal after the latter was involved in an accident while practising for the Spanish Grand Prix.

The Amiens public road circuit featured a series of tight corners broken up by a long straight. At 19.6 miles, it was

comparatively short by the standards of the early part of the
century. The 29-lap race (which meant a distance of 600 miles)
was scheduled to start at 5 a.m. A horse towed the cars into
position, but a thick mist which reduced visibility to a few
yards delayed the start by half an hour. With visibility now
around 300 yards, Gustave Caillois was sent away in the first
Sunbeam at 5.31. Some cars – among them Bablot's Delage –
stalled in the damp conditions but the Sunbeam team had
taken the precaution of filling their radiators with warm water.
On the very first lap Antonio Moriondo overturned his Itala.
He jumped out unhurt and, with considerable assistance from
his travelling mechanic Giulio Foresti, managed to manhandle
the car back into an upright position. The pair then changed a
broken wheel, straightened the bent steering column and set
off again. Having lost two minutes at the start, Bablot, one of
the favourites, stalled his cold engine again on a hill nine miles
into the race. He was able to restart only by putting the car in
reverse and running backwards down the gradient.

Up front, Boillot and Goux were setting the pace with
Chassagne back in third, the Sunbeams proving that their
strength lay in reliability rather than speed. Then on lap three
Boillot surprisingly dropped back to fourth. Six laps later
Guyot had moved into the lead from Goux while Bablot in the
other Delage had climbed the field to fifth. Boillot kept
plugging away and by the end of lap 16 he had risen to second
place, just 1min 16sec behind Guyot.

Then disaster. In the course of lap 17 Guyot had to stop out
on the circuit to change a wheel. In his haste, his mechanic
Semos jumped from the moving car and was run over by the
rear wheel of the Delage. By the time Guyot had himself
changed the wheel and driven the stricken Semos slowly back
to the pits, the lap had taken in excess of half an hour – twice
the usual length. Furthermore, the pit stop to take on a spare
wheel and a new healthy mechanic meant the next lap also
took a painstakingly slow 23 min 12 sec. Those two laps
wrecked Guyot's chances. Boillot made the most of Guyot's
misfortune and by lap 25 had established a four-minute lead

over team-mate Goux. He seemed assured of a comfortable victory but suddenly he ran out of water. The car clouded in steam, he spluttered into the pits where his mechanic wasted precious minutes in trying to locate the radiator cap. By the time Boillot returned to the race, the leaking radiator bound with rags and adhesive tape, his advantage had been drastically reduced to just six seconds. He regained his composure, however, and went on to win by two and a half minutes at an average speed of 72.2mph, in the process becoming the first man to capture the French Grand Prix twice. Goux was second, Chassagne third, Bablot fourth and the unlucky Guyot fifth. It can be tough when a Grand Prix car has to double up as an ambulance . . .

ACROSS THE LINE BACKWARDS

TARGA FLORIO, 23 NOVEMBER 1919

The brainchild of Count Vincenzo Florio, the Targa Florio was first run in Sicily in 1906. When the suggestion of staging a race on the mountainous island had initially been put to the Count, his response was that there were no roads. Undeterred by this minor obstacle, the organisers found a tortuous 90-mile loop which proved more than a match for man and machine. Following a 12-year absence, the race was revived in 1919 over the 67-mile Madonie circuit. This may have been of a lesser distance than the original but the mountain twists ensured that there was no shortage of hazards. Among the 25 starters were a number of interesting names. Enzo Ferrari was making his racing debut at the wheel of a CMN; graduating from hill climbs, Antonio Ascari, the new hope of Italy, was driving a Fiat; André Boillot, younger brother of Georges who had been killed in the First World War, was in a 2.5-litre Peugeot; and René Thomas was driving an Indianapolis Ballot car which had been entered so late that Thomas had been obliged to drive it all the way from Paris to Naples. At one point on the journey through Italy Thomas had to wait while scaffolding was erected to replace a stretch of road that had been washed away by torrential rain. Most of the starters were Italian, including the Alfa Romeos of Giuseppe Campari and Nino Franchini and the pair of 1914 Grand Prix Fiats driven by Ascari and Count Giulio Masetti.

Thomas may have been forgiven for thinking that he had

49

seen off the worst of the weather in Italy but on the eve of the race a raging storm deposited a two-inch covering of snow on the mountain section. The following morning at 7 a.m. Enzo Ferrari was first away, followed by Ascari, in a devilish combination of snow and high winds, swiftly followed by rain, hail, sleet and sun, although not always in that order. To cope with the conditions, the drivers wore gauze masks but discarded their goggles because of the snow. The principal casualty on the first lap was Ascari, whose Fiat skidded on the treacherous road, plunged down a 30-foot ravine and was not found until halfway through the race! André Boillot was proving a worthy successor to his illustrious brother and an opening lap of 1hr 54min 36sec gave him a lead of nearly four minutes over Thomas, with Domenico Gambino third in a Diatto and Count Masetti's Fiat in fourth. But starting the second lap Boillot's Peugeot skidded, struck a bank, leapt three feet in the air, dropped on two wheels and was only prevented from plunging 200 feet over a precipice by a handily placed pile of stones. A lesser driver might have been unnerved by this experience but Boillot pushed on regardless, maintaining a healthy lead over Thomas despite having a car which boasted just half of his rival's cubic capacity.

When Thomas came in for fuel at the start of the final lap, having driven flat out, he discovered to his horror that he was still seven minutes behind. Boillot's carefree approach to this treacherous circuit had seen him leave the road on no fewer than six occasions but between accidents he was by far the quickest driver in the race. He didn't even bother to stop for fuel when beginning the last lap. Instead his equally manic mechanic grabbed a can from the pits and refuelled on the move. Thomas pressed on boldly but couldn't hope to compete with such daredevil tactics and in the end he pushed too hard and crashed, leaving Boillot with a lead of around half an hour.

Others might have been content to coast home but the Frenchman continued to drive like a madman right to the finish. It very nearly proved his undoing. For as news reached the crowd in the stands of Boillot's impending arrival, knots of spectators began to trickle excitedly on to the circuit. Boillot came roaring round the final corner and suddenly saw hordes of people in front of him. He jammed on the brakes and swerved to avoid the clusters of well-wishers but merely succeeded in spinning into the grandstand . . . just ten yards from the finish. Perhaps feeling guilty at their part in the proceedings (although three of their number were injured in the collision), the spectators started to push Boillot's car back on to the track until a journalist helpfully pointed out that Boillot would be disqualified unless he and his mechanic did the pushing. Although in the latter stages of exhaustion, the pair succeeded in dragging the battered Peugeot back on to the road, from where Boillot rolled across the finish line backwards. But that wasn't the end of it. Ernest Ballot reminded them that reversing over the finish line was also illegal so they were lifted back into the car, drove down the road, turned round and this time crossed the line facing the right way. A yard or so over the line, Boillot collapsed over the wheel, muttering gloriously, 'C'est pour la France!'

His average speed of 34.2mph had spreadeagled the field. Antonio Moriondo's Itala finished second, half an hour adrift, and Gamboni was a further 12 minutes back in third. Enzo Ferrari completed the race (no mean achievement in itself) but was well down the field. On the day nobody could cope with the new Boillot.

A MESSAGE FROM ABOVE

BROOKLANDS 100 SHORT HANDICAP, 30 SEPTEMBER 1922

With road racing illegal in England, the Brooklands circuit, near Weybridge in Surrey, was built in 1907 in the grounds of landowner Hugh Locke-King's country home to cater for the burgeoning interest in motor sport. The lap distance was slightly in excess of three miles, the circuit's most famous features being the 30-foot-high cement banking sections at either end of the track which enabled cars to fly round at speeds of 120mph. It was not a circuit for the faint-hearted.

Brooklands quickly established itself as a highly popular venue, particularly with the London sporting fraternity, and a number of meetings were held throughout the year. Among the more colourful regulars was Count Louis Zborowski whose father, Count Eliot Zborowski, had been killed at a 1903 hill-climb when his sleeve caught in the car's hand-throttle. In the years following the First World War, Count Louis built up a string of huge Mercedes-Benz cars, which were affectionately known as Chitty-Chitty-Bang-Bangs because of the deafening noise made by their exhausts. Chitty I boasted a 23-litre airship engine, identical to that used in Zeppelins, and Zborowski used to drive the monster Merc over to Brooklands from his estate in Canterbury, probably frightening the life out of other road-users. He always dressed his crew in a uniform of black shirts and oversize check caps, specially imported from Palm Beach. He was, to put it mildly, an enthusiastic privateer... somewhat in the image of Mr Toad.

He and Chitty I trundled up from Kent for the 1922

autumn meeting but the combination had a nasty experience during one of the practice sessions. He was speeding around the track in familiar style when he suddenly lost control and the car struck a bridge parapet at the top of the banking, slid backwards down the concrete, went clean through the timing box and off the circuit. Zborowski was unhurt, but timekeeper Chamberlain hid behind the timing box when he saw Chitty about to leave the track and lost a number of fingers in trying to take belated evasive action. Another track official, Cann, threw himself into a ditch and was happy to see Chitty leap over him. Chitty I would never race again, but Zborowski already had a successor lined up . . . Chitty II.

In the meantime, fully recovered, he drove a Benz in the 100 Short Handicap. A field of 11 cars were started at intervals according to their engine capacity. John Duff's white Benz was on scratch while Zborowski set off 12 seconds earlier. Duff did a lap of 114.49mph and Zborowski lapped at 103.76mph but the handicap system – a familiar feature of races at Brooklands – meant that neither could match F.C. Clement's blue Bentley, which won from a Vauxhall driven by M.C. Park. Unfortunately Duff failed to pull up after crossing the finish line and flew over the top of the Members' banking, wrecking the Benz. Although Duff was taken to hospital, his passenger, an immaculately dressed young stranger who had begged a lift in the paddock, was unhurt until the car's petrol tank, which had lodged in a tree, fell on him and laid him out.

As for Zborowski, he was killed driving a Mercedes in the 1924 Italian Grand Prix at Monza. Eerily, he was wearing the same cufflinks that had caused his father's death.

A STROLL ALONG THE PROM

BLACKPOOL SPEED TRIALS, 16 JUNE 1923

For most of the summer English seaside promenades such as
Herne Bay, Southsea, Bexhill and Blackpool would echo to
nothing louder than the chattering of holidaymakers. But just
occasionally they would reverberate to a different sound – the
roar of engines and screech of tyres as cars and motorcycles
sped along at terrifying speeds of 60mph or more, all in the
name of sport.

The genteel Sussex resort of Bexhill-on-Sea staged the first
promenade speed trial in 1902, but perhaps this is not too
surprising in view of the fact that, the following year, it was
also the first English resort to permit mixed bathing. Clearly
the Bexhill councillors at the turn of the century were an
enlightened bunch. Strange as it may sound, in 1905 the world
land speed record was equalled on Blackpool promenade
when Clifford Earp's Napier reached a speed of 104.53mph.
Blackpool duly became one of the most popular venues for
speed trials because its promenade was sufficiently wide to
accommodate two cars or motorcycles at a time. Racing
against the clock (and each other) in pairs rather than singly
offered greater spectator appeal. However, the town's
promenade races were soon outlawed because of the danger
they posed – not least to the donkeys – but were revived in
1923 to mark the end of the town's carnival week. A total of
227 entrants – including some 80 cars – turned out in 1923 to
speed along the half-mile course on Queen's Drive between

Bispham and Uncle Tom's Cabin. Stands were erected on one side of the promenade, and the cliffs at the other side of the tram lines were also packed with spectators. In total there were 32 classes (15 for cars) spread over seven hours of head-to-head racing, the star attraction being Sir Malcolm Campbell in his 350hp V12 Sunbeam land speed record car. Fortunately for any competing Bentleys and Bugattis, the Sunbeam was there for exhibition as opposed to competition.

The day was a resounding success. Indeed some competitors were reported as saying that the track was better than Brooklands. There were only three unsavoury incidents. One motorcycle crashed into a marshal who had to be taken to hospital, and at the finish of one of the car sprints, Mr C.F. Temple, described as 'a noted Brooklands racer', skidded at speed and was hurled from his vehicle. But the sole fatality was a dog killed by a car. Then again, it wouldn't be a race meeting without a dog story.

FIFTY YARDS FROM GLORY

TARGA FLORIO, 27 APRIL 1924

Over 50,000 German fans travelled to Sicily for the 1924 Targa Florio in the hope of witnessing a triumph on foreign soil for the three-strong Mercedes team of Christian Werner, Alfred Neubauer and Christian Lautenschlager. Their journey was to prove worthwhile, but only after Antonio Ascari and Alfa Romeo had seen victory sensationally snatched from them in the last 50 yards of the 268-mile race.

Ascari was joined in the Alfa team by Giuseppe Campari, Louis Wagner and Count Giulio Masetti, while there was also strong opposition from the Fiats of Pietro Bordino, Carlo Salamano and Cesare Pastore plus the Peugeot of André Boillot and a 3-litre Ballot driven by Jules Goux. After the first of the four 67-mile laps, only half a minute separated the first five cars on time, Masetti leading from André Dubonnet in a Hispano-Suiza with its wooden body built by an aviation company, Werner, Boillot and Ascari. The cars became more spread out in the course of the second lap, which ended with Werner leading Ascari by two minutes. Boillot was a further 1min 20 sec back in third, followed by Masetti and Campari. On lap three, Goux left the road as did Boillot who, faced with a choice between skidding and wrecking his tyres or dropping 6 feet into a bean field, chose the latter option and was seen driving across the field hotly pursued by his mechanic waving the starting handle! Amazingly this detour only cost him one place.

At the end of the third lap Werner was forced to come in for a wheel change. His lead of 2min 53sec over Ascari was thus eroded despite a remarkable pit stop, in which two burly Germans lifted the Mercedes (with the driver still in it) while others slipped jacks under the axles. Ascari's lead was slender but appeared certain to be decisive. When he had just three miles to go, a gun was fired to let the crowd know that he was approaching. Celebrations for an Italian victory were already beginning, while the Germans consoled themselves with the thought that their man Werner had driven a fine race and would surely have won but for having to change that wheel. The crowd at the finish line gazed up the road waiting impatiently for the red Alfa to come into view. Finally Ascari appeared, but all was not well. The car was coasting. As the Italian fans held their breath, it struggled slowly towards the line before spluttering to a halt a mere 50 yards from the finish. The engine had seized. Ascari was eventually pushed over the line but the lost time had handed victory to a surprised Werner. The Germans were jubilant.

Werner's time of 6hr 32min 27sec was achieved at an average speed of 41.1mph. Third place went to Masetti, and Bordino finished fourth, 14 minutes behind the winner. Shortly after crossing the finish line, Bordino fainted, and not even ice or water could revive him at first. He was in a desperate way. Ascari knew how he felt.

A PIT STOP FOR LUNCH

EUROPEAN GRAND PRIX, 29 JUNE 1925

The first Grand Prix to be staged in Belgium was held at the 8.76-mile Spa circuit in 1925. A race had been scheduled for 1914 but by then a different sort of battle was being fought on Belgian soil. The 1925 event was run under the title of the European Grand Prix but a low turn-out and a monotonous race was scarcely the best advert for European motor racing. In fact the day was memorable for just one reason – the most amazing display of arrogance by the Alfa Romeo team. If you can imagine Michael Schumacher prolonging a pit stop to tuck into a picnic, you'll get the picture.

Twelve cars were supposed to take part but when the Sunbeams and Guyots scratched, that left four Delages against three Alfas. The Delage drivers were René Thomas, Robert Benoist, Albert Divo and Paul Torchy, while the Alfa team comprised Antonio Ascari, Giuseppe Campari and Count Gastone Brilli-Peri. There should have been everything to play for since, although the World Championship did not begin in earnest until 1950, a short-lived experiment did take place for manufacturers from 1925, and this was one of the races which counted, in company with the Indianapolis 500 and the French and Italian Grands Prix. The other innovation for the year was the abolition of riding mechanics in Grand Prix events. Most racing cars now became single-seaters.

Ascari led the way round the first lap from Campari, Benoist, Brilli-Peri, Divo, Torchy and Thomas but on the next circuit Benoist dropped out with a split fuel tank. Then on lap four Torchy stopped for new plugs and retired soon after. The Delage misery deepened three laps later when Thomas's caught fire. He burnt his left hand trying to beat out the flames and retired. So after little more than 50 of the 500 miles, there were already only four cars left running.

At half-distance Ascari was still showing the way to Campari, Divo and Brilli-Peri. It was hardly riveting entertainment for the Belgian crowd but it was to get much, much worse. For soon Brilli-Peri retired with a broken spring and Divo exited the race after making two long stops – one for tyres, the other for plugs. Now it was just the two Alfas. Round and round they went, separated by over a quarter of an hour. The crowd, partly disappointed at the lack of French involvement but even more disgruntled by the tedious procession, began to jeer and boo the Alfa drivers. Irked by this show of disapproval, Alfa team manager Vittorio Jano decided to rub in the Italian superiority by arranging for a sumptuous lunch to be laid out in the pits. Then, to a crescendo of boos and hisses, he called in his two drivers and they sat down to a leisurely meal while the mechanics polished the cars. The spectators could hardly believe their eyes.

Their stomachs satisfied, Ascari and Campari resumed the 'race', remaining in that order to the finish at which point Ascari was 22 minutes ahead of his team-mate. He had led from start to finish at an average speed of 74.46mph.

The joy of Ascari and Alfa was to be short-lived. He was killed in his next major event, the French Grand Prix, following which the Alfa cars withdrew from the race as a mark of respect. Alfa still won that inaugural World Constructors' Championship (beating Duesenberg and Bugatti), but the season had been tarnished by the death of their star driver. It was all a far cry from that picnic in the pits at Spa.

A CLASH OF THE GIANTS

BROOKLANDS MATCH, 11 JULY 1925

Parry Thomas knew every inch of Brooklands and particularly its famous banking. A wheel mark made by him in 1925 was just two inches from the top of the banking, while on another occasion he got so close to the edge that his car removed a shrub growing on the other side. His formidable Leyland-Thomas machine was a match for any vehicle over a short distance of the Surrey circuit and held the lap record at more than 120mph. In 1923 he issued a challenge to any driver for a race over three or four laps, but there were no takers. However a handicapped standing-lap contest was run one moonlit Thursday evening between Thomas, George Duller's Bugatti and Ernest Eldridge's mighty 21.7-litre Fiat 'Mephistopheles', which was fitted with an airship engine and had frightening speed and power in short bursts. With only the exhaust flames of the cars visible to spectators, the Leyland gave a five-second start to the Fiat and 30 seconds to the Bugatti but crossed the line 30 yards ahead of Duller with Eldridge just behind in third. Thomas reissued the challenge in 1924 and Eldridge was all set to race him at that year's autumn meeting until the Fiat broke an oil pump in practice.

The match was rescheduled for the West Kent Motor Club meeting in the summer of 1925 over three laps, for stakes of £500. Since it was just a small club meeting, fewer than 2,000 people turned up to watch one of Brooklands' greatest duels. Eldridge drove without helmet or goggles but did take the precaution of carrying a passenger to warn him when Thomas was trying to overtake. Thomas wore his customary fair-isle jersey, helmet and goggles. The two huge machines started together from the mile box on the railway straight with Thomas on the inside. *The Autocar* recounted the contest in less than glowing terms. 'A more horrid spectacle to sit and watch has probably never been seen in motor racing. Several well-known drivers hurried to the bar, at which they remained out of sight, full of apprehension, until the race was over.'

As the flag fell, the Leyland took a lead of a length, to the astonishment of most onlookers, but before the half-mile the chain-driven Fiat accelerated and had surged into a lead of 200 yards by the Byfleet banking, which it took in a typically flamboyant skid. When the Fiat again swerved near the Fork, trackside spectators fled for cover. Thomas closed a little but an attempt at passing was thwarted when the Leyland slid down the banking. Eldridge adopted the tactic of keeping the Fiat low on the banking sections and, despite a succession of hair-raising skids, was able to maintain his slender advantage starting the third and final lap. The Fiat still looked the likely winner but as it slewed across the Fork for the final time, the engine cut out, allowing the Leyland to thunder past. Any doubt regarding the outcome was settled on the Members' banking when the Fiat's off-side rear tyre blew, sending chunks of rubber flying over the tree tops. Eldridge pressed on but Thomas claimed the spoils at an average of 123.23mph as opposed to the Fiat's 121.19mph. Thomas also set a new lap record of 129.70mph. Brooklands had never seen anything quite like it.

WHEN THREE WASN'T A CROWD

FRENCH GRAND PRIX, 27 JUNE 1926

The death of Antonio Ascari at the 1925 French Grand Prix had brought about renewed concerns over motor racing safety. Two-litre cars were now capable of attaining speeds in excess of 130mph, which was considered dangerously fast, and so for 1926 the sport's governing body introduced a new formula which restricted engine capacity to 1.5-litres. The opening Grand Prix of the season was in France and entries were received from Delage, Talbot, Sima-Violet and Bugatti, but unfortunately the first three marques did not have their new 1.5-litre cars ready in time and had to scratch, leaving the showpiece race in the calendar to be contested by just three Bugattis.

For the first time the French Grand Prix was being staged at Miramas, near Marseilles. The brainchild of veteran driver Paul Bablot, the circuit was a 3¼-mile oval with slightly banked turns at either end. Set in a windswept desert area, it was unpopular with competitors and spectators alike. The drivers found the layout dull and the surface unreliable, while spectators were faced with a four-mile walk from the nearest railway station. Miramas struggled to attract entries or crowds at the best of times so to hold the Grand Prix there in a year of transition for the sport was an inspired decision!

The Automobile Club de France soon realised it had blundered badly. Aware that a meagre feast was about to be set before the French public, the ACF added a 1,500cc cycle car race to the programme of events in the morning, but hardly anyone was present to appreciate the gesture. Lured outdoors by the heat, more spectators arrived for the Grand Prix in the afternoon, but most were soon wishing that they had chosen an alternative form of entertainment.

The three Bugattis lined up on the grid in ridiculous isolation. At the wheels sat Pierre de Viscaya, Bartolomeo Costantini and Jules Goux, who had not won a major race for 13 years. Ahead of them lay 100 laps of the most boring circuit in Europe. De Viscaya set the early pace, unaware that both he and Costantini were carrying the wrong type of fuel due to a mistake by the Bugatti crew. Well before half-distance the problem became so acute that de Viscaya had to retire and Costantini lost many laps in the pits. This left Goux to motor round and round by himself. In fairness, he did his best to entertain the crowd, treating it as if it were a real race, and averaging a respectable 68.16mph. He was the only finisher, Costantini finally giving up 16 laps from the end. The fiasco cost the ACF £2,500 and a lot of face. Not surprisingly, the French Grand Prix never returned to Miramas.

A MOST PECULIAR MATCH

BROOKLANDS, 15 JULY 1926

The indefatigable Parry Thomas took part in another bizarre Brooklands match in 1926 – a three-lap handicap race between his Leyland-Thomas, George Duller's supercharged Austin Seven, Paul Dutoit's Alvis and R.M. Hanlon driving a Greenbat electric truck of the type used for transporting luggage on railway stations! Whereas the Leyland-Thomas had a top speed of around 130mph, the Greenbat could barely manage 6mph with a following wind. It promised to be quite a contest.

Hanlon, formerly Dunlop's competition manager, received a start of 1hr 25min 38.4sec; Duller had a start of 1min 24sec; Dutoit was given a start of 59sec; and Thomas was on scratch. Before the start Dutoit treated the crowd to a series of spectacular skids at the temporary hairpin bends which had been laid out on the track in readiness for the next race. Hanlon then set off, his truck handicapped further still by being laden with two tons of wet sand ballast tied up in bags. He was expected to lap at around 5mph and to get progressively slower as his vehicle's batteries ran down. In fact he speeded up, lapping at 5.42, 5.43 and 5.48mph, which proved sufficiently speedy to secure victory by 32.4sec from the Alvis which lapped at 91.22mph. The prospect of an exciting finish was marred somewhat when Duller and Thomas, their engines misfiring, retired after just one lap.

With the race won, the Greenbat truck continued trundling

around the track to see how far its batteries would last, but after covering 13 miles and 1,055 yards in 2hr 50min 28sec, a transmission shaft was damaged when braking for a mechanic to take his turn at the tiller. It had made its point.

A GRAND DAY OUT

MIDDLESEX GYMKHANA, 17 JULY 1926

In its round-up of club news, *The Autocar* carried a report of the Middlesex County Automobile Club's annual gymkhana, held at Potters Bar. There were eight novelty events, pride of place going to the Blindfold Driving Competition in which, as the title implies, entrants had to drive blindfold to a certain point in the fastest time possible and without assistance from passengers. Happily this contest did not take place on public roads, but anyway if a car appeared to be following a dangerous course – such as towards the beer tent – a bell was helpfully rung as a warning.

The star performer was one R.C. Sharpe who notched a notable double. He won the Letter Box race, where a lady passenger had to post a card in each of four boxes without alighting, and followed it up with victory in the Lightning Artist race, where his passenger had to name correctly the animal drawn on a blackboard to which the car had first been driven. Well, it was more entertaining than the French Grand Prix.

Other events included the Steady Hand race, which required a passenger to fill a tumbler with water and carry it in the car to the end of the course without spilling the contents, and the Potato Putting event. Alas, there was no description of the rules for this last-named competition, but the imagination can fill in the blank spaces.

THE PAIN IN SPAIN

EUROPEAN GRAND PRIX, 18 JULY 1926

Driving a racing car has never been a particularly comfortable experience at the best of times, but never more so than in the cockpit of a Delage. The problem lay in the car's design, notably in the location of the exhaust pipes at the driver's side which created excessively high temperatures around the driver's feet and legs, making it necessary to stop at the pits at least once during a race purely to cool down. The design of the exhaust system also created a vacuum which sucked the exhaust fumes into the cockpit. So if the heat didn't get you, the fumes would. The situation became so intolerable that Delage withdrew the car from competition towards the end of 1926 in order that it could be redesigned for the following season. The cylinder-head was turned around to move the exhaust pipes from the driver's side. The Delage now became bearable as well as successful and lifted the 1927 World Constructors' Championship. Ironically, at the end of that year the company announced its retirement from Grand Prix racing. It left behind memories of pain and pleasure in almost equal measure. This was particularly true of the 1926 European Grand Prix held at the Spanish circuit of San Sebastian.

The Spanish sun was unforgiving that day. *The Autocar* wrote: 'A hot sun and a scorching sirocco blowing down the course and bringing with it, from time to time, blinding clouds of white dust, were the weather conditions prevailing just before the start of the race. It would have been difficult to imagine more strenuous conditions for the men, and events, indeed, were soon to prove the terrible nature of the ordeal through which the drivers had to pass.' A total of 21 entries were submitted for the race, but, in keeping with this chaotic year for Grand Prix racing, only six cars actually started – the three Bugattis of Bartolomeo Costantini, Jules Goux and Nando Minoia, and the three Delages of Robert Benoist, Edmond Bourlier, and Morel, with Louis Wagner as spare driver.

Goux nearly missed the start of the 45-lap race but got away first to lead from Minoia, Benoist, Costantini, Morel and Bourlier. On lap two Benoist overtook the two Bugattis and retained his advantage until lap seven, when he came into the pits for what were euphemistically known as 'supplies'... in other words a drink. This dropped him down to fifth ahead of Minoia, who was already having difficulties with both himself and his car overheating. Morel was now in the lead but on lap ten the searing heat got to him. Semi-delirious, he staggered into the pits and was hauled out of the car to receive treatment for sunstroke and burnt feet before being taken to hospital. The experienced spare driver, Wagner, took his place. After 14 laps Benoist again succumbed to the heat and the fumes from the Delage and stopped for relief. The crowd called for Delage team manager René Thomas to take the wheel but he was none too keen at the prospect of, as he later put it, 'roasting one's lower members, being asphyxiated by the exhaust gases and of being roasted by the sun... not at all enticing for a man of middle age'. Thomas was spared by the intervention of Robert Sénéchal who had been watching the race from the Bugatti pit and now offered his services as a Delage driver. When he climbed into the baking hot cockpit, it was the first time he had ever sat in a Delage. He would not be there for long.

By now, Wagner, in Morel's car, was also suffering and managed to come up with various excuses for stopping. After just one lap he came into the pits for gloves and two laps later he pitted for a soak with water. Wagner was a tough competitor but he was in a state of collapse and after five laps he gave up.

Sénéchal fared little better, managing just six laps before calling it a day. His exhaust box had blown and when his shoes started to burn, he came into the pits and stood in a bucket of water. So after 20 laps only one Delage – that of Bourlier – was still going, the other two being parked in front of the pits. Bourlier was battling on gamely in third place behind Costantini and Goux but ahead of Minoia. To relieve the temperatures of 110 degrees, the mechanics bored holes in the cars but the real salvation arrived, after the two Delages had been stationary for an hour, in the form of a change in the wind direction. Now blowing in from the sea, it freshened the circuit to such an extent that it roused Benoist to take over Morel's original car from Wagner. The last-named was also galvanised into action and, suitably refreshed after a nice long rest, he took the seat in the Benoist/Sénéchal car. Benoist and Wagner were so rejuvenated that they even managed to break the lap record, although it was immaterial in terms of the race result. The gallant Bourlier eventually could carry on no longer and slumped in the pits, his legs covered in burns. Sénéchal stepped into the breach once more and drove on to the finish. Towards the end Costantini was plagued by mechanical problems and slipped back to third behind the winner Goux and the Bourlier/Sénéchal car. The race officials, however, took a dim view of the unauthorised driver changes and disqualified all three Delages, only for the decision to be reversed later in the year. So the original result stood.

The weary drivers trudged – or in some cases were carried – away from San Sebastian that afternoon in the knowledge that most would be back at the same circuit the following week for the Spanish Grand Prix. Mercifully, the weather was kinder on that occasion.

THE RIOT AT MIRAMAS

GRAND PRIX DE PROVENCE, 26 MARCH 1927

Following the débâcle of the 1926 French Grand Prix at Miramas, the 1927 race was moved to Monthléry, leaving the exposed Camargue circuit to content itself with staging the lesser Grand Prix de Provence. The event was for cars with engine capacities ranging from 1.1 to 3 litres and was divided into four preliminary heats, the highest finishers progressing to the final. The heats were run in torrential rain and produced a major surprise in the 1.5-litre race where Robert Benoist's Delage, which would carry all before it that summer with wins in the French, Spanish, European and British Grands Prix, was beaten over 15 miles by Jules Moriceau's Talbot. The other heat winners were, in ascending order of engine size, Arthur Duray (Amilcar), Marcel Lehoux (2-litre Bugatti) and Louis Chiron (2.3-litre Bugatti), producing 17 finalists.

It was still raining heavily when the cars came out for the final. Benoist was last away for his warming-up lap and set off from the pits while the others were being marshalled to the grid. Coming around the final corner into the start/finish straight, Benoist was alarmed to discover a number of cars stretched across the track. He braked hard but on the slippery surface the Delage slewed sideways, hit Duray's Amilcar and put both vehicles out of the final. In the wake of this accident, the Talbot team immediately withdrew its three cars on the grounds that the track was too dangerous.

The remaining cars were then flagged away, with Chiron

and Lehoux at the head of affairs, but the unruly Marseillaise crowd, soaked to the skin and deprived of the leading French entries, suddenly stormed the barriers and invaded the circuit. They then proceeded to attack the Talbot pit and angrily damaged other cars which had been forced to pull up. With the rioters showing no signs of dispersing, the race was abandoned. The incident did nothing for the reputation of Miramas. The entrants vehemently criticised Miramas officials for failing to control the crowd and vowed never to race there again. They were as good as their word, and the unloved circuit lay idle for the next ten years.

THREE CAR TRICK

LE MANS 24-HOUR RACE, 18 JUNE 1927

The cathedral city of Le Mans in north-west France had been to the forefront of European motor racing since staging the inaugural French Grand Prix in 1906, on a circuit to the east of the city. Between 1911 and 1913 the Grand Prix de France (an event not to be confused with the French Grand Prix) was held on a long, triangular circuit to the south of Le Mans and after the war sections of this route were incorporated in a new 10.73-mile layout. This track, which consisted of public roads including part of Route Nationale 158 (the main Le Mans-Tours highway), provided a splendid setting for the 1921 French Grand Prix and encouraged thoughts of a long-distance race to demonstrate the reliability of touring cars. The Bol d'Or 24-hour race for light cars had been held at St Germain, near Paris, in 1922, proving that it was possible to stage night races other than in floodlit stadiums. And so in 1923 the Le Mans 24-Hour Race was born.

For the 1927 event, the British challenge was spearheaded by three big green Bentleys whose noisy exhausts shook the surrounding French countryside. Bentley had won in 1924 and had come so close two years later, only for S.C.H. (Sammy) Davis to drive the car into a sandbank when trying to regain second spot with just half an hour remaining. Given a lift back to the pits, he was faced with the unwelcome task of reporting the mishap to W.O. Bentley. Davis later wrote: 'I went for a long walk alone, and wished I was dead.' But Davis was back in the same 3-litre car – the famous 'Old No. 7' – and was joined in the team by Leslie Callingham (in a powerful 4.5-litre model) and George Duller. Only 22 cars lined up for the start, partly because tougher regulations regarding refuelling had deterred the leading French teams of La Lorraine and Chenard-Walcker from taking part, and also because the entire Tracta team had gone joy-riding the night before, resulting in a crash which put most of them in hospital. One of the team who was passed fit, Grégoire, was conspicuous for two reasons: his Tracta was the first front-drive car ever to appear in a competition, and he drove with a huge bandage around his head, a legacy of the inadvisable night out.

Four o'clock sharp saw the traditional Le Mans start (introduced in 1925) whereby the drivers ran across the track to their cars. Those whose vehicles possessed convertible tops had the added chore of having to raise the hood before driving off. As expected, Callingham's monster Bentley set the pace and was comfortably ahead of his two team-mates when, an hour after dusk, a single crash at White House took out the entire Bentley team.

Callingham came roaring into the corner at over 70mph to find a Schneider broadside across the track. Unable to avoid it, he crashed into it, spun and rolled across the road into a ditch on the far side. Seconds later, Duller, who was two laps behind, appeared on the scene. A noted amateur steeplechase jockey, he chose to jump for his life when he saw what was about to happen. He managed to avoid the Schneider but smashed into Callingham's car. Davis, in the third Bentley, had deliberately dropped back a little as darkness fell to avoid dazzling Duller with his headlights. He saw Duller's car ahead rush down the hill, jump the bridge and disappear round the bend. Davis wrote: 'As I swung around that right hand turn, on the road was a scatter of earth, a piece or two of splintered wood. The thing flashed an immediate warning ... but even then it did not occur to me to do more than slow down a little and be ready. The car swung round White House Corner almost at full speed. I jammed down the brake pedal, tried to spin the wheel and skidded broadside on, for, white and horrible in the headlights' beam, an appalling tangle of smashed cars appeared right across the road in front! With the rending crash of riven metal, we slid right into the mess, with a shock that threw me hard against the wheel. All the lights went out.' As Davis clambered out, he saw that the 'mess' was one Bentley on its side with the other on top of it. The three Bentley drivers, dazed but otherwise unhurt, stood there momentarily in the finest British stiff upper-lip tradition discussing the best course of action. The cars of Callingham and Duller were beyond redemption but Davis managed to extricate his machine from the tangled heap of metal and limp back to the pits. Moments after he had left White House, another car ploughed into the wreckage.

The damage to Davis's car included a bent front axle and frame, a smashed mudguard and running board, and a broken headlight. By the time a wheel had been replaced, a new headlamp had been fitted, the battery box had been secured firmly and the running board had been strapped up, half an hour had elapsed. With co-driver Dr Dudley Benjafield at the wheel, the patched-up Bentley set off in pursuit of the new leading car, the 3-litre Aries of Jean Chassagne and Laly. In pouring rain, Benjafield made considerable inroads, gaining a whole lap. But at 2.30 on the Sunday afternoon – with just 90 minutes to go – the Bentley was still a lap behind when 'Doc' Benjafield spotted the Aries stopped at the side of the road near Mulsanne. The following lap it was still there. The Aries was out of the race with fuel pump failure. Incredibly, magically, the battered Bentley was in the lead. And there it stayed, Davis bringing it home – mudguards flapping in the wind – to a memorable triumph by 217 miles. Only seven cars finished. After the winners had been deluged with flowers and soaked in champagne, Davis discovered that the link arm to the steering had all but sheared through and that a mere quarter-inch of damaged metal had stood between victory and tragedy. For had the link arm parted at 90mph, the driver would almost certainly have been killed.

The Bentley legend was confirmed at the celebration dinner at London's Savoy Hotel. With a straight face, chairman Sir Edward Iliffe rose to announce that a lady who was entitled to be at the dinner was waiting outside, and invited her to enter. The folding doors were swung back and, with her one headlamp blazing, No. 7 roared into the room for the grandest of entrances. The only people not amused were the Savoy management who had reacted in horror to the sight of the famous Bentley Boys manhandling the old lady up the hotel stairs!

CHIRON BEATEN BY AN AMBULANCE

FORMULA LIBRE RACE, MONTHLÉRY, 2 JULY 1927

As a supporting race to the French Grand Prix at Monthléry, a Formula Libre (free formula) contest was staged the day before the main event. This free-for-all was open to cars of all sizes and attracted a diversity of entrants, including Albert Divo in a 1.5-litre Talbot, Louis Wagner and W.G. Williams in a pair of 4-litre Sunbeams, Louis Chiron and George Eyston in 2.3-litre supercharged Bugattis, and Mme Devancourt in a little 1,100cc Salmson. But in the end the vehicle which governed the result was an ambulance.

Heavy rain deprived the big Sunbeams of their power advantage and although Williams led on the first of the ten laps, he and Wagner soon retired with transmission trouble. Divo took over at the front, hotly pursued by Chiron, but then tragedy struck when a Guyot left the road, killing its driver, de Courcelles. An ambulance rushed to the scene but it broke all regulations by going round the track in the wrong direction. As it pulled off, it blocked the fast-approaching Chiron who was forced to swerve on to the outer circuit, narrowly avoiding a second disaster.

But for having to execute this highly dangerous manoeuvre, Chiron might well have caught the leader. Instead Divo held on to beat Chiron by 32 seconds at an average speed of 74.75mph. Eyston was third and Mme Devancourt fourth in what must surely be the only race to have been decided by an ambulance driver.

BENOIST ALL IN A SPIN

SPANISH GRAND PRIX, 31 JULY 1927

French ace Robert Benoist subsequently described his win in the 1927 Spanish Grand Prix at San Sebastian as the most memorable victory of his career. That could have something to do with the fact that but for the swift intervention of the marshals, Benoist, disorientated by a spin, would have driven off along the track the wrong way – head-on into oncoming traffic. The consequences of such an error do not bear thinking about.

The 40-lap, 430-mile race developed into a duel between Bugatti and Delage, and in particular between Emilio Materassi's Bugatti and Benoist's Delage. The Bugatti seemed to handle the tricky circuit better, its faster cornering offsetting the Delage's speed on the straights. Materassi lost time early on with a spin but Benoist surrendered the lead when he had to come into the pits to change plugs. However, a stop for refuelling reduced Materassi's lead to 27 seconds with Benoist closing all the time. Soon they were running nose to tail with the cool, composed Frenchman exerting tremendous pressure on the volatile Materassi. It was a question of whether or not Materassi would crack.

The answer came with nine laps to go when Materassi overdid it at Bascardo's Corner and slammed into a wall. Following close behind, Benoist saw nothing but a thick cloud of dust. He slammed on the brakes and went into a violent spin, missing the Bugatti by a matter of inches. The spin, however, had caused him to lose all sense of direction and he resumed racing the wrong way. Scarcely able to believe their eyes, the marshals frantically waved him down, and he turned the Delage around and headed off in the right direction, recovering his composure to win by over two minutes at an average of 80.5mph from Count Carlo Alberto Conelli's Bugatti and Edmond Bourlier's Delage. But Benoist knew that he had come close to causing a major catastrophe, not to mention forfeiting his hard-won lead.

The race also marked the Grand Prix debut of Louis Chiron, who took over André Dubonnet's Bugatti and would have finished a creditable second had the car not broken down five laps from the finish.

THE ACTRESS AND THE OPERA SINGER

MILLE MIGLIA, 13 APRIL 1929

Count Aymo Maggi had dreamed of making his home town of Brescia the focus of the world's greatest motor race. Together with fellow Brescia residents, Count Franco Mazzotti, Renzo Castegneto and Giovanni Canestrini, Maggi conceived the idea of a 1,000-mile race through Italy, starting and finishing in Brescia, and taking place on public roads which would not officially be closed for the duration. The ambitious proposal appealed to Italian leader Benito Mussolini, who saw motor racing as the way forward, and in 1927 the first Mille Miglia was held. It quickly lived up to its billing as the finest road race in the world.

The first two Mille Miglias had been a resounding success, happily free from the accidents which had plagued the inter-city races at the turn of the century and which some had predicted would blight this charge through the towns and villages of northern and central Italy. Not only did the races attract sizeable entries but they made the sport accessible to the Italian people, who turned up in their thousands along the route to cheer on their favourites. The 1929 race attracted a more modest 72 entries, mainly because it clashed with the Monaco Grand Prix, which was considered the major event by the motoring world. With eight Bugattis at Monte Carlo, there were none left for the Mille Miglia. Indeed there were no foreign works entries, making the strong Alfa Romeo team hot favourites, their challenge spearheaded by the victorious 1928 pairing of Giuseppe Campari and Giulio Ramponi. Campari was a larger than life character. A frustrated opera singer, he loved to sing at the top of his voice while roaring along the road. Alfa's chief rivals were the Brescia-based OM team, whose drivers included Antonio Brivio and the up-and-coming Tazio Nuvolari. The smaller classes were expected to be dominated by the Fiat 509s who made up more than a quarter of the total entry. The most colourful competitor was actress Mimi Aylmer, who arrived at the start wearing a smart red dress and fur jacket, with her chauffeur at the wheel of a Lancia Lamba. Everyone assumed that the chauffeur would do the driving but at the last minute she took the wheel, relegating him to the passenger seat where he was to stay for the entire race. Ahead of them all lay 1,018 miles spread over two days, the route descending as far south as Rome. At least one third of the race would be run on dirt roads, additional hazards including 67 level crossings, many of which were unmanned.

Surprisingly it was the lone Maserati of 'Baconin' Borzacchini and Ernesto Maserati which led to Bologna, by which time the OM driven by two of the race founders, Maggi and Mazzotti, had been forced to retire with transmission trouble. Another early casualty was Nuvolari, who crashed out in what would subsequently prove to be typically spectacular style. Four minutes behind the Maserati was Campari, pursued by Achille Varzi, Count Brilli-Peri and Carlo Pintacuda, all in Alfas. On the run down to Rome Varzi was delayed for half an hour by having to stop and put out a fire, and Brilli-Peri dropped out with engine trouble. Borzacchini and Maserati were still ahead at Rome but on the notoriously tricky drive up to the Adriatic, they dropped out with transmission trouble. This seemed to leave the way clear for Alfa and by the time they reached the Adriatic coast Campari and Ramponi held a lead of over 20 minutes. Back at Bologna, with just a fifth of the race to go, Campari still had a commanding advantage over the OM of Giuseppe Morandi and Archimede Rosa, which had moved up into second ahead of Varzi. Although Campari's car suffered two punctures on the final section, he reached Brescia to win by ten minutes from Morandi and Rosa with Varzi and Colombo two minutes behind in third. The Alfa's winning time was 18hr 4min 25sec, an average speed of 56.05mph. Forty-two of the 72 starters were still going at the finish.

Among them was Mimi Aylmer, but not until she had made one last gesture to her adoring fans. Way down the field in 29th place and some seven hours behind the winner, she pulled over on the outskirts of Brescia and stopped for five minutes to attend to her hair and make-up. After putting on fresh lipstick, she felt able to face her public once more and drove on to the finish where she received a rapturous welcome. She then stepped out of the car with a radiant smile, immaculately groomed, and showing no sign whatsoever of fatigue. The expression on her chauffeur's face told a different story. Looking a nervous wreck, the poor man was later given a special award at the prize-giving for being the most courageous man of the race. Without doubt he had earned it.

THE ICE-MAN MELTETH

TARGA FLORIO, 4 MAY 1930

Achille Varzi was known as the ice-man of Italian motor racing. Whereas fellow countryman and fierce rival, Tazio Nuvolari, typified the explosive Latin temperament, Varzi remained cool and calculating, a breed apart. This approach had brought Varzi a number of victories in minor races but he had yet to establish himself in the very top flight of world drivers. At the 1930 Mille Miglia the flamboyant Nuvolari had revelled in emphasising his superiority. Well ahead on time as dawn was about to break on the second day, he spotted Varzi ahead of him on the road. Switching off his lights, he crept up on Varzi unawares, then flashed them on again as he swept past on his way to victory. For Varzi it had been a humiliating experience. Nuvolari was the top dog . . . and both men knew it.

Three weeks later the pair met again in the Targa Florio, run over five laps of the intimidating Madonie circuit. The Alfa Romeo team was managed by Enzo Ferrari, who had cars for Nuvolari, Giuseppe Campari and Varzi. The last-named had driven a modified Alfa P2 to victory in the Bordino Prize at Alessandria but, with a top speed of 140mph, it was considered unsuited to the twisting Madonie course. Ferrari certainly thought so and warned Varzi that the car was too dangerous for the Targa Florio, but Varzi put his foot down. Campari and Nuvolari were not exactly renowned for erring on the side of caution but even they steered clear of the P2 for this race, preferring instead to drive two of the new 1,750cc

82

sports cars. Bugatti sent a strong four-man team, led by Louis Chiron and Albert Divo, and there was also stiff opposition from the Maseratis of Luigi Arcangeli, Baconin Borzacchini and Ernesto Maserati, but this was to be the day that Achille Varzi came of age.

He announced his intentions from the off, putting in a blistering opening lap to break the track record and lead the way from Nuvolari and Campari in the other Alfas and the Bugatti trio of Chiron, Divo and Count Carlo Alberto Conelli. Chiron upped the tempo to overtake Nuvolari and Campari on elapsed time but, at the end of the second lap, was still losing ground to the seemingly unstoppable Varzi. On the third lap, however, Varzi suffered a fuel leak which allowed Chiron to close the gap to less than two minutes, and when the Italian came into the pits for a wheel change at the end of lap four, he was actually half a minute behind. Having started 12 minutes behind Chiron, he was unaware of the problems that the Monegasque driver was encountering out on the circuit, for Chiron had skidded on some loose stones on a downhill section and had been forced to change two wheels. But for Varzi back in the pits every second counted. There was no time for a longer stop to take on fuel so his riding mechanic snatched the can and proceeded to pour the fuel into the tank as the car sped off along the road. In doing so, he spilt some on to the exhaust. Within an instant, flames were licking around Varzi's neck but he had come too close to victory to be denied now and, keeping his legendary cool, he drove on defiantly while the mechanic valiantly tried to beat down the flames with a seat cushion. Somehow they negotiated that final lap safely and speedily, and took the chequered flag to wild cheers from the patriotic Sicilian crowd. Chiron was nearly two minutes back in second with Conelli third, Campari fourth and Nuvolari only fifth. Varzi had well and truly proved his point. Both he and the car had been up to the task. He was now able to join the world's racing élite.

PASSING MANOEUVRES

RELAY GRAND PRIX, 25 JULY 1931

Ever keen to welcome ingenious new ideas to brighten up their meetings, the Brooklands committee adopted a suggestion from the Light Car Club to run a team relay race for amateur drivers. The event was restricted to cars of 1,500cc or under, each team of three being handicapped according to engine capacity. Each car had to do 30 laps, the fastest car in the team starting first, followed by the next fastest and finally the slowest. When the first car completed its 30 laps, the driver came in, handed a sash to the team's next driver who then sprinted to his car and continued for another 30 laps. If a car retired, the next car could still take over but it had to cover the extra distance as well as its own 30 laps. Thus if the first car ground to a halt after 12 laps, the second car would have to complete 48 laps.

Twenty-two teams took part in the 270-mile race and, in addition to the rules, had to contend with torrential rain which flooded part of the track. More than one team had to push its first car over the start line before immediately summoning the second car to run 60 laps. The race proved a triumph for the new racing Austin Sevens, the team of Leon Cushman, J.D. Barnes and Charles Goodacre winning at an average speed of 81.77mph. A mixed team of a Lea-Francis, a Riley and an Austin Seven finished second at 80.14mph with another Austin Seven team in third.

The Morgan team adapted its cars by holding the hand

throttles open with rubber bands so that their drivers could concentrate solely on steering – a tactic which resulted in some hairy excursions around the banking. Ultimately it proved of minimal benefit, the team finishing no higher than 12th. The race produced plenty of chaos during changeovers with drivers bumping into officials and photographers, while one driver was in such a hurry to get away that he tried to start with the handbrake on.

FAGIOLI BRINGS THE BRIDGE DOWN

CZECHOSLOVAKIAN GRAND PRIX,
27 SEPTEMBER 1931

The 18.2-mile Masaryk circuit at Brno in Czechoslovakia was used occasionally during the 1930s and was the setting for a remarkable national event in 1931 which featured just about the most unusual accident in Grand Prix history.

A sizeable crowd turned up to watch the 308-mile race, among them Czech driver Elisabeth Junek, whose participation in the 1928 Targa Florio had created a sensation when it became known that the race leader for a short while was a woman. She also raced in that year's German Grand Prix, sharing the driving with husband Vincenz (the owner of one of Prague's premier banking houses), but he suffered a fatal accident in the race, after which his wife retired from competitive driving.

Luigi Fagioli was first away at Brno in a Maserati, pulling out a useful lead on the opening lap from Baconin Borzacchini, Achille Varzi, Rudolf Caracciola, Louis Chiron and Tazio Nuvolari. Fagioli was still in the lead on lap two when the rear hub cap of his car struck one of the pillars of a temporary wooden bridge which had been erected across the circuit and brought the entire bridge crashing down on to the track in front of his pursuers. Varzi, who had moved up to second, took the main brunt but managed to bulldoze his way miraculously through the fallen timber. However, his efforts proved in vain, having caused so much damage to the front axle of his Bugatti that he had to retire. Nuvolari collided with the timbers a few seconds later and broke the rear axle of his Alfa. While Varzi drove Nuvolari back to the pits, Fagioli also had to drop out on the next lap as a result of the curious collision, which mercifully did not result in any injuries to drivers or spectators.

Shortly afterwards Marcel Lehoux hit a boundary stone and broke a wheel rim. Changing the wheel, he set off again to such good effect that he broke the lap record, only to retire immediately afterwards with a bent differential shaft. Next to suffer was Caracciola, whose big Mercedes hit a marker post and wrecked the near-side wheel. This chapter of accidents left Louis Chiron's Bugatti with an unassailable advantage and, although Fagioli switched to a second Maserati and Nuvolari replaced Borzacchini, neither could catch the leaders. Chiron eventually won by nearly a lap from Hans Stuck's Mercedes, with German driver Heinrich-Joachim von Morgen third in a Bugatti. Chiron's third win of the season had certainly been his most eventful.

VICTORY AT 1½ MPH

MONTE CARLO RALLY, JANUARY 1932

After travelling the length or breadth of Europe through snow and ice as quickly as was humanly and mechanically possible, competitors in the 1932 Monte Carlo Rally found that the entire event would be decided by a crazy final test in which they had to drive as *slowly* as they could over a distance of 100 yards. The rules stipulated that during the test the wheels had to be moving at all times. Although nobody else liked the innovation, it seemed to suit M. Vasselle, whose 3.5-litre Hotchkiss saloon covered the 100 yards in 2min 35.51sec at a speed of 1.5 mph to win the most coveted prize in rallying. No wonder the next day's headlines were along the lines of: 'FARCICAL TEST RUINS MONTE CARLO RALLY'.

The Monte had first been run in 1911 and each winter saw cars converging on Monaco from all over Europe. For 1932 there was a new starting point, Umea in northern Sweden, 2,231 miles from Monte Carlo. Since the object of the exercise was for competitors to cover the greatest distance possible within the time limits, Umea became a popular choice, with over half of the 116 entrants opting to start from there. In the end, the top 18 all started from Umea. Among them were Vasselle and the 1931 winner, Donald Healey, who was driving an Invicta. By contrast, only eight crews decided to set off from Athens even though it was actually 21 miles further from Monaco. But no driver had yet managed to battle his way through the snows of Yugoslavia in January. Other starting points that year included Frankfurt, Gibraltar, John O'Groats, Lisbon, Stavanger, Jassy, Palermo and Glasgow. The most unusual starter from Glasgow was Rootes PR man Dudley Noble in a Hillman Wizard 75 . . . towing a caravan.

Although the Umea starters had to cope with black ice and three ferry crossings, 28 made it to Monte. Even Vasselle's car, which had a top speed of just 50mph, went off the road at one point. The conditions in the Balkans were no better than usual, yet five cars from Athens managed to force their way through. Indeed the starters who fared worst were those who had set off from John O'Groats. They were severely hampered by widespread flooding.

Of course reaching Monaco was one thing. Now they had to face the deciding test. The previous year's braking and acceleration test had been scrapped and replaced by this new curious examination of driving skills. Cars had to be driven as slowly as possible, in top gear, for 100 yards, then as fast as possible (still in top gear) over the next 100 yards, at the end of which they had to be stopped within 40 yards. Many competitors prepared for the test by calling in at local garages for wheels or axle ratios to be changed. This apparently took the rally organisers by surprise. Healey had small spare wheels fitted to his Invicta immediately before the test so that the rear of the car almost scraped along the ground. It had the desired effect, enabling Healey to record a slow time of 1min 54.91sec – good enough for second place overall. However, he was too quick for Vasselle who thus became the first – and only – man to win the Monte by driving slowly. For the following year the ill-conceived go-slow test was unceremoniously dumped.

CAMPARI'S HAMMER BLOW

MILLE MIGLIA, 9 APRIL 1932

Giuseppe Campari was the undisputed king of the Mille Miglia. The winner in 1928 and 1929, third in 1930 and second in 1931, he was expected to make another bold show in the 1932 race, particularly since he was at the wheel of one of the all-conquering Alfa Romeos. In recent years the event had virtually turned into an Alfa benefit and in 1932 the company provided almost half of the entire 88-car entry. There were works cars for Campari, Rudolf Caracciola, Baconin Borzacchini and Tazio Nuvolari, supplemented by several Scuderia Ferrari Alfas entered by Enzo Ferrari and driven by the likes of Pietro and Mario Ghersi, Giulio Ramponi, Carlo Trossi, Antonio Brivio and Piero Taruffi. One man sadly missing from the Alfa line-up was Luigi Arcangeli who had been killed at Monza while practising for the previous year's Italian Grand Prix. The serious opposition to Alfa was pretty much confined to Achille Varzi in a Bugatti and the Lancia Lambda of Strazza and Gismondi, although there were interesting entries from a couple of English aristocrats – Lord de Clifford in a 750cc MG Midget and the Hon. Brian Lewis (later Lord Essendon) at the wheel of a Talbot 105.

On the first section to Bologna, Nuvolari led from Varzi and Caracciola, with just five seconds covering them, and all three averaging over 100mph for the stage, but as the cars took to the mountains Varzi sustained a hole in his petrol tank and retired. Approaching Florence, Pietro Ghersi tried to take a sharp bend too fast and skidded into a lamp-post, wrecking the car. A few minutes later the cheering crowd welcomed the 1930 winner Nuvolari but, spotting the bent Alfa, his attention wandered for a split second, which was long enough for him to crash into a tree, his car coming to rest a matter of yards from Ghersi's. The impact of the accident was so severe that Nuvolari's co-driver, Gianbattista Guidotti, was thrown from the car and knocked unconscious. When Guidotti eventually came round, there was no sign of Nuvolari, but he was vaguely aware of being carried on a stretcher by four sinister-looking figures wearing long, flowing cloaks with hoods over their heads. Dazed and confused, Guidotti feared he was being abducted by the Ku Klux Klan, so he closed his eyes and pretended to be dead. Only later did he discover that his 'abductors' were dedicated Florentine monks who were taking him to the monastery hospital for treatment. Another early casualty was Giacomo Ragnoli, who was making his race debut in a Fiat. Heading south from Bologna on the road to Florence, his car veered off the road on a bend. Ragnoli was unharmed and walked into an inn, conveniently located on the offending corner, and downed several brandies. In the following year's race he went off at the same corner...

At Florence it was Caracciola who led from Campari and Taruffi, and the positions remained unaltered down to Rome except that Campari and Taruffi swapped places. Crossing the Apennines, Caracciola lost valuable time when he was forced to stop to adjust his brakes and by the time he reached Terni, the German's lead over Taruffi had been cut to a minute with Campari a further minute adrift in third. Campari began to scent another famous victory and overhauled Taruffi, so that by Perugia he was just 35 seconds behind Caracciola with Borzacchini moving up to third. Building up a veritable head of steam, the burly Campari powered on and had surged into the lead as he approached the Adriatic coast. However, such flat-out driving over winding roads had taken its toll and Campari decided to let his mechanic, Sozzi, have a turn at the wheel so that the great man could take a breather in preparation for the final assault. No sooner had Sozzi taken over than he crashed the Alfa into a wall near Ancona and put himself and Campari out of the race. Perhaps understandably, Campari was not best pleased and chased the tearful Sozzi down the road brandishing a hammer from the tool kit. Fortunately for Sozzi, while he may not have been the faster driver, he was the faster runner.

Campari's mishap left Borzacchini in the lead and he pulled out a ten-minute advantage over the ailing Caracciola, who was soon to retire with a cracked chassis. The Alfa of Taruffi and Eugenio Siena gave chase before falling victim to a broken piston near Bologna. This allowed Trossi and Brivio to claim second place, eventually finishing 15 minutes behind the winning car of Borzacchini and Bignami. A total of 42 cars made it back to Brescia with Alfa filling nine of the first ten places, only being denied a clean sweep by the Strazza/ Gismondi Lancia which came seventh. Down in 25th was the Hon. Brian Lewis who, after already losing time by taking a wrong turning, had to resort to patching up a holed fuel tank with a piece of chewing gum.

So Borzacchini was the toast of Brescia that night...but Campari maintained with some justification that victory should have been his.

CORTESE'S QUICK FIX

MILLE MIGLIA, 9 APRIL 1933

The greatest drama in the 1933 Mille Miglia actually occurred on the eve of the race. While a Scuderia Ferrari-entered Alfa Romeo was being prepared for the following day, a stray electric spark ignited petrol vapour and the whole car went up in flames. Although one of the team mechanics was badly burnt, nobody thought to tell the driver, Franco Cortese, about the incident. So when he arrived just four hours before his scheduled start time expecting to see a car in pristine condition, he was horrified to discover that it had been severely damaged. Participation in the race looked unlikely to say the least, but Cortese refused to panic and instead patiently supervised the rebuilding of the car. For three hours Cortese and his crew toiled away fixing the rear of the Alfa, where most of the damage had occurred, but just when they appeared to be on top of things one of the mechanics accidentally poured a can of water into the fuel tank. As a result the tank had to be completely dismantled and cleaned. Against overwhelming odds, the car was repaired in the remaining hour and Cortese was able to set off just a few seconds later than his scheduled starting time.

Cortese was only one of another huge Alfa entry, the principal opposition to the Italian team expected to come from Manfred von Brauchitsch in a Mercedes-Benz. This year's race also saw the first Mille Miglia entry from a British works team, MG sending over three K3 Magnettes driven by Earl Howe and

Hugh Hamilton, Sir Henry 'Tim' Birkin and Bernard Rubin, and Captain George Eyston and Count 'Johnny' Lurani. The Italians were so delighted to welcome the Britons to their race – particularly at a time of heightening European political tension – that the MG team was greeted by King Victor Emmanuel of Italy, Mussolini and the British Ambassador. An unusual entry was General d'Agostini's eight-cylinder Alfa which was powered by gas generated from a charcoal burner. This was part of an initiative by the Italian government to seek out alternative fuels in the event of an oil crisis.

The previous year's runners-up made an early exit when Carlo Trossi skidded his Alfa into a wall, the crash propelling co-driver Antonio Brivio through the air en route to what was happily a relatively soft landing. Baconin Borzacchini's Alfa was first at Bologna and was still in the lead at Rome, hotly pursued by Tazio Nuvolari in another Alfa. Last away, Nuvolari had endured a noisy drive after losing a silencer, he and mechanic Decimo Compagnoni being forced to wear cotton wool in their ears to deafen the din. Nuvolari was three minutes behind at Rome but shortly afterwards, close to Borzacchini's home at Terni, the leader retired with a cracked cylinder head, allowing Nuvolari to seize an advantage which he would keep to the finish. He completed the 1,022-mile round trip to Brescia in 15hr 11min 50sec (at an average speed of 67.9mph), over half an hour ahead of the remarkable Cortese and Castelbarco who, after all their pre-race drama, had driven an inspired race. Alfa not only filled the top ten places but won four different classes, although Eyston and Lurani did gain a popular victory for MG in the 1,100cc category. In any other event the domination by one manufacturer could have led to accusations of tedium, but there was never any danger of the Mille Miglia becoming dull as long as there were people like Franco Cortese taking part.

A FIERY FINISH

MONACO GRAND PRIX, 23 APRIL 1933

The first Monaco Grand Prix in 1929 had been hailed by
bewildered observers as 'the nearest approach to a Roman
chariot race that has been seen of recent years'. With its
glamorous Riviera backdrop and spectators afforded
unrivalled, close-up views of the action, it quickly became an
immensely popular addition to the racing year, and in 1933
broke new ground by being the first Grand Prix at which grid
positions were decided on practice times rather than by ballot.
The race itself would go down in history as the scene of one of
the greatest duels of all time, between those old foes Achille
Varzi and Tazio Nuvolari, and one which, even after 99 laps of
non-stop cut and thrust, still managed to provide a sensational
sting in the tail.

The practice sessions were dramatic enough. Rudolf
Caracciola ploughed into a wall, badly injuring his right leg –
an accident which kept him out of racing for over a year and
left him with a permanent limp. And Nuvolari completed only
11 practice laps before bending his car so badly at Ste Devote
that it was not repaired until race day. The all-important times
produced a front row of Varzi (Bugatti), Louis Chiron (Alfa
Romeo) and Baconin Borzacchini (Alfa Romeo). Nuvolari's
Alfa was on the second row. The Alfa was faster than the
Bugatti in a straight line but there aren't too many of those at
Monaco, where the Bugatti's superior cornering was expected
to come into its own. From the inside berth, Varzi shot into the

lead on the first of the 100 laps, ahead of Borzacchini, Marcel Lehoux and Nuvolari. On lap two Nuvolari moved up into second and next time round he edged into the lead. For the next 50 laps the pair exchanged leadership of the race with bewildering regularity, there rarely being more than a second between the two cars. The pace they set was so furious that the first of the back-markers was lapped after just seven circuits. Behind the two leaders was an equally ferocious scrap for third spot between the Alfas of Borzacchini and Philippe Etancelin, but then the flamboyant Frenchman skidded at the chicane, allowing Borzacchini to pull clear. Etancelin pressed on and broke Varzi's lap record on lap 51, eventually catching Borzacchini seven laps later. But then on lap 65 Etancelin's axle shaft broke, putting him out of the race.

This battle, however, paled into insignificance alongside the one which continued unabated for the lead. Nuvolari was driving in typically demonic fashion, taking corners with just one hand on the wheel because the other was almost constantly occupied with the gear lever. Although he had managed to maintain his narrow advantage for much of the race, the lead continued to change hands frequently and on lap 80 Varzi got past once more. On lap 83, Nuvolari led; by lap 93, it was Varzi; on lap 98 – with just two remaining – it was Nuvolari. With no more than a car's length separating them, they sped around the world's tightest and trickiest circuit as if joined by an invisible piece of string. Before the end of lap 99, Varzi had seized the initiative (setting a new lap record in the process), only to be re-passed at the beginning of the final lap. Surely now Nuvolari would hold on, but as the pair went up the hill to the Casino for the last time, smoke was seen pouring from the Alfa's bonnet. An oil pipe had burst as a result of Nuvolari over-revving on the hill. Varzi gratefully accepted the invitation and shot by to record a memorable victory.

Meanwhile Nuvolari coasted grimly on towards the finish until the hot oil caused a fire. As flames shot out from beneath the Alfa's bonnet, he jumped from the burning car and pushed it across the finish line, hotly pursued by irate officials waving fire extinguishers. Unfortunately one of the Alfa crew also lent a hand, which resulted in Nuvolari being disqualified, second place going to Borzacchini and third to René Dreyfus in a Bugatti. So the little man had nothing to show for what was, even by his standards, an inspired drive. Of the 100 laps, he had led for 64 and Varzi for only 36, but on the vital last lap Lady Luck had chosen to side with Varzi.

ON THE BEACH

SOUTHPORT SANDS 50-MILE RACE,
29 APRIL 1933

Throughout the 1920s and 1930s race meetings and record attempts were popular fixtures on spacious beaches all over Britain – notably at places such as Pendine, Porthcawl, Saltburn, Weston-super-Mare, Skegness and Southport where the tide being out guaranteed miles of sand on which to lay out a course or attain extraordinarily high speeds. That is not to say that beach racing was all plain sailing. The tide came in so fast at a Skegness meeting in 1924 that the last race of the afternoon was reported as being run with the course awash. Another hazard was that in races of several laps the sandy corners would become badly churned up by successive cars, making it difficult for drivers to pick a smooth path or maintain control of their machines. At Southport one year May Cunliffe became 'tramlined' in such ruts in her super-charged Sunbeam, as a result of which the car rolled over and over, killing her father who was acting as riding mechanic.

Southport Motor Club called itself the World's Premier Beach Racing Club and regularly attracted crowds in excess of 15,000, all kept under control by mounted police. Among its finest coups was attracting a visit from speed king Sir Henry O'Neal de Hane Segrave for a meeting in September 1925. Segrave, winner of the 1923 French Grand Prix, drove a 2-litre red Sunbeam and proved just as unbeatable on Birkdale Sands as he had at Tours. At the end of the day he had won 11 races and four cups, including the prestigious ten-mile event. And in one of the speed trials for which he would later become famous, he thrilled the spectators by reaching a speed of over 100mph. He did, however, lose out in a match with C.M. Needham's Brough Superior motorcycle, run over a mile from a standing start. Needham won by inches after Segrave had hit a soft patch of sand while trying to accelerate away from the start. Such were the vagaries of beach racing.

In April 1933 Birkdale Sands staged a 50-mile race over 100 laps of a short circuit divided down the middle by a row of flags so that the cars had to negotiate a hairpin bend at either end. With some 3,000 cars parked on the beach to watch, the race developed into a battle between the Bugattis and the smaller, more manoeuvrable, supercharged Austin Sevens which, on account of their lesser engine capacities, were given four credit laps. This proved decisive as W.L. Thompson's Austin Seven held on gamely to win from the early leader, Jack Field's Bugatti. As the mighty Bugatti crossed the finish line, the exertion of so much tight cornering took its toll and the piston collapsed, sending clouds of smoke into the air. Marshals ran amok with fire extinguishers and Field emerged unharmed, none the worse for his day on the beach.

A DIFFERENT CORNER

INTERNATIONAL TROPHY, 6 MAY 1933

By the 1930s Brooklands was in decline. The track had become worn through constant use and the banking was in a state of disrepair, heavily patched in places. It was in grave danger of being left behind by the high-speed racers of the era. So the search was on for new ways to bring out the best in the circuit, especially through races where speed could be contained to a reasonable level in order to prevent additional wear and tear. Handicap races had been a staple diet of the Brooklands programme for many years. In the early days, these necessitated cars starting at different points on the track, but this method was somewhat impractical since, from their particular vantage point, the drivers frequently struggled to see the starter's flag. For its 200-mile race in 1925 the Junior Car Club had introduced artificial corners to the oval track, which not only reduced speed but also provided a more interesting spectacle. For 1933 the JCC decided to take things a step further and replace its 1,000-mile sports car race with a 100-lap novelty handicap for the International Trophy.

At Brooklands there was a vast area of track at the section known as the Fork where the old finishing straight joined the outer banked circuit. 'Bunny' Dyer, secretary of the JCC, had the idea of dividing the track into three separate channels at this point – one channel going straight on, the second channel taking a chicane formed of hurdles, and the third channel tackling a more difficult chicane. The result was a handicap race with a difference. All of the cars started together, the smallest-engined (supercharged up to 750cc and non-supercharged up to 1,500cc) going straight on at the Fork, the next group (supercharged up to 1,750cc and non-supercharged up to 3,000cc) taking the easier chicane, and the biggest cars (supercharged over 1,750cc and non-supercharged over 3,000cc) negotiating the tougher chicane. Any car taking the wrong channel was penalised. To slow the cars further on their exit from the Byfleet banking before coming face to face with the obstacle course, an additional chicane was inserted halfway down the finishing straight.

The race certainly captured the imagination, 33 cars practising for a week to get used to the handicap corners. Ultimately 28 set off for the first prize of £500. There were 15 cars in the small vehicle group, mainly Austins, MG Midgets and Riley Nines; seven in the medium section, including Mille Miglia K3 MG Magnettes, a pair of Amilcar Sixes, and an Avis driven by Sir Ronald Gunter and Le Mans hero Dr Dudley Benjafield; and six in group three, among them Sir Malcolm Campbell, returning to Brooklands after his land speed record attempts, in a 4-litre V12 Sunbeam, and the Hon. Brian Lewis in an Alfa Romeo – the first time an Alfa had raced in the UK. Another interesting entrant in the fast car section was 21-year-old American millionaire Whitney Straight in a black and silver Maserati. Straight had sat an exam at Cambridge that morning and had flown down to Brooklands for the race. Each group had the tails of their cars painted a distinguishing colour so that drivers knew which channel would be taken by the car ahead.

The cars were flagged off in a massed start at 2.30 p.m. Jim Elwes in an MG Midget was first away but was quickly overhauled by the more powerful cars, and at the end of the first lap Campbell led from Lewis and Straight. Flashing past the pits to start lap three, George Eyston's 'Magic' Midget lost its off-side rear wheel at 80mph and the bouncing wheel struck a pit marshal, knocking him unconscious. Straight then began to assert his authority, lapping at over 90mph so that the ribs soon vanished from the Maserati's tyre treads and its wheels spun wildly at every corner. After 30 laps he had lapped the entire field but two circuits later the car blew up and he had to retire. At four o'clock Campbell led from Lewis and Kaye Don's Bugatti, only to lose almost a minute to his nearest rival through a tardy pit stop. Lewis cornered faster than Campbell but the Sunbeam had the greater acceleration, making for a close contest.

Campbell let his co-driver Staniland take over for a few laps while he took a well-earned rest, but the inexperienced pilot overdid it and had to come in to change plugs. Seeing the race slip away, Campbell discarded his helmet and, still smoking a cigarette, jumped back behind the wheel. Fortunately his fuel tank didn't leak. However, he was forced to retire shortly afterwards, having completed 80 laps.

Campbell's departure left Lewis in charge. Don was a distant second until he, too, dropped out with just eight laps remaining. Lewis went on to win by a comfortable 11 minutes from Eddie Hall's MG Magnette, with Mrs Bill Wisdom third in a similar car. So although the Alfa had emerged triumphant on its British debut, the smaller cars had also fared well. All in all, the unique handicapping system was adjudged to have been a great success.

THE FIXED RACE

TRIPOLI GRAND PRIX, 7 MAY 1933

The 1933 Tripoli Grand Prix should be remembered for a gallant – and ultimately tragic – final drive by that dashing Englishman Sir Henry 'Tim' Birkin. Instead it is better known as being the subject of the great Grand Prix fixing scandal, the result of the race allegedly rigged by the leading Italian drivers so that they could profit from the State Lottery.

The newly opened Melaha circuit at Tripoli was 8.5 miles long and the fastest in the world. Speeds of up to 140mph were commonplace. With Libya then an Italian colony, that great motor racing fan, Mussolini, wanted maximum publicity for the circuit and the race. To this end, Marshal Balbo, the new governor of Libya, organised a national lottery in conjunction with the Grand Prix. Tickets went on sale in Italy months before the race. For the layout of no more than a few lire, there was the prospect of winning seven and a half million lire, the equivalent of around £80,000. This was serious money. Three days before the race, 30 lucky tickets were drawn – one for each of the starters.

On the eve of the race a stout, bald-headed gentleman called at Achille Varzi's hotel room. He introduced himself as Enrico Rivio, a timber merchant from Pisa, and explained that he had drawn the lottery ticket bearing the number of Varzi's car. He asked Varzi to win the race. Varzi promised to do his best but was puzzled as to why Signor Rivio had flown all the way from Pisa to Tripoli to make such a basic request. Then

103

Rivio put all his cards on the table: if Varzi won, he could have half of the lottery prize money. Moreover Rivio produced a document to that effect, drawn up by his solicitor. Varzi apparently made no firm promises, but as soon as his unexpected guest had departed, he is said to have telephoned his old adversary but new-found friend, Tazio Nuvolari.

Race day saw temperatures of over 100 degrees in the shade. The new circuit was described as running like a white ribbon between the palm trees and the yellow sand. The grandstand was resplendent with a mixture of Italian officers and Arab sheikhs while nearby, in a special box, sat the 30 people from all walks of life, clutching the slip of paper which could prove their passport to riches. There was a Milan butcher, an old lady from Florence, a student, a baron who had fallen on hard times...and there was Signor Rivio, his bald pate beaded with perspiration, his face ruddy from a combination of the heat and the anticipation.

In a display of pomp and ceremony, Marshal Balbo flagged away the 30 starters, but instead of the expected Italian domination, it was Birkin's privately entered green Maserati who led them round followed by Nuvolari (Alfa), Giuseppe Campari (Maserati) and Varzi's Bugatti. On lap five of 30, Campari took the lead and Nuvolari also got past Birkin. At that stage Varzi was already 57 seconds behind the leader. Signor Rivio was observed mopping his brow. By lap 12 Campari was nine seconds ahead of Nuvolari, with Baconin Borzacchini up to third and Birkin hanging on gamely in fourth. Varzi appeared to be making little impact.

On lap 14 Campari came into the pits to refuel, allowing Nuvolari into the lead. Then Campari had to stop again because the Maserati's oil tank had worked itself loose. He lost 15 minutes while the tank was bound tight with rope and, although he rejoined the race, he dropped out shortly afterwards. He was soon spotted drowning his sorrows with a bottle of Chianti. Meanwhile from second place, Birkin had come in to refuel on lap 16. Maserati had sent only one mechanic to service both Birkin's car and Campari's and since the Englishman was a private entry, Campari took precedence and commandeered the mechanic. This left Birkin to enlist the services of a local garageman, who was such a drunk that he spent the entire race asleep under a palm tree. Heroically performing his own pitwork, Birkin lost two places through the prolonged stop, dropping down to fourth.

At two-thirds distance, Nuvolari's lead had been greatly reduced by Borzacchini with Louis Chiron not far behind in third. Then Varzi made his move, and by lap 25 he was up to third as Chiron and Birkin started to falter. The Bugatti was making ominous noises, however. Two cylinders were dead and the car was slowing. To stop for a change of plugs would have seen the end of any realistic chance he had of winning the race. Signor Rivio must have been about to tear up his ticket, especially with Nuvolari seemingly on the brink of lapping Varzi.

Until now, everything on the track had appeared above board, but the closing laps were decidedly irregular. First, on lap 27, Borzacchini inexplicably slowed and kept looking over his shoulder. Then he cut a corner so fine that he hit one of the empty oil drum markers. The car skidded to a halt with a burst tyre. Borzacchini was out of the race, but appeared none too concerned. Nuvolari began the last lap 30 seconds ahead of Varzi, but with half a mile remaining the Mantuan, too, began looking anxiously over his shoulder. The Alfa slowed alarmingly until, just 100 yards from the finish, it ground to a halt. Nuvolari jumped out and screamed: 'No petrol! No petrol!' Mechanics rushed to his assistance, but the delay allowed the ailing Varzi to loom into view. Nuvolari suddenly got going again but not in time to prevent Varzi crossing the line, almost in slow motion, the winner by one-tenth of a second. Exhausted, Varzi was carried shoulder-high by the crowds. Among the first to congratulate him was Signor Rivio.

That evening, as Varzi, Nuvolari and Borzacchini sipped the finest champagne, rumours began to circulate that the race had been fixed. These three were named as the prime suspects with Campari and Chiron also suspected of being fringe players. At a hastily convened meeting of the country's supreme sporting authority the following morning, there were calls for all five to be disqualified and for their competition licences to be withdrawn. The demand was rejected. To have thrown out five of the most famous drivers in Europe might have dealt a fatal blow to the image of motor racing. Instead they escaped with a mild warning. However, in future the lottery system was changed so that ticket numbers were drawn just five minutes before the race when the drivers were already in their cars and were therefore immune to temptation.

If Borzacchini and Campari did profit from the race, they did not enjoy their good fortune for long. Four months later both were killed at the Monza Grand Prix when their cars hit an oil patch dropped by Count Trossi's Duesenberg on the South Curve.

The controversial Tripoli Grand Prix was also to prove Birkin's last race. In finishing an honourable third, he had reached out of the Maserati for a cigarette and had burned his arm on the hot exhaust pipe. He paid no attention to the burns until they flared up a few weeks later. Blood poisoning set in and he died on 22 June.

LE MANS VICTORY SEALED BY CHEWING GUM

LE MANS 24-HOUR RACE, 17 JUNE 1933

More than a few eyebrows were raised when Alfa Romeo announced its pairings for the 1933 Le Mans Endurance Race. Raymond Sommer and Tazio Nuvolari in the same team? Neither was exactly fond of playing a supporting role. What were Alfa thinking of?

The Frenchman had won the previous year's race in partnership with Luigi Chinetti, but had insisted on driving 20 of the 24 hours himself as he had infinitely more confidence in his own ability than that of his co-driver. Chinetti was probably not in a position to argue too much with this high-handed approach, but Nuvolari was a different matter altogether. He would not act as anyone's chauffeur. The potential clash of egos was frightening.

True to form, Sommer loftily declared that he would be doing most of the driving in 1933 since Nuvolari was not as familiar with Le Mans as he was, and anyway the Italian was a known car-wrecker. If Nuvolari was allowed to remain at the wheel for more than a few hours, he would be sure to blow the Alfa's engine. No, the only hope of success was for Sommer to take the lion's share. For once, Nuvolari exercised considerable restraint, pointing out politely but firmly that he was a leading Grand Prix driver who knew his way round every circuit in the world and would not be troubled by a simple configuration such as Le Mans. Sommer backed down and, albeit reluctantly, agreed that they should divide the driving equally.

In the end this unlikely arrangement worked, but for all the merging of two great talents, it was a simple piece of chewing gum that won the day.

Sommer and Nuvolari's short-wheelbase Mille Miglia type Alfa was one of 29 starters. Others included a noisy 6.8-litre V8 Duesenberg, entered by Prince Nicholas of Romania. The American car was popular with European royalty, but was too cumbersome for Le Mans where its high fuel consumption led to its downfall, it being disqualified after just 22 laps for refuelling sooner than was permitted.

Sommer took first turn in the favourites' car and got away to a good start, leading at the end of the first lap from the fellow Alfas of Louis Chiron and Franco Cortese, Chinetti and Varent, and the English duo of Brian Lewis and Tim Rose-Richards. By 24 laps Sommer had established a healthy advantage, at which point he was persuaded to hand over to Nuvolari. Contrary to fears, Nuvolari did not break the car and when he handed it back to Sommer that night, they had a lead of more than two laps over Chinetti and Varent. Everything seemed to be going smoothly until half-distance, when Sommer came in to the pits because the front wing had broken loose and the petrol tank had developed a leak through the constant vibration. Hasty repairs were carried out, the hole in the tank was plugged with chewing gum, and 15 minutes later Nuvolari rejoined the race, now over a lap behind the Chinetti/Varent car. Such a deficit was nothing to a man of Nuvolari's stature and over the next few hours he set about catching and eventually overhauling the lead car. By ten o'clock on the Sunday morning – when little more than half of the field were still running – Nuvolari and Sommer led by a lap. This position was strengthened by the departure of Cortese, who rolled his car out of the race at the Esses.

Until now the chewing gum had done its job admirably, but suddenly the makeshift fuel tank repair gave way and Sommer was forced to make another unscheduled pit stop. With no satisfactory means of sealing the leak, it was evident that more stops might be necessary and so, being the faster driver,

Nuvolari took the wheel in the hope that he could minimise the effect of the frequent fuel stops. How Sommer reacted to this order is not documented.

With less than an hour to go Nuvolari was barely two minutes ahead of Chinetti, but then another wretched fuel stop allowed Chinetti to take the lead. It seemed that Nuvolari's valiant efforts would be in vain. With just one lap remaining Nuvolari moved up into a challenging position and swept past Chinetti. But the latter was not about to surrender and surprised Nuvolari by regaining the lead. Then at Arnage, Chinetti, under intense pressure, missed a gear change, allowing Nuvolari through once more and he held on to win by 400 yards, the lead having changed hands three times in the final eight miles of a classic 24-hour race.

Encouragingly for the British contingent, of the 13 finishers, they filled the next five places. Lewis and Rose-Richards were third, 287 miles ahead of a 1.1-litre Riley driven by Peacock and van der Becke. Aston Martins finished fifth and seventh, sandwiching a new 750cc MG.

But the day belonged to Nuvolari, who had broken the lap record no fewer than nine times. It is doubtful whether Sommer ever questioned the little Italian's driving skills again.

THE WRONG PIT SIGNAL

LE MANS 24-HOUR RACE, 15 JUNE 1935

Back in the 1930s the pit board was a driver's sole means of communication with his team. So when the Alfa team signalled to Frenchman René-Louis Dreyfus that he was comfortably leading the Le Mans 24-Hour Race in the closing stages, he eased off accordingly to preserve the car. Imagine his horror therefore when at 4 p.m. as the cars crossed the finish line, Dreyfus discovered that his crew had blundered. Instead of winning, he was five minutes behind in second place and had missed the opportunity to close the gap. The Alfa camp would not have been a happy place that Sunday night.

There were 58 starters, 36 of them British, including six Rileys and seven Aston Martins. Alfa Romeo had won the previous four races but the team proved less reliable this year... and not only in terms of their pit signals. Nevertheless it was the four supercharged Alfas who set the early pace, the Brian Lewis/Earl Howe car leading for the first six laps before stopping for a change of distributor. The Luigi Chinetti/ Gastard Alfa then took over but dropped back after the first hour, having been delayed by a wheel change. This opened the way for a third Alfa with the experienced Raymond Sommer at the wheel. Sommer was having to drive solo as his co-driver, de Sauge, had been conveniently taken ill! Sommer built up a lead of two laps but as a wet evening gave way to a wet night, he lost seven laps due to a blocked fuel line and eventually retired early on Sunday morning. At midnight there was a new leader – the 4.5-litre British Racing Green Lagonda driven by John Hindmarsh and Louis Fontes – but both the Lewis/Howe and Dreyfus/Stoffel Alfas were on the same lap, as was a 4.9-litre Bugatti.

The Alfas' tale of woe continued when the Chinetti/Gastard car retired after twice going off the road and Earl Howe's car broke a piston. This left just one Alfa running. Dreyfus and Stoffel lost valuable time, too, having their shock absorbers changed, and by midday on the Sunday appeared to have little chance of catching the Lagonda. A British victory to end the run of Italian domination seemed a foregone conclusion at the start of the final hour, only for the Lagonda to hit trouble. Fontes was forced to make several stops with fading oil pressure, allowing the Alfa to close right up. When Dreyfus passed the stricken Lagonda as it sat in its pit, the Alfa team signalled that he was now in the lead. In fact he was still a lap behind and, making no attempt to speed up, remained in that position at the chequered flag.

With a British victory and 22 of the 28 finishers being British, there was much celebration in the bars and cafés of Le Mans that night. But for Alfa, Italy and an unhappy French driver, it was the race that got away.

NUVOLARI VERSUS THE GERMANS

GERMAN GRAND PRIX, 28 JULY 1935

By the summer of 1935 German nationalism was reaching its height. The self-styled master race could not countenance defeat in any shape or form – in the political arena, on the battlefield, or on the football pitch or running track. This sense of superiority applied equally to the motor racing circuit, where the sleek silver Mercedes and Auto-Unions were sweeping all before them. Germany not only had the fastest cars, but also the finest drivers – men like Rudolf Caracciola, Manfred von Brauchitsch and Bernd Rosemeyer, the new sensation who, like so many of his predecessors, had risen from the ranks of motorcycling. In their spotless white overalls, the Germans appeared clinical and efficient, and their public came to view them as unbeatable.

The march to power had begun in 1934 when, after Alfa Romeo victories in Monaco and France, Mercedes and Auto-Union had carved up the rest of the season between them, notching wins in Germany, Switzerland, Italy, Spain and Czechoslovakia. They carried on the good work in 1935. Luigi Fagioli won the Monaco Grand Prix for Mercedes; Achille Varzi (Auto-Union) triumphed in Tunis; and Caracciola's Mercedes won in Tripoli, France and Belgium. Nothing was expected to stand in the way of the silver machines on home soil, and a regiment of dedicated Nazis marched 350 miles to the Nürburgring in anticipation of another German clean sweep. The line-up was headed by five Mercedes (Caracciola,

Fagioli, von Brauchitsch, Hermann Lang and Hans Geier) and four Auto-Unions (Rosemeyer, Achille Varzi, Hans Stuck and Paul Pietsch). The best the Italians could muster by way of competition were three Alfa Romeo P3s, driven by Tazio Nuvolari, Louis Chiron and Antonio Brivio. But even on a circuit with 176 corners, the Alfas' 265bhp would surely be no match for the Auto-Unions' 350bhp and the Mercedes' 400bhp.

Despite the drivers' preference for starting positions on the grid to be decided by practice times, the organisers insisted on a ballot, which put the crowd favourite, Caracciola, back on the fourth row. Any spectator apprehension was quashed immediately when Caracciola, shooting off almost before the flag had fallen, stormed straight into the lead. Fagioli lay second but before the end of the first of the 22 laps had surrendered that position to the slender figure of Nuvolari who, in his familiar uniform of sky blue trousers and yellow sweater, had steered the Alfa around the outside of the pack in a daring manoeuvre. At the end of that opening lap, Caracciola sped past the pits at 170mph, followed 12 seconds later by Nuvolari who clocked 150mph, and Fagioli close up in third. On the second lap it was Rosemeyer's turn to force his way through the field, relegating Nuvolari to fifth behind Caracciola, Rosemeyer, Fagioli and von Brauchitsch. Soon Chiron passed Nuvolari and moved up to fourth when Rosemeyer had to stop for a wheel change. But by lap five both Chiron and Brivio had retired, with transmission trouble and a broken differential respectively, leaving Nuvolari alone against the might of the Germans.

The situation certainly seemed to appeal to the little Italian, who took the fight to the Germans in inspirational fashion. By oversteering round each corner in a four-wheel drift (a technique which he pioneered), Nuvolari was able to gain precious seconds and work his way back up through the field. By lap ten only Caracciola remained ahead, but even he could not hold off the irresistible Nuvolari who, to the horror of the German crowd, swept past him into the lead. Then came the high drama of the race. At the end of the 11th lap – half-distance – the leading five cars came into the pits to refuel and change wheels. Von Brauchitsch got away in 47 seconds but in the Alfa pit a pumping device broke and, amid much panic, the refuelling operation had to be completed by hand with a funnel. Excitable at the best of times, Nuvolari went spare and, in his frustration, downed an entire bottle of mineral water, pausing only to swear at his hapless mechanics. The stop took a calamitous 2min 14sec and when he eventually rejoined the race, Nuvolari had fallen back to sixth. It was nothing short of a disaster.

The efforts of von Brauchitsch's pit crew had hoisted him into the lead from Caracciola, Rosemeyer and Fagioli, but Nuvolari quickly began to make up some of the lost ground and in the course of one lap – the 13th – he passed Stuck, Fagioli, Caracciola and Rosemeyer to rise to second place, just 69 seconds in arrears. Von Brauchitsch responded by setting a new lap record of 10min 30sec and by 14 laps had increased his advantage to 1min 26sec. He then appeared to ease off in the belief that victory was a foregone conclusion, and this enabled Nuvolari to make renewed inroads into the lead, cutting it back lap by lap – to 63 seconds, then 47, 43 and, starting the final circuit, 35. Such a lead should still have been sufficient for the German to take the chequered flag in first place, but as he passed the pits he could be seen pointing frantically at his left-side rear tyre. The same tyre had begun to show alarming signs of wear at the start of the previous lap, but Mercedes team boss Alfred Neubauer had overridden his mechanics' pleas to bring von Brauchitsch in for a tyre change. 'Brauchitsch will make it,' he snapped, 'and so will the tyre. It's only a question of a few minutes.' The tyre didn't make it. Coming out of a corner less than six miles from the finish, the Mercedes' tyre collapsed. Von Brauchitsch skilfully managed to retain control but could do nothing more than grind home slowly on the rim. Nuvolari swept past imperiously to win what the world's press described as 'a historic triumph of man over machine'. Stuck was nearly two minutes behind in second with

Caracciola, who later complained of having felt unwell during the race, third, Rosemeyer fourth and von Brauchitsch fifth.

The 250,000-strong crowd were stunned by this blow to German supremacy. The loudspeakers, which had been prepared to announce another German victory, remained ominously silent. The organisers eventually conducted a search for the Italian flag, which was then half-heartedly raised but without the accompaniment of the Italian national anthem, for the simple reason that nobody had bothered to bring the record. Except Nuvolari, that is. He always carried a record of the anthem in his suitcase for good luck, so he sent his mechanic to fetch it and the spectators were finally able to listen to the least popular tune in Germany that afternoon. It must have been a bitter pill to swallow, but for Nuvolari it was probably his finest hour. One of motor racing's strangest races was also one of its greatest.

KEEP RIGHT ON TILL THE
END OF THE ROAD

LE MANS 24-HOUR RACE, 18 JUNE 1938

In the illustrious history of the Le Mans 24-Hour Race, there have been few more surprised winners than the coupling of Eugene Chaboud and Jean Tremoulet. Barely eight hours into the race their 3.6-litre Delahaye was beset by so many gearbox problems that it could only be driven in top. Such was the despair of the team's mechanics that they were ready to call it a night and wheel the stricken car back to the paddock, but Chaboud wanted to carry on for as long as was humanly and mechanically possible. Even he must have thought the car would only hold out for a few more hours at the most, but, defying the odds, it kept going and, with rivals falling by the wayside, the pair who had been all but written off before midnight became the toast of France at 4 p.m.

Forty-two cars lined up for the traditional Le Mans start on a Saturday afternoon which was hot and oppressive, with more than a hint of a storm in the air. Over half of the entrants were French, led by a pair of new 4.5-litre Delahaye type 145 V12 models, driven by René Dreyfus and Louis Chiron, and G. Comotti and Albert Divo. They were opposed by five smaller, 3.6-litre Delahayes plus a new 4.5-litre Talbot, the latter in the hands of Luigi Chinetti and 'Phi Phi' Etancelin, and, from Italy, the Alfa Romeo of Frenchman Raymond Sommer and his Italian co-driver Clemente Biondetti. After the last of the cars had roared away, the long six-minute wait began to see which would be first to reappear at the end of the opening lap.

116

The answer was Dreyfus, who flashed past the stands ahead of Comotti and Sommer. By the end of lap two, Sommer was up to second and fanning himself with his hat, either an indication of extreme confidence or extreme heat, or possibly both. Next time round he was in the lead.

The race now developed into a battle between Sommer and Dreyfus until the Delahaye fell back through overheating. Comotti's Delahaye suffered a broken gearbox in the first hour and, at the two-hour mark, Dreyfus's car finally gave up the ghost and was retired. So both of the new Delahayes had failed miserably. After five hours the Chinetti/Etancelin Talbot retired with valve trouble, allowing the Alfa to establish a healthy lead over the nearest Delahaye – that of Chaboud and Tremoulet. Meanwhile the Delahaye of Mongin bit the dust when it caught fire. Trackside helpers threw dirt into the engine to extinguish the flames, but arguably did more harm than good as the car flatly refused to restart.

At the halfway point 23 cars were still running and Sommer and Biondetti had built up a commanding ten-lap advantage over the ailing Delahaye of Chaboud and Tremoulet. They soon stretched this lead to a seemingly insurmountable 13 laps. Surely only mechanical failure could rob the Alfa of victory.

Although the action on the track became somewhat lacklustre for the next few hours, there was plenty of interest off it. *The Autocar* noted: 'Some humour enlivened the spectators when a chart-keeper suddenly made himself a box seat outside on the pit counter, sat himself down in all solemnity, called on all persons to give him full view, then kept falling asleep, so that he never succeeded in recording the full number of cars running, and once lost his pencil, having forgotten its lodgment behind his ear.' Then at 12.45 p.m. a tent in the spectators' enclosure suddenly caught fire... happily without casualties.

At around the same time, the race took off as dramatically as the spectators in the enclosure. Biondetti brought the leading Alfa into the pits with a broken valve. He slowly restarted but two laps later spluttered to a halt at White House.

After leading for the best part of 21 hours – with Sommer doing the fastest lap of over 96mph – the Alfa was out of the race. This shock exit left the way clear for Chaboud and Tremoulet, who kept plugging away to limp home ahead of another Delahaye which had actually sustained a leak in its fuel tank before the start! All in all, the 1938 Le Mans was a triumph for the walking wounded.

LADIES' DAY

LADIES' CUP RACE, 25 JUNE 1938

Right up until its closure in 1972 (following complaints from local residents about the noise), the tight two-mile circuit at Crystal Palace was a great favourite with Londoners. Its major event of the year was the splendidly titled London Grand Prix, although it has to be said that the quality of driver and car did not always live up to the billing. It was no Monte Carlo. To attract greater interest for the 1938 London Grand Prix, clerk of the course Harry Edwards organised a five-race card beginning at 3.30 p.m. and which included a special race for lady drivers only. He knew that this would generate tremendous publicity, and so it proved as a huge crowd turned out to watch some of the leading lady drivers of the day slug it out around five laps of the track.

What the line-up lacked in quantity – there were just five starters – it made up for in quality. Mrs Bill Wisdom, a regular at Brooklands, drove a supercharged Alta while Kay Petre, arguably the best-known lady driver of the time, took to the wheel of a Riley. *The Autocar* expressed considerable interest in the presence of the diminutive, flame-haired Mme Itier, an experienced French driver. Perhaps its correspondent merely happened to like small redheads. Unfortunately Mme Itier's car – a little 995cc Simca-Fiat – was no better suited than a milk float to the cut and thrust of motor racing, and was hopelessly outgunned by the Altas. The circuit announcer did his best to enlist sympathy for the overseas challenger by declaring that her car was 'undercharged' and 'not suited to the circuit'. A trip to the shops, yes; a race track, no.

Although Mrs Wisdom and Mrs A.C. Lace drove identical Altas, the former surrendered her chances with a hairy skid at Stadium Dip. With the remainder of the cars being of such diverse power, the race turned into little more than a procession. Mrs Lace, wrote *The Autocar*, 'drove this very fast machine with due respect to score an easy win'. It then added, somewhat ominously: 'Mrs Lace is a much improved driver, as she would be the first to confess when reminiscing about some of her past drives in rally special tests.' Mrs Petre drove a 'careful' race to finish second, ahead of Mrs E.M. Thomas in a Delahaye, the underpowered Mme Itier, and the struggling Mrs Wisdom. Immediately after being presented with the Ladies' Cup, Mrs Lace hurried off to BBC Broadcasting House to be interviewed on the radio programme *In Town Tonight*. Such was media fame, 1930s style.

In the following week's edition, *The Autocar* had more to say about the race in an editorial under the heading 'The Weaker Sex?'. It wrote: 'The quite exciting race for women drivers at Crystal Palace last meeting revives a small controversy, anent which I personally think that any race or event organised for women drivers only is wrong. Nowadays a woman driver ought to be able to compete on even terms with men, and there should be no suggestion that she has to have special arrangements made which in themselves suggest that she is not a good enough driver.'

Equality had finally arrived at that great male bastion, the race track.

AN ENCOUNTER WITH A STAG

DONINGTON GRAND PRIX, 22 OCTOBER 1938

In an era when motor racing had a disturbingly high mortality rate, most drivers regarded serious injury – or worse – as an occupational hazard. But few treated it in quite as cavalier a fashion as Tazio Nuvolari. From the moment he first arrived on the scene on two wheels back in the 1920s, the Italian ace had made it clear that in the event of a pre-race accident, only a formal death certificate was likely to prevent him competing. Doctors despaired of him. A crash in the 1925 Italian Grand Prix at Monza put him in hospital, where he was swathed in bandages like an Egyptian mummy. Yet seven days later he took part in a motorcycle race, having persuaded medics to bandage him in such a manner that he could be placed on his machine in a riding posture.

Having moved up to four wheels on a regular basis, he broke a leg at Alessandria in 1934 when his Maserati skidded into a tree on the wet road. After four weeks in hospital as the world's most impatient patient, Nuvolari defied the advice of the doctors and entered to drive a Maserati in the Avus Grand Prix in Germany. He had the pedals of the car specially adapted so that all three could be operated with one foot (the other still being in plaster), and before the race he was presented by a local gymnastic club with a chunk of the tree which he had hit in Alessandria. The inscription read: 'To Tazio Nuvolari, intrepid ace of the wheel as a record of the providential obstacle which though preventing a sure victory saved a precious existence.' The sight of him hobbling out on crutches for practice sessions and having to be helped in to and out of the cockpit must have done wonders for his opponents' confidence but, despite being plagued by cramp, he managed to finish a gallant fifth. The fourth-placed Earl Howe said of Nuvolari's drive: 'Let any who say it was foolhardy at least be honest and admit it was one of the finest exhibitions of pluck and grit ever seen. By such men are victories won!'

Two years later, while Nuvolari was practising for the Tripoli Grand Prix, a wheel of his Alfa Romeo caught a marker stone at over 125mph. The tyre burst, the car turned over and ended up in the sand which bordered the circuit. For his part, Nuvolari was flung into the air like a doll and landed in a heap of parched grass. Helpers who rushed to the scene found the smoking car but no sign of its driver until, ten minutes later, the stricken Nuvolari was located deep in the grass, lying unconscious with damaged ribs and severe bruising. In hospital he was put into plaster and ordered to rest for several days. 'But of course,' came the reply. 'After the race I shall do so!' The next day, although scarcely able to move in his plaster corset, he drove a replacement Alfa into seventh place. It was the stuff of which legends are made.

The Donington Grand Prix had first attracted the mighty German teams in 1937 and had proved such a success (Bernd Rosemeyer winning in an Auto-Union) that they returned in force to the tree-lined Leicestershire circuit for the 1938 race. It was scheduled to be the last major event of the season, listed for 2 October, but when the German teams arrived a week earlier to start practice, they found themselves slap in the middle of the Munich crisis. In case war was about to break out, the Germans hurried home and the race was cancelled, but once Chamberlain had returned with his promise of 'peace for our time', the contest was rearranged for 22 October and the Germans returned.

Three days before the race the 45-year-old Nuvolari took his Auto-Union out for a practice session. That he was now at the wheel of a German car was the result of a considerable fall-out with his Italian employers. He was approximately halfway round the circuit when a huge stag emerged from some woods and ran straight across the track, ploughing into Nuvolari's car. Nuvolari stopped 200 yards further on and limped back to attend to the animal which was lying in a pool of blood. Back at the pits ambulance men were worried by Nuvolari's non-appearance and so they drove off to search for him. They found him stroking the dead stag. 'You cannot take anyone to the hospital,' he said gravely, 'not even this unfortunate one. He died on the spot.' In fact Nuvolari was in need of hospital treatment, having fractured a rib in the collision, but he no longer wanted to be bothered with doctors and nurses. He was not prepared to risk being told he could not drive in the race. Instead he asked for the stag to be taken away and prepared himself for the race. After persuading the organisers to agree to his request to have the stag's head stuffed and mounted, he got out his lucky corset, which he had improvised for himself using tight bandages, and set out to thrill the British public in the same way that he had captivated spectators all over mainland Europe.

In the absence of Rudolf Caracciola, who had burnt his foot during the Italian Grand Prix and in any case was said not to like Donington as a circuit, Hermann Lang took pole in a Mercedes from Nuvolari, Manfred von Brauchitsch in a second Mercedes and the great British hope, Richard Seaman, in a third. Near the back of the grid was an ERA driven by band-leader Billy Cotton. A crowd of 60,000 turned up to watch the Duke of Kent start the 80-lap race with a Union Jack. From the off, Nuvolari shot into the lead from his Auto-Union team-mate Hermann Müller and the Mercedes trio of von Brauchitsch, Seaman and Lang, and stayed at the head of affairs until lap 20 when he went into the pits for a change of plugs. Emerging in fourth spot behind Müller, Seaman and Lang, Nuvolari was about to lap Hanson's Alta when the tail-ender dropped a sump full of oil on the descent to the hairpin. Nuvolari picked his way through the hazard but Seaman was not as fortunate and spun off the road, promoting Nuvolari to third. He was still third after the mid-race refuelling stops but Lang had now taken over pole position from Müller. Driving with typical verve and flair and, according to contemporary reports, a huge grin on his face, Nuvolari proceeded to reel in the front two. He passed Müller and on lap 67 overtook Lang for a lead he was never to relinquish. Showing no ill effects from his severely restricted movement, he pulled away to win by 32 seconds from Lang, Seaman, Müller and von Brauchitsch.

Nuvolari received a rapturous welcome from all except some of the serious punters in the bookmakers' enclosure. They had torn up their tickets when he had looked to be out of the race following his practice accident and now they were furious with themselves. Two days after crossing the finish line the 'Maestro', as he was known, was presented with the Grand Prix trophy along with the mounted stag's head, which he intended to take with him to other tracks as a lucky mascot. It would be another 16 years before a German Grand Prix car would again race on English soil, but in the meantime Nuvolari's epic drive under unbelievably difficult circumstances would provide a lasting memory through the dark days of the Second World War.

THE TIED MONTE

MONTE CARLO RALLY, JANUARY 1939

The 1938 Monte Carlo Rally had seen the introduction of a mountain section through the French Alps, thereby providing an exacting new test and further establishing the event as an all-round examination of driving skills. In particular the ascent and descent of the treacherous Col des Leques had proved such an attraction that the Alpine route from Grenoble was retained for the following year. The Alpine route was divided into five sections and had a target average speed of 31mph. The first section went from Grenoble over the Col de la Croix Haute to St Julien en Bouchène, where the relatively straightforward second section began. Section three was short and sharp – an eight-mile sprint from Barrème to Castellane via the twisty, and invariably icy, Col des Leques. Section four from Castellane to Grasse took the drivers over the Col de Luens, and finally section five was the run through Nice to Monte Carlo.

For 1939, a total of 500 bonus points were awarded to starters from Athens, 498 points from Bucharest or Tallinn, 497 from Stavanger or Palermo, and 496 from John O'Groats or Umea. With every point vital in the final reckoning, 42 of the 121 starters chose Athens, although aviator Amy Johnson was one of 24 setting out from John O'Groats. While the Scandinavian routes were badly hit by snow, a series of landslides near Salonika were cleared in time for the Athens starters to get through. The conditions on the Alps were less severe than had been anticipated – even the Col des Leques was clear – with the result that the majority of the competitors were able to keep within the time limits and not incur penalty points. Since the Alpine route had failed to thin out the field, everything rested on the final two sections – the driving test and the speed hill climb, the latter a new feature for that year. The driving test consisted of a 200-yard sprint, a fast reverse over a line, then another 100-yard dash to the finish.

The joint leaders going into the test were Jean Trevoux and co-driver M. Lesurque (the 1938 runners-up) in a 3.5-litre Hotchkiss, and Jean Paul and co-driver M. Contet in a 3.5-litre Delahaye. Both had started from Athens and both had been unpenalised between Grenoble and Monte Carlo. Moreover, they recorded the same time – 25.8 seconds – for the driving test. They were actually beaten in the driving test by the 1938 winner Bakker Schut in a Ford V8, but he had started from Tallinn where there were fewer bonus points to be earned. So this left Trevoux and Paul still tied for the lead with just the corkscrew hill climb at Eze remaining. Incredibly, they again recorded identical times – 72.6 seconds – in being the fastest up the hill, and so for the first and only time in the history of the Monte Carlo Rally, the event ended in a tie.

THE WRONG SIDE OF THE ROAD

GRAN PREMIO INTERNACIONAL DEL NORTE, 27 SEPTEMBER 1940

This South American marathon produced one of the first major victories in the glorious career of Juan Manuel Fangio, but it so nearly ended in disaster following a horrendous blunder by his mechanic who, disorientated by being in a strange country, forgot which side of the road he was supposed to be driving on and smashed into a private car.

In 1939 the Argentine Automobile Club started work on an ambitious project to link Buenos Aires and New York by road. Hoping that road racing might persuade the relevant authorities to construct a network of paved roads through South America, the AAC conceived the Gran Premio Internacional del Norte, a 5,868-mile race to be run over 13 stages, starting and finishing in Buenos Aires and taking the competitors as far north as the Peruvian city of Lima. Precious little of the route was paved – only the first 400 miles or so to Cordoba – much of the journey through Peru being on mountainous dirt tracks with alarming drops to one, or sometimes both, sides. The climb across the Andes reached altitudes of over 13,000 feet – a daunting prospect for drivers who were not equipped with such essential items as oxygen cylinders. It was to be a tremendous test of stamina and driving skill, the sole respite being a two-day break at Lima.

The 29-year-old Fangio was just starting out in motor sport. Driving a Chevrolet coupé, he faced stiff opposition from brothers Oscar and Juan Gálvez; Ernesto Blanco,

Argentine champion driver of 1936; and Angel Lo Valvo, the 1939 Argentine champion. Familiarising himself with the route before the actual race, Fangio recalled pulling into a remote Bolivian village for the night and asking for the toilet. He was somewhat taken aback to be shown to a patch of waste ground where a pig was rooting around. That was public convenience, Bolivian style.

The race started at one minute past midnight from the stadium of River Plate Football Club, the starting order having been determined by drawing lots. The first stage – between Buenos Aires and the Argentine town of Tucuman – covered 847 miles, a stage distance never before attempted in that type of racing. Enrique Valiente (who drove under the name of 'Patoruzu') led on the initial stretch to Rosario but by Cordoba, the Gálvez brothers had taken over, chased by Boris Afanacenco, Pedro Cavacevich and Fangio. Slowly but surely, Fangio's reconnaissance trip began to pay off and at the end of that long first stage he found himself in the lead. The Gálvez brothers won the second and third stages (to La Quiaca and Potosi respectively), a number of the crews being affected by the altitude on the plains of Bolivia. Among the casualties was Lo Valvo, who had to return from La Quiaca to his native Arrecife when his co-driver and brother-in-law, Antonio Spampinatto, was taken ill as a result of a lack of oxygen. With only one doctor competing in the race, there was little chance of medical attention en route.

Having arrived safely in La Paz at the end of the fourth stage, Fangio was nearly put out of the race through no fault of his own. His mechanic, Héctor Tieri, went to fetch the Chevrolet but forgot that whereas in Argentina they drove on the left, in Bolivia they drove on the right. Setting off on the wrong side of the road, he ploughed straight into another car. The accident left the Chevrolet with a bent chassis and a twisted axle and necessitated hasty repairs before it could set off on the next stage.

Then on the way to Lima a fan blade broke and made a hole in the radiator. The gap was plugged with a handkerchief and a piece of rag, and Fangio continued on his way. The delay meant that he was only 11th on that stage, but he still led overall.

On the return from Lima, the Gálvez brothers went off the road at night, Oscar breaking his shoulder-blade and he and Juan finishing up at the bottom of a ravine with the Ford coupé. Julio Pérez went off at the same corner, leaving his car balancing precariously on the edge of the precipice. Hearing cries, he shone his spotlight into the dark depths of the ravine and located the Gálvez brothers!

The elimination of his closest rivals left Fangio with a lead of some 90 minutes and although he contrived to hit a large rock on the penultimate stage between La Quiaca and Tucuman, he ended up winning as comfortably as anyone could in a race where he never quite knew what was around the next corner and where his mechanic couldn't be trusted to drive more than 100 yards.

RACING ON ICE

SWEDISH WINTER GRAND PRIX,
22 FEBRUARY 1947

Motor racing on ice had been a popular spectator sport in Scandinavia since 1931, when the first Swedish Winter Grand Prix was run on the frozen Lake Rämen. Among the entrants that year was German ace Rudolf Caracciola, but he was unable to master the surface as expertly as the Finnish drivers. For the following year's event a crowd of 60,000 turned up. Lake Vallentuna, north of Stockholm, became a regular venue of ice races from 1934 and it was there, 13 years later, that Reg Parnell and the ERA team swept all before them in the first post-war Swedish Winter Grand Prix.

Manufactured between 1935 and 1939, the ERAs (it stood for English Racing Automobiles) raced with some distinction either side of the war even though only 17 were ever made. Three fell into the hands of Reg Parnell, George Abecassis and Leslie Brooke, who took them to Sweden for the Grand Prix at Rommehed on 9 February 1947. The race turned into an ERA walkover because their chief rivals – the French – were stranded miles away on a ship stuck fast in ice. So it was decided to rerun the event 13 days later on Lake Vallentuna, by which time the French challenge was expected to materialise. Indeed it did, led by Raymond Sommer, but he proved no match for the wily Parnell.

Between the two races Parnell had to arrange for spare parts to be sent over from England after his engine had blown. He also had the idea of fitting twin rear wheels to the ERA to improve its road-holding on the ice of Lake Vallentuna. As a frequent competitor in hill climbs, he owned a set of extra-long hubs to facilitate the fitting of twin wheels, but unfortunately they were at home in England, and he was in Sweden. So he phoned his nephew and instructed him to get the hubs and a spare set of wheels to London Airport and over to Gothenburg that night. When Parnell fitted them to the ERA, Sommer immediately objected but the Englishman had checked the rules beforehand and had found that there was nothing to preclude twin rear wheels.

The race began in temperatures of minus 15 degrees Fahrenheit, most of the drivers wearing RAF flying jackets to keep out the cold. A 3¹/₂-mile circuit had been snowploughed across the lake, the surface of which was sheet ice. Since nobody was permitted to use studded tyres, the organisers had spread fine gravel over the entire course and then sprayed it with water to give it a texture like sandpaper. This certainly improved the grip, but it was Parnell's extra rear wheels which really made the difference. No car could match the road-holding of his ERA and he skated to victory at an average speed of 68.16mph – a triumph of British ingenuity.

THE SILVERSTONE SHEEP

MUTTON GRAND PRIX, SEPTEMBER 1947

It is a sobering thought that Silverstone may never have become the venue for the British Grand Prix but for an animated drinking session in a Worcestershire public house. Fresh from a satisfactory day's competition at the nearby Shelsley Walsh hill climb, a group of drivers were in good spirits at the Mitre Oak, Ombersley, one evening in September 1947 and were discussing where they might be able to race next. Their options appeared strictly limited, Brooklands having been sold and Donington Park still being cluttered with military vehicles. Then one of their number, an enthusiast by the name of Maurice Geoghegan, happened to mention a virtually disused airfield near his home village of Silverstone in Northamptonshire. He said that he had tested a Frazer Nash on the airfield the previous year and had mapped out a perfectly satisfactory two-mile circuit along the perimeter roads and one of the runways. Why didn't they go the next day?

After drinking to what was clearly an excellent idea, the owners of 11 Frazer Nashes and a Bugatti set off for Silverstone the following morning, where they were joined, so the story goes, by the pilot of a passing Tiger Moth who landed on the runway and tried his luck at the wheel of one of the cars. During practice one driver ran over an old garden fork, the impact causing the implement to spring up and stab him in the arm. Although there were reportedly no fewer than four doctors present, none bothered to attend the wound, which finally stopped bleeding of its own accord.

Precious few details are known about the race itself other than that Geoghegan was on the approach to Stowe when his Frazer Nash hit an errant sheep. It was the end of the road for both car and sheep, the latter receiving the scant consolation that the race would be known thereafter as the Mutton Grand Prix. The meeting finished in the time-honoured tradition – at the Saracen's Head, Towcester.

Word got around. Within a year of Geoghegan's pioneering race, Silverstone airfield was staging its first British Grand Prix. Then in 1949 it adopted the familiar perimeter-only layout which remained in use for many years and helped establish Silverstone as the home of British motor racing.

ORANGES AND LEMONS

MILLE MIGLIA, 1 MAY 1948

With petrol still in short supply following the war, the 1948 Mille Miglia was predominantly an Italian affair. Apart from a quartet of Healeys – from the new factory of British rally driver Donald Healey – the 167 starters were mainly Fiats, Ferraris, Alfa Romeos and Cisitalias. Ferrari's competitive debut had been less than a year earlier but the company had made such great strides in that short time that it was able to provide three works Tipo 166 models for Clemente Biondetti, Franco Cortese and the old warhorse, Tazio Nuvolari. At 55, Nuvolari was no longer in the best of health, still suffering the after-effects of inhaling exhaust fumes during a race in Paris two years previously. He had spent several months recuperating in a convent on the shores of Lake Garda, but when Ferrari gave him the opportunity to come out of his semi-retirement, it was an offer he could not refuse. Even so, he did not finally agree to drive until a few days before the race.

The first drivers were flagged away at midnight on 1 May, a process which continued at one-minute intervals until shortly before dawn. The first stage, from Brescia to Padua, saw young Alberto Ascari (son of Antonio) leading in a Maserati from Cortese's Ferrari, Consalvo Sanesi's Alfa Romeo and Nuvolari. Although he was literally spitting blood because of his lung condition, Nuvolari drove like a man possessed and while crossing the Apennines forced his way into the lead. At Rome he was 12 minutes ahead of Ascari with Cortese third,

Sanesi fourth and Biondetti fifth, but the wiry little Mantuan's frantic pace soon began to take a toll of his rivals. Ascari retired soon after leaving Rome on the return journey, as did Cortese and Sanesi.

Nuvolari was flying but, piece by piece, the bodywork of his Ferrari started to object to the rigours to which it was being subjected. He lost his front near-side mudguard in a minor altercation and then, while speeding along, his bonnet somehow became unfastened before a sudden gust of wind blew it over Nuvolari's head and down the mountainside. 'That's better,' shouted Nuvolari to his mechanic. 'The engine will cool more easily.' Next his seat began to come adrift, probably as a result of the vibration from going around tight corners. Nuvolari could feel himself sliding – a sensation which was making him seasick – so he jettisoned the seat and continued the race sitting practically on the frame of the car, using a bag of oranges and lemons as an improvised cushion. Disregarding his ashen-faced mechanic, he gave no thought to slowing down despite the fact that the car was disintegrating around him, and paid the price when a spring shackle broke after the Ferrari had taken a huge hole in the road at over 100mph. Although the car was now virtually reduced to a bare chassis, Nuvolari arrived at Bologna with a healthy lead over Biondetti. There the Ferrari team signalled to him to stop, but he answered with a derisive gesture and sped off into the distance. Further up the road at Modena, Enzo Ferrari watched in despair as Nuvolari flew past. He knew that the car could not possibly hold out much longer and, sure enough, between Reggio Emilia and Parma Nuvolari's brakes failed and the car skidded off the road at a succession of corners. Nuvolari was not one for giving up, but even he realised that it was futile to continue. Utterly exhausted, both mentally and physically, he went to a nearby church to ask the priest if he could lie down for a couple of hours. While he slept, the mechanic telephoned through the news of the Ferrari's retirement.

Biondetti went on to win the race for the third time, by a

record 47 minutes from the Fiat of Comirato and Dumas. Fiats were also third and fourth. However, not for the first time – but sadly for the last – the race was all about the incredible exploits of Tazio Nuvolari.

FARINA IN A HUFF

ITALIAN GRAND PRIX, 11 SEPTEMBER 1949

The usual practice among teams running three or four cars in a race when the drivers were evenly matched was to allow them to sort out the placings for themselves over the opening laps and then to signal to them to maintain those positions for the duration. No team wanted its drivers cutting each other's throats by risking needless overtaking manoeuvres, so it made sense to have an arranged finishing order. And it was equally desirable for the drivers to play some part in reaching that decision. Alfa Romeo, however, had its own ideas. Alfa insisted on picking the winner itself and often signalled the leading Alfa driver to slow down so that a team-mate could overtake him. Not surprisingly, this policy did not always go down well with the drivers.

The first signs of rebellion occurred at the 1946 Turin Grand Prix when the Frenchman Jean-Pierre Wimille was instructed by the Alfa pit to ease off and allow team-mate Achille Varzi through to win. This resulted in a huge post-race row, as a result of which Wimille was dropped from the Alfa team for the forthcoming Milan Grand Prix, an event which was run over two heats and a final. Alfa driver Giuseppe 'Nino' Farina, an Italian doctor of engineering, finished first in his heat but was subsequently relegated to third for jumping the start. As far as Farina was concerned his moral victory in the heat had earned him the right to be allowed to win the final, but instead Alfa announced that Count Felice Trossi was to be given preferential treatment. Obeying team orders, Varzi let Trossi through to the front after a

137

few laps. Farina was now close up in third, but there was no way that Varzi was going to give way this time. Instead the pair were locked in a ferocious duel with Varzi seemingly desperate to prevent Farina from going after Trossi. Eventually the battle took its toll and Farina's brakes started to give him trouble. When he spun at a corner, instead of rejoining the race in third place, he simply retired in a huff because he hadn't been permitted to win. That evening at a local café, his behaviour was described as 'aloof and sulky'.

In the wake of his temper tantrum at Milan, Farina was told that his services were no longer required by Alfa. He did not compete anywhere in 1947, raising speculation that he had retired, but he was back in 1948, and the following year's Italian Grand Prix at Monza found him at the wheel of one of the new Maseratis. The race was eagerly anticipated in Italian circles since it marked the Grand Prix debut of Ferrari and was expected to herald the return to competitive action of Alfa Romeo. The Alfa presence failed to materialise, however, leaving the Ferrari boys to have matters pretty much their own way. Although running in third place, Farina soon realised that his Maserati was no match for the two leading Ferraris. The further into the distance they disappeared, the more despondent he became until finally he once again dropped out for no obvious reason. There was nothing mechanically wrong with his car – he had just given up because he was unable to catch the Ferraris. One of these subsequently retired, meaning that Farina could have finished second, but he was never interested in being second best. Alberto Ascari went on to gain a comfortable victory in his Ferrari from Philippe Etancelin's French Talbot and the Maserati driven by Prince Bira of Siam. Piero Taruffi in the other works Maserati struggled on to finish seventh, 16 laps behind the winner. Farina could not be bothered.

Ironically, following the deaths of Varzi and Wimille in crashes and Trossi from cancer, Farina was given another chance by Alfa in 1950 and went on to win the inaugural World Drivers' Championship. For once he was happy.

THE HELPFUL SPECTATOR

ENDURANCE RECORD ATTEMPT, MONTHLÉRY, 29 SEPTEMBER 1951

At the end of September 1951, Porsche sent a team of five drivers and three cars to the Monthléry autodrome near Paris with the intention of setting a succession of new endurance records over a period of four nights. Despite paying every attention to detail in their preparations, the team only achieved their goal thanks to the intervention of a spectator with a can of petrol.

The five drivers – Petermax Muller, Walter Glockler, Huschke von Hanstein, Hermann Ramelow and Richard von Frankenberg – arrived on the 29th with an 1,100cc coupé, a 1,500cc coupé, and a sports two-seater which Glockler himself had built. On the first night they set about breaking the medium distance records in the 1,100cc class – at 500 miles, 1,000 kilometres and six hours. The existing record speed was 98.16mph but the Porsche averaged over 100mph to establish a new mark.

The main challenge began the following night – an attempt on the world 72-hour endurance record in the 1,500cc class. The previous record of 80.71mph had been set by a 3-litre Citroen as far back as 1935. For over 24 hours the Porsche lapped at a steady 103 to 105mph which, when taking into account stops for refuelling, new tyres and fresh drivers, worked out at an average of around 99mph. Everything was progressing according to plan until the car came in for one of its routine fuel stops and driver changes. As the drivers swapped, the engineer held the fuel hose, the valve was turned on and ... nothing. Not a drop of fuel came out.

For a moment there was stunned silence. Then the mechanics dashed over to the huge fuelling tank wagon which had been specially built for the record attempt. Valves were fiddled with, stopcocks turned, but still not a drop of petrol came out. The man in charge of the tank climbed on to the top to make sure that it wasn't empty. It was half full with 400 gallons. Its reluctance to share it with the car was a mystery.

All the while valuable seconds were being lost. The car had been stationary for over half a minute and the delay was threatening to wreck the record attempt. Just then a Porsche owner, who had driven over from Germany to watch the proceedings, announced that he had a four-and-a-half-gallon canister of petrol in his car. To sighs of relief, he sprinted over to his car and back, and the fuel was safely deposited in the Porsche. The record attempt was back on course.

As the 1,500cc coupé set about making up the lost time, the problem with the tanker was traced to a faulty valve. But no sooner had one problem been overcome than another cropped up. Shortly after 2 a.m., with Muller at the wheel, the gearbox went. Following a ten-minute stop, one of the mechanics managed to engage third gear but no other. Aware that any further delay would be fatal, the decision was taken to drive the remainder of the 72 hours in third gear only! This emergency measure worked reasonably well on the track but was a major headache at the two-hourly pit stops. Starting up in third gear was eventually achieved by the crew pushing the car from 20 yards behind the start line and all letting go simultaneously just before it crossed the line. If so much as one hand had touched the car beyond the starting line, all of the hard work over the previous hours would have been wasted.

In spite of the various misfortunes along the way, Porsche did go on to break the 72-hour record at an average speed of around 95mph. Yet it would all have been so different but for that bystander with his can of petrol.

LEVEGH GOES SOLO

LE MANS 24-HOUR RACE, 14 JUNE 1952

The name of Levegh had been familiar to French motor racing
enthusiasts since the sport began. Once the chosen name of
driver Pierre Velghe (of which 'Levegh' was an anagram), it had
subsequently been revived as a pseudonym for his nephew,
Pierre Bouillon, a seasoned campaigner who, at 46 years of
age, was approaching the veteran stage by 1952.

At Le Mans, Levegh and his young co-driver Marchand
carried the hopes of the French nation at the wheel of a 4.5-litre
Talbot Lago. But they faced formidable opposition from three
Mercedes 300SL sports coupés, six Ferraris and three C-type
Jaguars. In the event, only the Mercedes challenge materialised
since four of the Ferraris went out with assorted clutch,
transmission and electrical problems (and Luigi Chinetti was
disqualified for refuelling one lap early), while Jaguar succeeded
in shooting itself in the foot before the race had even started.
After that year's Mille Miglia, Stirling Moss had observed that
the Mercedes cars had outstanding speed in a straight line.
Mindful of the long Mulsanne Straight at Le Mans, Jaguar tried
to increase the speed of the C-types by restyling their bodywork
with smaller apertures to the radiators. The Jaguars ran hot in
practice, but the lesson was not heeded, and all three cars
dropped out of the race within the first three hours due to
overheating. Ironically, the Mercedes did not turn out to be that
quick at Le Mans after all, and owed their success more to the
failings of others ... which brings us back to Levegh.

In the early stages Talbot found itself second best to a French rival, the 2.3-litre Simca-Gordini of Robert Manzon and Jean Behra which led until just before half-distance when its brakes failed. This left Levegh in control, but he made the mistake of trying to drive the entire race single-handed, flatly refusing to hand over to Marchand even for a short time. Levegh's excuse was that the Talbot's rev counter had broken and he feared that Marchand was too inexperienced to be trusted with the car in that state. But others felt that he was hell-bent on breaking Louis Rosier's record stint of 23 hr 40 min at the wheel on his way to victory in 1950. American owner/driver Briggs Cunningham nurtured similar ambitions but after making it single-handed through to the Sunday morning, he stopped for a call of nature, and in his absence, co-driver Spear seized the opportunity to put in a few laps. They eventually finished fourth.

By midday on Sunday Levegh had a commanding four-lap lead over the two surviving Mercedes (Karl Kling having retired with a broken dynamo), but his driving was becoming increasingly erratic as fatigue started to take its toll. On several occasions, all four wheels were off the track. But still he refused to take a rest. Then with just 50 minutes to go, his stubbornness proved costly. Having driven 2,330 miles without once getting out of the car, and nursing a lead of 25 miles, he made the mistake of selecting first gear instead of third in the pre-selector gearbox, causing a connecting rod in the Talbot's engine to snap. His folly let Mercedes through to score a German one-two (courtesy of Hermann Lang and Fritz Riess, a lap ahead of Helfrich and Niedermeyer), making Levegh the least popular sportsman in France that evening. For the following year new rules were introduced to prevent any driver at Le Mans doing over 80 laps at a time or taking the wheel for more than 18 of the 24 hours. The crazy antics of the likes of Levegh would happily become a thing of the past.

Tragically, that was not the last to be heard of the name Levegh. Returning to the scene of his solo attempt, he was killed in the 1955 24-Hour Race, along with 83 spectators, in a crash for which he was widely – if perhaps unfairly – held responsible.

A TRAGIC INVASION

ARGENTINE GRAND PRIX, 18 JANUARY 1953

The opening race of the 1953 season was the inaugural Argentine Grand Prix in Buenos Aires, a contest which saw local hero Juan Manuel Fangio return to action following a crash at Monza the previous year. But at the end of a disastrous afternoon, it was Giuseppe Farina, not Fangio, whom everyone was talking about.

Farina was driving a Ferrari, along with Alberto Ascari, Luigi Villoresi and the young Englishman, Mike Hawthorn, whose driving in a Formula Two Cooper-Bristol had so impressed the Maranello hierarchy in 1952. With the new Maseratis not yet ready, Fangio, Froilan Gonzales, Felice Bonetto and Oscar Gálvez all had to rely on old models. In trying to keep up with the Ferraris, Fangio twice spun off the wet circuit in practice but still managed a creditable second on the grid to Ascari, with Villoresi and Farina third and fourth fastest respectively.

Argentina loved its motor racing, and the reappearance of Fangio plus fellow countryman Gonzales ensured a bumper crowd in excess of 90,000. However, crowd control left a great deal to be desired and as the circuit threatened to overflow with spectators, several drivers voiced their concerns. Despite this, the organisers remained adamant that everything was under control, and the start was delayed by just four minutes.

Ascari led into the first corner with Gonzales and Fangio disputing second, but Hawthorn started slowly and had

143

dropped from sixth to 13th at the end of the first of 97 laps. Fangio moved into second on lap two but Ascari's Ferrari was proving the faster car and started pulling away by almost a second per lap. Behind these two, the prime movers were Villoresi (who had lost several places through an early pit stop) and Hawthorn, both of whom began to carve their way through the field into the top six.

Then on lap 32, tragedy. A spectator suddenly ran across the track in front of Farina and, in trying to avoid the trespasser, Farina lost control of the Ferrari and ploughed into the crowd. Farina escaped serious injury but ten spectators were killed and 36 injured. With spectators running all over the circuit, it seemed certain that the race would be stopped, but the chaos gradually abated and the racing continued uninterrupted.

Four laps after the fatal crash, Fangio retired when a universal joint on his Maserati broke. This allowed Robert Manzon, driving superbly in a Gordini, to move up to second ahead of Villoresi, Hawthorn, Gálvez and Gonzales. On lap 43 Manzon stopped for a tyre change, but the tyre proved difficult to remove and he lost over two minutes in the pits. He eventually resumed in sixth place, only for his left rear wheel to fly off on lap 68. His gallant race was over.

Ascari went on to win pretty much in his own time from Villoresi, Gonzales and Hawthorn. But the result was of minor importance on what had been a black day for Argentine motor racing.

CALLED FROM THE BAR

LE MANS 24-HOUR RACE, 13 JUNE 1953

The preparation for an endurance race such as Le Mans is all-important. Drivers need to be at the peak of physical fitness with a clear head and razor-sharp reactions. What they do not need is a hangover, which is why the triumphant 1953 drive of Tony Rolt and Duncan Hamilton has entered Jaguar folklore.

Following the 1952 débâcle at Le Mans, Jaguar was anxious to make amends the following year. And this time it boasted an innovation which worked – disc brakes. The inclusion of these at the expense of the traditional drum gave the Jaguar drivers a crucial advantage, allowing them to brake later into corners. The team, which had won in 1951 with Peter Walker and Peter Whitehead, entered three works C-types – to be driven by Walker and Stirling Moss, Whitehead and Jimmy Stewart, and, as reserves, Rolt and Hamilton. The last-named pair would only be able to race if one of the 60 accepted starters dropped out beforehand. Rolt and Hamilton waited more in hope than expectation but by the Friday evening nobody had withdrawn. They were duly informed that their services would not be required.

So they did what most sportsmen would have done in such circumstances – they went out and got drunk... very drunk. Rolt, a former army officer, and Hamilton, an ex-fighter pilot and generally larger-than-life character, drowned their sorrows with a vengeance, and by the early hours of Saturday morning they were suitably mellow. It was then that Jaguar team manager 'Lofty' England finally caught up with them, sitting on a pavement, and informed them that a team had made a late withdrawal from the 24-Hour Race. They were in the race after all. The news that in just over 12 hours' time they would be haring around Le Mans at 100mph should have had an instant sobering effect, but so much alcohol had been consumed that they were still feeling decidedly the worse for wear on the Saturday afternoon. Neither relished the prospect of taking the first stint at the wheel so they tossed a coin to decide who would *not* start. Rolt lost the toss.

Fortunately the fresh air soon cleared their hangovers and after an hour Rolt found himself in third place behind Moss/Walker and the Ferrari 375MM of Luigi Villoresi and Alberto Ascari. During the second hour Moss made two stops to clear a blocked fuel pipe, thereby dropping to 21st and allowing Villoresi to take the lead. But Rolt responded to the challenge by passing the Ferrari and setting a new lap record at 4min 30sec (115mph), over ten seconds faster than Ascari had gone the previous year. Ascari's reply was equally emphatic, lowering the lap record to 4min 27.4sec and instigating a battle with the Jaguar which would last right through the night. But the Jaguar's superior braking always gave it the upper hand and by dawn on Sunday it had a two-lap advantage. After both cars had made routine stops around 8.30 a.m., the Ferrari was heard to have a slipping clutch. Within two hours it had retired, leaving the way clear for Rolt and Hamilton to proceed to an unlikely win.

Although tired following their Friday night excesses, they managed to drive 2,540 miles at an average speed of 105.84 mph – the first time a Le Mans winner's speed had topped 100mph. In fact the first seven cars home all averaged over 100mph. Moss and Walker fought their way back up the field to finish second, with Whitehead and Stewart fourth behind a Chrysler-engined 5.5-litre Cunningham.

As the Jaguar team toasted its success, two of its number were observed celebrating rather more gingerly than usual.

HELL IN BUENOS AIRES

ARGENTINE GRAND PRIX, 16 JANUARY 1955

With echoes of the energy-sapping 1926 European Grand Prix, this race was run in unbearably hot conditions. At the start of the three-hour ordeal, the temperature in the shade at Buenos Aires stood at 100 degrees Fahrenheit while ground temperatures exceeded a staggering 125 degrees. Only the strong or the acclimatised could hope to survive and in the event only two drivers – Juan Manuel Fangio and Roberto Mieres – were able to last the distance. Not surprisingly, both were Argentinians. Everyone else either gave up altogether or had to stop at some point for a rest, enabling a fresher driver to take over, so that in the course of the 96-lap race there were 16 driver substitutions among the 21 starters and more than 50 pit stops.

Froilan Gonzales put his Ferrari on pole, and back on the third row was up-and-coming British driver Stirling Moss, new to Mercedes-Benz for 1955, having been with Maserati. There was a typically mad rush into the first bend and when things sorted themselves out at the end of the opening lap Fangio's Mercedes had a slender advantage over Alberto Ascari (Lancia), Moss, Gonzales and Nino Farina (Ferrari). On the second lap a multiple crash involving Jean Behra and Karl Kling reduced the number of participants to 16, and on the following lap Ascari moved to the front, only to be overtaken soon after by Gonzales. The battle between Ascari and Gonzales raged until lap 22, when Ascari spun on a patch of oil and crashed into the fence.

147

As early as quarter-distance, drivers were coming into the pits in a state of extreme fatigue. After Ascari's retirement, Gonzales stopped for a rest, his car being taken over by Farina who himself had been relieved a matter of a few laps earlier by the Ferrari spare driver, Umberto Maglioli. When Farina soon found the going too tough, he was replaced for a time by Maurice Trintignant who, in a distinction shared with Behra, would go on to drive three different cars in the race. Meanwhile Moss retired on lap 30, too exhausted to continue, and abandoned his Mercedes at the side of the track. Four laps later Fangio, the new leader, stopped for refreshment and the welcome opportunity to pour cold water over himself. The delay allowed Harry Schell's Maserati to seize the initiative but soon the American, too, was affected by the heat and was substituted by Behra. Mieres had a stint in front until he was kept in the pits for ten minutes with fuel pump problems.

It was so hot in the stands that halfway through the race all of the soft drinks supplies had run out, forcing parched spectators to buy wine bottles filled with tap water which were brought in by an emergency fleet of lorries from the surrounding area. An indication of the debilitating nature of the heat was that one Ferrari actually had five different drivers, the car standing idle in the pits for an entire lap because none of the drivers was fit enough to take the wheel. Finally it was Gonzales who, after a prolonged rest and an injection to alleviate back pain, climbed into the cockpit, earning the nickname of 'Cabezon' (the stubborn one) from his home crowd.

Gonzales resumed the struggle a considerable distance behind Fangio but began closing at the rate of five seconds per lap. Fangio was now on the brink of collapse himself and on more than one occasion contemplated giving up. He later recalled: 'Once or twice I felt as if my Mercedes-Benz had caught fire. I turned right round to look, but there was nothing to be seen. It must have been the wind carrying the hot air from below the car, and up round the cockpit to burn my shoulder and neck.' A few laps from the finish Mercedes team boss Alfred Neubauer signalled to Fangio to come into the pits to hand over the car to Moss, who was now suitably refreshed by a shower, but Fangio pretended not to understand and pressed on. He kept going by imagining that he was lost in the snow. His predicament was helped by an accident to Gonzales who pressed so hard that he spun off, bending the Ferrari's front suspension. He was more than happy to hand the car back to Farina, who drove on to the finish. With one supreme last effort, Fangio came home almost two minutes ahead of the Gonzales/Farina/Trintignant/Gonzales/Farina Ferrari with the Farina/Maglioli/Trintignant/Maglioli Ferrari in third. When it came to the prize-giving, Fangio was so tired he could hardly stand. It had been that sort of a race.

HELPING HANDS

ITALIAN GRAND PRIX, 2 SEPTEMBER 1956

The 1956 Formula One World Drivers' Championship all boiled down to the last race of the season, at Monza. The destiny of the title lay between two men with hitherto contrasting careers – Juan Manuel Fangio, the brilliant Argentinian who had been world champion in each of the past two seasons, and Peter Collins, the young British driver who was just beginning to make his mark in Formula One. Fangio had won that year in Argentina, Britain and Germany, while Collins had triumphed in Belgium and France. Under the complicated points scoring system of the time, which took into account a driver's best five finishes, Fangio had 30 points from his best five. In order to add to his total, he had to finish first or second at the Italian Grand Prix. Going into that race, Collins had 22 points from four finishes. So if he were to win at Monza, set fastest lap (which earned an extra point) and Fangio were to finish outside the first two, Collins would snatch the title by 31 points to 30. There was everything to play for.

To complicate matters, Fangio and Collins were team-mates at Lancia-Ferrari. In the absence of Mercedes, who had withdrawn from Formula One in the wake of the 1955 Le Mans tragedy, Lancia-Ferrari had swept virtually all before them in 1956 and Monza looked like being no exception. Fangio took pole position from team-mates Eugenio Castellotti and Luigi Musso, but Collins could do no better than row three. Before the race Fangio had expressed concern about tyre wear, believing that it was the only thing which stood between his team and victory. He suggested to Castellotti and Musso that they carve up the race between them. Fangio offered to set the pace and then towards the finish, to allow the other two through to fight out victory. Fangio was perfectly content with third place so long as Collins wasn't in with a chance of winning. Fangio hoped that the idea of tucking in behind him and thereby conserving their tyres for much of the race would appeal to the two Italians but they wanted no part of it, preferring to go their own way.

As the flag fell, Fangio moved smoothly into the lead but was passed almost immediately by Musso and Castellotti, who seemed to be treating the race as one of five laps rather than 50. Their pace was suicidal and after just five laps, exactly as Fangio had predicted, both dived into the pits with their tyres in shreds, leaving the front four as Fangio, Stirling Moss in a Maserati 250F, Collins, and Harry Schell in a Vanwall. Further down the field, Jo Bonnier, in his first championship race, had taken over Luigi Villoresi's Maserati after four laps but had to retire himself just three laps later with valve trouble. And on lap six the Marquis de Portago's Lancia-Ferrari slid dramatically down the banking after losing a tyre and quit the race with a bent suspension.

Back at the sharp end, Castellotti lost another tyre on lap nine and retired after spinning wildly into the barrier, and two laps later Collins had to stop for a new tyre when lying in fourth. Then on lap 19, sensation. Fangio pulled into the pits with a broken steering arm. The damage could be repaired but the delay would wreck any chance Fangio had of winning the race. The pit signalled for Musso, who had moved up to third, to come in and hand over his car to Fangio so that the championship quest could be resumed, but Musso ignored the instruction and drove on. Eventually, after four laps had been lost, Castellotti drove away in Fangio's repaired car, there being no point in Fangio returning to the fray so far adrift. As each lap passed the Argentinian could see his title hopes disappearing a little further. A world champion without a car.

151

Moss was now in the lead and pulling away from Schell. By half-distance the Englishman's advantage was 13 seconds. On lap 28 Schell stopped to refuel, promoting Musso to second, but two laps later Musso came in for a tyre check. Everyone expected that Fangio would take over, but Musso insisted on continuing. To Fangio's credit, he bore no malice.

Collins managed to get past Schell (who then retired on lap 32 with transmission trouble) and was still in third place on lap 35 when he came in for a tyre check. With Fangio seemingly out of the running, Collins had a very real chance of taking the title but when asked by Fangio's manager if he would consider handing his car over to the world champion, Collins did not hesitate. He jumped out of the cockpit, allowing Fangio to inherit third place. Fangio threw his arms around Collins in sheer exuberance and gratitude and sped off, hell-bent on making the most of his good fortune. Moss was still half a lap ahead of Musso until on lap 45 he ran out of fuel on the back straight. As the car slowed to around 120mph, Moss spotted Luigi Piotti's privately entered Maserati coming up behind in seventh place and gestured to the Italian to give him a shove. The compliant Piotti tucked in behind Moss and proceeded to nudge the works Maserati round the curve to the pits, where Moss was able to refuel!

Moss rejoined in second place behind Musso but with only a ten-second margin over Fangio. Three laps from the finish, however, the steering arm on Musso's car broke as he was exiting the banking and he coasted to a halt in front of the pits. Despite a tyre that was almost bald, Moss held off Fangio's challenge to win by 5.7 seconds.

Moss took the race, Fangio the title, both having received a helping hand in different ways. Afterwards, track officials tried to disqualify Moss because he had been given a push, but Moss protested that Piotti was his team-mate and was therefore permitted to give him a push. In fact, Piotti was a privateer, but the officials swallowed the argument and allowed Moss's victory to stand. As for Collins, was his decision to throw away the chance of the championship an illustration of supreme sportsmanship or sheer stupidity? Collins tried to explain it away by saying that Fangio deserved the title and hinted that he (Collins) would never have been able to cope with the adulation anyway. Whether that would have been the case, we were never to know. For two years later, Collins was killed at the German Grand Prix before ever realising the chance to be world champion.

MONZANAPOLIS

RACE OF TWO WORLDS, 29 JUNE 1957

Seeking a showdown between the different worlds of European and US track racing, the Milan Automobile Club devised this short-lived contest which brought Indy Car racers to Italy. It was staged at Monza, the feeling being that the Americans would be at home on a banked circuit, but proved such a flop that it was scrapped after just two years.

The principal reason why the event failed to live up to its star billing was that the European manufacturers shunned it, the sole opposition to the Indy roadsters coming in the form of three Ecurie Ecosse D-type Jaguars. Jean Behra had intended to race a Formula One Maserati, but the huge tyres with which the American cars were fitted turned out to be a disaster on the Italian entry and had a detrimental effect on its handling. A second Maserati was also withdrawn, leaving the three Jaguars to take on nine Indy cars. The D-types did have a good pedigree. The car driven by John Lawrence was the one in which Ron Flockhart and Ivor Bueb had won at Le Mans the previous weekend, where Jack Fairman's car had finished second. The third car was driven by Ninian Sanderson. But they had little chance against the Indy cars, not least because, fitted with smaller tyres, they were under strict orders from Jaguar team bosses not to exceed 150mph around Monza for fear of tyre failure. With the American cars averaging speeds of over 160mph, it did not take a genius to calculate which team was likely to come out on top.

The race was divided into three 63-lap heats, making a total distance of 500 miles. The cars had to attain a speed of 140mph just to qualify for the race and the writing was on the wall when the three Jaguars found themselves on the last two rows of the grid. On a typically hot Italian summer's day, events got away Indianapolis-style, the cars keeping station 20 yards apart and being led round by a pace car. At the end of the pace lap Fairman took advantage of the Jaguars' four-speed gearbox (the Indy cars had only two gears) and managed to weave his way through the field to the front. He was so surprised that when he looked in his mirror and saw no other cars, he thought there must have been a false start. The illusion was only fleeting. By the end of the next lap three Indy cars had used their superior acceleration to scorch past the D-type, relegating it to fourth. That was as good as it got for the Jaguars. Fairman came eighth in that first heat and followed it up with a fifth and a fourth to finish fourth overall – the highest-placed European. Victory went to Jimmy Bryan in a 4.2-litre Dean Van Lines Special (winner of the first two heats) from Troy Ruttman's John Zink Special (which won the third heat) with Johnny Parsons' Agajanian Special in third.

Despite the poor response from the European teams, the event was repeated the following year when Jim Rathmann won for the US in a John Zink Leader at an average speed of 166.72mph. Stirling Moss drove a Maserati sponsored by the Eldorado ice cream company, but could only finish a distant seventh. Maybe he shouldn't have stopped on every corner...

After another indifferent showing from the Europeans, the Race of Two Worlds was finally put out of its misery through lack of interest.

THE DAY THE TRACK MELTED

FRENCH GRAND PRIX, 5 JULY 1959

Apart from two excursions to Rouen, the fast, triangular circuit at Reims was the home of the French Grand Prix throughout the 1950s. Never a place for the faint-hearted, Reims provided a greater challenge than usual in 1959 when temperatures soared so high that on race day the surface of the circuit started to melt.

The third race of the season following Monaco and Holland, Reims was expected to suit the Ferraris of Tony Brooks, Phil Hill and Jean Behra, and so it proved in the Wednesday practice session with Brooks setting a time of 2min 19.4sec which only Stirling Moss in a BRM could get near. Brooks and Moss were so content with their times that they sat out Thursday practice, during which Brabham's Cooper and Phil Hill nipped ahead of Moss to record the second and third fastest times respectively. These positions remained unaltered on the Friday and, with Saturday free, race day on the Sunday saw Brooks, Brabham and Hill line up on the front row with Moss and Behra on row two. Friday had been hot, but Sunday was even worse and by lunchtime the tarmac on parts of the circuit was beginning to melt in the extreme heat. How it would stand up to 50 laps remained to be seen.

The start was at 2 p.m., and from the flag Brooks went straight into the lead with Moss surging through from the second rank. As the cars passed the grandstands for the first time Brooks still led from Moss, the American Masten Gregory

(Cooper-Climax), Brabham and Phil Hill. Already the surface at Thillois hairpin was starting to break up and soon big stones and lumps of tar were being thrown up by the tyres. As the drivers suffered, Innes Ireland (Lotus) was the first to stop for replacement goggles. On lap eight Graham Hill brought his Lotus into the pits with a stone through the radiator and on the next lap Gregory stopped with a badly cut face and the effects of heat exhaustion.

By the tenth lap Brooks had a four-second lead over Maurice Trintignant's Cooper, followed by Brabham, Moss, Phil Hill and crowd favourite Behra, who had fought his way through the pack after stalling on the starting grid and having to be push-started. On lap 20 Trintignant spun at Thillois and stalled. Although he managed to push-start the car he was so tired that he had to stop at the pits for refreshment before resuming in 12th place. By halfway Behra had worked his way up to fourth, but he had to retire on lap 32 when his engine blew.

All of the drivers were struggling in the intense heat. Brabham recalled: 'I was almost at the stage of collapsing at the wheel, so I broke all the windscreen away with my hand to try to get some air. Every car I got near showered me with bricks and stones. I was coasting into the corners rather than braking, because my feet were so badly burnt that I could hardly put any pressure on the pedals.'

Brabham's discomfort was heightened when Phil Hill passed him as, on lap 38, did Moss. However five laps later Moss stalled at Thillois and, unable to restart without outside assistance, was automatically disqualified. With the circuit continuing to disintegrate, Brooks picked his way around to win from Phil Hill and Brabham, the Australian having to be lifted out of the cockpit at the end of the race. The scene in the pits afterwards was likened to a hospital, with nearly every driver suffering from cuts and bruises caused by flying stones and tar, as well as the heat.

THE FINAL PUSH

UNITED STATES GRAND PRIX,
12 DECEMBER 1959

The final race of the 1959 Formula One season was the United States Grand Prix at Sebring, Florida – the first time that race had counted towards the World Drivers' Championship. Going into it, three drivers still had a chance of winning the title – Jack Brabham (in the revolutionary, rear-engined Cooper-Climax), Stirling Moss (Cooper-Climax) and Tony Brooks (Ferrari). With the best five finishes from the nine races counting, Brabham was six points ahead of Moss and eight ahead of Brooks, but the permutations were such that Moss could snatch the championship with a win and a fastest lap (provided Brabham didn't finish second) and Brooks could tie with the Australian if he won and Brabham failed to score.

During qualifying Brabham was unhappy with his car and decided to swap with his team-mate, 22-year-old New Zealander Bruce McLaren. But this car also needed some fine tuning and Brabham and the mechanics were up until one o'clock on the morning of the race. Grid position was all-important, but here the colourful American Harry Schell threw a spanner into the works by recording what appeared to be an unfeasibly fast time in his very moderate Cooper. Rumours circulated that he had taken a short cut along the back stretch of the bland airfield circuit, but Schell pleaded his innocence. His time of 3min 5.2sec (the third fastest, just ahead of Brooks) seemed too good to be true and Ferrari, who naturally wanted Brooks on the three-car front row, immediately protested. After much argument, Schell insisted on taking his place on the front row alongside Moss and Brabham, thereby relegating Brooks to the second rank. Ferrari were not happy.

The race was to be run over 42 laps (218 miles), and as the flag fell Brabham roared into the lead, only to be quickly passed by Moss. On the first lap Taffy von Trips accidentally rammed his Ferrari team-mate Brooks going into a corner and both went off. This was not the start Ferrari wanted and, after coming into the pits for a precautionary check, Brooks rejoined in a lowly 15th. Of course, if Brooks had been allowed to start on the front row he would, in all probability, have been well clear of von Trips, who started from row three. But for the time being, speculation could wait for another day.

By the fifth lap Moss had increased his lead to ten seconds but the next time round he coasted to a halt with a broken transmission. It would not be the first or the last time that Moss would stand accused of wrecking a car by setting off too quickly, but more important than the whys or the wherefores was the fact that he was now out of the championship equation. Brabham and McLaren proceeded to pull well clear with the race – and the title – seemingly sewn up. By the end of lap 24 there were only seven cars still running. Brooks did his utmost to make up the lost ground, but the deficit was too great and he was left languishing over a minute behind the leading pair in fifth. Although the race appeared to be in his pocket, Brabham was taking no chances and let McLaren slipstream him so that if anything should happen to the leading car, the New Zealander could take over at the front and still beat Brooks to the finish.

Starting the final lap, less than five seconds separated the front three of Brabham, McLaren and Maurice Trintignant, also in a Cooper. Then about a mile from the finish and with victory almost in sight, Brabham's car suddenly began to run on two cylinders. The engine went dead. He was out of fuel. McLaren slowed in sympathy, but Brabham frantically waved him on, fearing that Brooks might somehow snatch an unlikely win. McLaren got the message. Trintignant sped past moments afterwards as Brabham's car crawled around the track, eventually grinding to a complete halt some 500 yards from the finish. He took off his helmet and goggles, climbed out of the car and started to push. 'Why must home straights always be uphill?' he later lamented.

With McLaren and Trintignant already finished, the crowd wondered anxiously what had happened to Brabham. All eyes looked down the track. Then in the distance they spotted a hunched figure in blue overalls pushing his car up the straight. Brooks flashed by to take third and Brabham inched slowly but surely towards the line, encouraged in his efforts by the man waving the chequered flag. Police on motorcycles kept back the excited spectators, who were all too eager to give the weary Australian a helping hand which would probably have resulted in his disqualification. As Brabham himself remarked: 'It must have been the first time the new world champion was escorted to the line by a motorcycle escort.' After five minutes of pushing, he made it across the line and slumped to the ground in exhaustion...safe in the knowledge that he had won the World Championship by four points. It was a most unusual end to a season.

BRABHAM GOES BY TRAM

PORTUGUESE GRAND PRIX, 13 AUGUST 1960

After a faltering start to the defence of his title with disappointments in Argentina and Monaco, Jack Brabham struck a rich vein of form in mid-season, steering the Cooper to victories in four successive Grands Prix – Holland, Belgium, France and Britain. With three races left and Brabham in a commanding position, the championship moved to the street circuit of Oporto for the Portuguese Grand Prix. Each 4.6-mile lap presented a variety of challenges for driver and car, not least cobblestones and tramlines. It was likely to be a bumpy ride.

Among the 15 starters for the 55-lap race were Stirling Moss, recovered from a crash at Spa when a wheel came off, and world motorcycle champion John Surtees in only his second four-wheel Grand Prix. To the surprise of many who thought he would struggle to make the transformation to cars, Surtees put his Lotus on pole, ahead of Dan Gurney's BRM, Brabham and Moss. On the third row, Scotsman Innes Ireland was puzzled to see an Irish flag fluttering above his Lotus, the race organisers having deduced from his surname that he was Irish!

Having stalled his engine on the grid in the previous race (the British Grand Prix), Graham Hill was determined not to miss out again and edged the BRM forward from the second row while waiting for the flag to fall. Finding Hill at their shoulder, the drivers ahead also inched forward so that by the

161

time the flag eventually fell, the entire front row plus Hill were a good car's length over the line. Gurney shot into the lead, only for Brabham to overhaul him at the first corner. Undaunted, Gurney fought back immediately and regained the lead under braking at the end of the straight. And so it was Gurney out in front at the start of a highly eventful lap two.

'After the straight and the left-hander,' remembered Brabham, 'you go uphill and along the tramlines. Then you have to turn left but the tramlines go straight on. I came up and moved inside to overtake but I got myself into the tramlines going straight on like a tram and it was obvious I wouldn't be able to stop. I thought, I'll have to stay in the tramlines all the way to the depot, wherever that is.' Finally he slowed and managed to extricate the Cooper before turning round and heading back towards the circuit. The crazy detour had cost him six places, plunging him from second to eighth.

After five laps Gurney led Surtees by five seconds with Moss in third, but on lap 11 Gurney spun and fell back to fifth. He later retired on lap 25 with engine trouble. Moss was hampered by similar problems which required a number of pit stops, so that at halfway Surtees held a comfortable lead from Phil Hill and Brabham. These two had been enjoying quite a scrap until, on lap 29, Hill missed a gear and ended up among the straw bales which had been spread liberally around the edge of the course as a safety feature.

Almost from the outset fuel had been seeping on to Surtees' canvas driving shoes and on lap 36 this caused his foot to slip off the brake pedal as he was approaching a twisty section. The car hit a kerb, the collision bursting the radiator. With Surtees out of the race, Brabham now led by a minute from his team-mate Bruce McLaren and, after his earlier adventures, the reigning champion was not going to let it slip. The Coopers came home in that order for Brabham's fifth Grand Prix win in a row and his second successive World Drivers' Championship. Fighting food poisoning to finish third at Oporto (which must have made every cobblestone a particularly unpleasant experience) was young Lotus driver Jim Clark in his first full season.

162

Meanwhile Moss ensured that the race concluded in almost as much chaos as it had started. He was lying in fifth on lap 51 when his brakes locked entering a corner. After stalling the car, he tried to restart, but while he was struggling the race finished. Realising this, he turned the car in the opposite direction, restarted it downhill, did a U-turn and crossed the line to finish what he thought was an ingenious fifth. Alas, his initiative was not rewarded and he was subsequently disqualified for driving in the wrong direction.

THE GRAND PRIX WITH NO RETIREMENTS

DUTCH GRAND PRIX, 22 MAY 1961

If the measure of an exciting motor race is frequent pit stops and retirements, then the 1961 Dutch Grand Prix was the most tedious of all time. For the 75-lap, 195-mile race through the sand dunes at Zandvoort passed without a single retirement or indeed a pit stop, making it unique in Formula One history. Fifteen cars started and fifteen finished, the first eight all on the same lap.

The front row of the grid was filled by three rear-engined Ferraris, the Maranello team being the only manufacturer properly prepared for the new 1.5-litre formula so early in the season. American Phil Hill and Germany's Count Wolfgang 'Taffy' von Trips – one of the sport's great characters – recorded identical times in practice, with Richie Ginther (another American) just 0.2 seconds slower. Von Trips jumped into the lead from the flag, followed by Hill, but Ginther got away slowly and dropped back to seventh. Jim Clark challenged Hill for second spot in the early stages, the Lotus making up for its relative lack of speed on the straights by being quicker than the Ferrari at cornering. Clark, however, dropped back a little as the race progressed, the handling of his car deteriorating with a reduced fuel load. Up front, von Trips continued merrily on his way, leading from start to finish, Hill tucking himself in second behind his team-mate. Clark finished third and, after an ongoing battle, Stirling Moss passed Ginther at the hairpin on the final lap and crossed the line in fourth, a wheel ahead of the Ferrari. The top five were covered by just 22 seconds.

Sadly the inactivity of Zandvoort was not repeated through the rest of the season. In the penultimate race at Monza, championship leader von Trips – and 15 spectators – were killed after the Ferrari tangled with Clark's Lotus. This left Phil Hill to become world champion in the most tragic of circumstances.

THE F1 TRACTOR

OULTON PARK GOLD CUP, 23 SEPTEMBER 1961

Every now and again a car comes along that is so unorthodox it stops the motor racing world in its tracks. Such a vehicle was the Ferguson tractor company's P99 which, in 1961, became the first four-wheel drive car to win a Formula One race.

Everything about the P99 was different. Not only did it have four-wheel drive, but its engine was at the front at a time when all other Formula One cars had switched to rear engines. It was the brainchild of Fred Dixon and former Jaguar driver Tony Rolt, who teamed up with Harry Ferguson to develop a four-wheel drive prototype. It showed such promise that it was entered for the 1961 British Grand Prix at Aintree. Stirling Moss drove it in practice but Jack Fairman took over for the race itself. Its outing ended prematurely when, following a pit stop to rectify ignition trouble, mechanics had to push start it. The Cooper team were particularly vociferous in their complaints, as a result of which the Ferguson was black-flagged and disqualified.

Its third public appearance was at the 1961 Oulton Park Gold Cup, the last major race of the British season. Although the car had failed to finish in its two previous starts, with Moss back at the wheel it took an instant liking to the picturesque Cheshire circuit and clocked the second fastest practice time – just 0.2 seconds behind Bruce McLaren's Cooper-Climax. Making up the four-car front row were Graham Hill (BRM) and Jim Clark (Lotus). The race started badly for the

Ferguson, Moss struggling to engage first gear off the grid, as a result of which it was Clark who led into Old Hall Corner on the first of the 60 laps. When they passed the stands again, Moss was down in fourth.

The wet track, however, suited the Ferguson and its superior traction, allied to its unique transmission which enabled it to out-brake every other car, allowed Moss to make rapid progress. Hill had taken the lead on lap three but by lap six he was forced to yield to Moss. Hill, whom *The Times* said had 'become a most skilful and determined driver', managed to stay with Moss for a few laps but the BRM's engine then began to lose power and he dropped back. Clark retired with a broken front suspension and Hill now found himself under attack from the Cooper of Jack Brabham, who had moved up into third ahead of McLaren. Hill gallantly kept the Australian at bay for almost 20 laps until Brabham got past along the Avenue. Shortly afterwards Hill retired with a broken piston.

For all the activity behind him, Moss remained unflustered, even finding time on more than one occasion to wave to an acquaintance as he negotiated the left-hander at Cascades. As the track dried out, he set a new lap record, proving the car to be no 'wet-road freak' as *Motor Sport* put it. At an average speed of 88.83mph, he went on to win by nearly a minute from Brabham with McLaren in third – sweet revenge on the Coopers for the Aintree incident. It was Moss's fourth Gold Cup success and one which was welcomed enthusiastically by delighted members of the Ferguson research team.

Yet the P99 was never able to fulfil its potential. It later took part in the Tasman series of races in Australia and New Zealand and in 1964 Peter Westbury drove it to victory in the British Hill Climb Championship. It became used as a test vehicle for Ferguson Research and ended up at the Donington Museum. But its day of glory was not forgotten and as recently as 1997 Moss named it as his favourite Formula One car. High praise indeed for the bastard son of a tractor!

THE POST-RACE COLLISION

FRENCH GRAND PRIX, 8 JULY 1962

It is virtually unheard of for two Grand Prix cars to crash into each other *after* the race has finished, but that is precisely what happened at the end of an eventful 1962 French Grand Prix.

The race was returning to Rouen for the first time in five years, but without the Ferraris because of a strike in Italy. For this, the fourth race of the World Championship season, Jim Clark put the new Lotus 25 on pole, ahead of Graham Hill's BRM and Bruce McLaren's Cooper. The three drivers each had a win to their credit that year. Hill crossed the line first in the Dutch Grand Prix at Zandvoort, McLaren emerged victorious in Monaco and, three weeks before Rouen, Clark had picked up his first championship win, at Spa. And now just 0.6 seconds separated the three different marques on the front row in France.

Hill got away first from Clark and McLaren but his BRM team-mate Richie Ginther stalled on the grid and had to be pushed to the pits, finally joining the race almost a lap in arrears. By lap three of 54, John Surtees' Lola had moved up to second and was threatening Hill but a pit stop through fuel starvation on unlucky lap 13 dropped Surtees back to eighth. The Coopers were also proving surprisingly unreliable. Jack Brabham had to retire on lap 11 with a collapsed rear suspension and McLaren's car was plagued with the same problem. Although the New Zealander was able to rejoin the race, the delay had cost him any realistic chance of victory.

Up front, Hill had pulled out a healthy 22-second lead over Clark by lap 30. He had just lapped Jack Lewis for the second time when the Cooper's brakes failed and the car rammed Hill's BRM under braking for the next corner, sending Hill in a spin. This mishap enabled Clark to sneak through, only for the Scot to retire three laps later with a faulty front suspension.

With 12 laps remaining and a 25-second advantage over Dan Gurney's Porsche, Hill seemed assured of his second win of the year, but then the BRM developed a fuel-injection difficulty and came to a halt at the hairpin, allowing Gurney to go on and gain his and Porsche's first championship victory. Having fought his way back up through the field, Surtees slipped down again with gearbox trouble, and so South African Tony Maggs was able to finish a surprise second in a Cooper, a lap behind the winner. Ginther was a further lap back in third.

But the real drama of the race was yet to come. As Surtees crossed the line in fifth and headed for the pits, he found his way blocked. At that point, Maurice Trintignant's Rob Walker-entered Lotus came rushing through in seventh and, swerving to avoid Surtees, left eighth-finisher Trevor Taylor in a works Lotus with nowhere to go. Taylor smashed into Trintignant at 80mph, wrecking both cars but fortunately causing no lasting damage to either himself or the Frenchman. It was an expensive end to the day for both Rob Walker and Lotus.

THE GREAT ESCAPE

MONACO GRAND PRIX, 30 MAY 1965

Graham Hill and Monaco were made for each other. That raffish air, the fast life, the glitz, the glamour, no wonder it was his favourite circuit. Of his five wins there, he always rated his 1965 victory to be the finest – largely because he achieved it despite finding himself up an escape road a quarter of the way through the race.

Precision is the key to Monte Carlo. As Hill himself once remarked, there is nowhere to spin. If you get a corner slightly wrong, you run the risk of bouncing off hotels, nightclubs, telegraph poles or street lamps. Every yard of the 195 miles requires absolute concentration.

The 1965 World Championship was a stuttering affair. The first race had been on New Year's Day in South Africa where Jim Clark had won in a Lotus. The second race – at Monaco – was five months later, but Clark was absent on Indianapolis 500 duty. Having won there for the two previous years, Hill was hot favourite and sure enough he put the BRM on pole from Jack Brabham, now driving a car bearing his name. Both Brabham and Hill had new team-mates, of whom much more would be heard in years to come. With Dan Gurney also at Indianapolis, the second Brabham-Climax was driven for the first time in a championship race by New Zealander Denny Hulme. And Hill was partnered by a young Scotsman, Jackie Stewart, who excelled himself to go third fastest in the BRM in only his second Grand Prix. Indeed on Friday practice

Stewart had announced his arrival in no uncertain terms by actually going 0.2 seconds faster than Hill, but the BRM team leader regained the initiative in final qualifying on the Saturday afternoon. At the back of the grid – on their Grand Prix debuts – were two Hondas. Since the team had been guaranteed two starting places, the unlucky Jochen Rindt in a Cooper was excluded despite having lapped faster than Richie Ginther's Honda. Ironically, Ginther retired at the end of the first lap with a broken driveshaft. Rindt's time would come.

Hill led from the start, pursued by Stewart, Lorenzo Bandini and John Surtees in the two Ferraris, and Brabham. The BRMs began to pull away from the Ferraris at the rate of about a second per lap and appeared to have everything in control. Then on lap 25, Hill came out of the tunnel at around 120mph and as he started to brake in readiness for the chicane, he saw Robert Anderson's Brabham approaching the chicane at a crawl, a universal joint having broken. Realising to his horror that Anderson was going to be occupying the chicane at precisely the same time that he intended to fly through it at 95mph and that there was only room for one car, Hill slammed on the brakes as hard as he could. He later wrote: 'I made as if to go through the chicane and I left things until the point of no return, and then I saw that there was just no way I could get through without clobbering him. I came off the brakes for a second so that I could steer and changed direction down the escape road. Then I stood on them again and I left some rare old skid marks.'

The BRM ground to a halt well up the escape road. Hill quickly jumped out of the car, pushed it backwards on to the track, climbed in again and restarted the engine, all of which took some 35 seconds and dropped him back to fifth behind Stewart, Bandini, Surtees and Brabham.

Cursing his luck, Hill set off in hot pursuit of the leaders. 'I was a bit cheesed off over the whole business,' he remarked. 'If I had come by a second later I would have been able to get through, but as it was, I just couldn't get down to a sufficiently slow pace to follow Anderson through the chicane at his speed.

171

It was bad luck that he just happened to be in that position.'

On lap 30 Hill caught Stewart, who had spun away his lead at St Devote, and four laps later the youngster moved over and waved his team leader through. Meanwhile Brabham passed both Ferraris to take the lead, only to drop out with engine trouble on lap 43. Hill was now third behind the two Ferraris and began attacking them for all he was worth, repeatedly shattering the lap record. He got past Surtees on lap 53 on the short downhill stretch leading from Casino Square, and after sitting patiently on Bandini's tail for 12 laps, he pounced on the Italian at the same spot. Surtees, too, overtook Bandini and actually closed to within two seconds of Hill but Hill reacted by setting another new lap record to reaffirm his position. Surtees' plucky drive came to an untimely end on the penultimate lap when he spluttered to a halt having run out of fuel, but as only Hill, Bandini and Stewart completed the full race distance, he was still classified fourth.

So Hill recorded an improbable victory, born out of adversity, and one which emphasised why he was the uncrowned King of Monaco. Overshadowing even his own little excursion, the most spectacular moment of the race occurred at the entrance to the chicane on lap 80 when Paul Hawkins' Lotus spun through the straw bales, went over the edge of the quay and ended up in the harbour in much the same manner as Alberto Ascari ten years earlier. Hawkins was unhurt, but as Hill could have testified, there were more practical ways of getting through the chicane in moments of crisis.

THE DEMOLITION INDY

INDIANAPOLIS 500, 30 MAY 1966

The Americans were hell-bent on revenge. They were still smarting from the previous year when Jim Clark had the effrontery to become the first British driver to win the Indianapolis 500. The US press had poured scorn on the Scotsman's chances before that race and had afterwards been forced to eat humble pie, never the most popular American dish. They were adamant that there would be no repeat performance in 1966. The Brits were going to be put in their place.

In the build-up to the world's largest single-day sporting event (attracting a crowd in excess of 400,000), the Americans were full of confidence despite a three-pronged British assault from Clark's Lotus, and the Lolas of Graham Hill and the emerging Jackie Stewart. Both Hill and Stewart were making their debuts at the Brickyard – in Stewart's case it would be his one and only appearance – but their drives would leave a lasting impression after a hugely eventful race in which most of the drama was packed into the start and finish.

The American talent on show included five cars from Dan Gurney's new Eagle team, but it was young Mario Andretti who took pole in a Brawner-Ford. Alongside him on the front row was Clark's Lotus, Hill qualifying a disappointing 15th. Right at the back of the grid was Bobby Grim's Watson-Offy, the only front-engined car in the race. The start could scarcely have been more sensational. Indianapolis was no stranger to

173

spectacular pile-ups but this was extraordinary even by its standards. After just 100 yards Billy Foster and Gordon Johncock collided going into Turn One and 14 more cars piled into the wreckage, wheels flying in every direction. Some spectators were slightly hurt by flying debris but when the dust settled, the only permanent damage was to the 11 cars – a third of the field – which were eliminated. An hour and a half later the race was restarted. Andretti shot into the lead from Clark, while further back Hill had a tricky moment on Turn One when his car hit a patch of oil left over from the multiple crash. Andretti maintained his advantage until he was black-flagged with smoke pouring from his car, caused by a defective valve. Clark took over at the front but his hopes of a repeat victory were dashed by a spin on Turn Four on lap 62 which cost him 25 seconds and allowed Lloyd Ruby's Eagle to step into top spot. When Clark spun again on lap 84 and lost the best part of a minute in the pits, Stewart, who was enjoying a remarkable drive, went second. All three Brits were now very much in contention, Hill having moved steadily through the field, but at 350 miles, Ruby looked the likely winner, only to be black-flagged himself due to the appearance of ominous clouds of smoke. Suddenly Stewart found himself in the lead, and there he stayed until just ten laps from the finish when he dropped out with engine failure. It was a cruel blow and he walked back to the pits to a tremendous ovation from the crowd who, in spite of their partisanship, were appreciative of what had been a courageous debut on arguably the world's most intimidating race track.

With Hill and Clark now vying for the lead, it seemed certain that victory would go to a British driver...but which one? At the end of the race, by which time only seven cars were still running, both men thought they had won. Lotus team boss Colin Chapman told Clark that he was the winner and the Scot duly completed a lap of honour. However, Hill was equally sure that he had won and both cars headed for Victory Lane. The dispute concerned lap 175, on which Hill had passed Clark. Lotus insisted that Hill had merely unlapped himself but Lola thought Hill had been moving into second. Clark's sponsor, the forthright Andy Granatelli, stormed: 'How could Hill win when they were announcing and showing on the scoreboard that Stewart and Clark were running one-two and Hill was half a lap away on the backstretch? If that was the case, Hill had been leading all the time and Stewart was never in front. We lapped Hill on the 47th lap and we were running faster than him the rest of the way.' When it was put to Hill that there had been a mix-up in the timekeepers' box, he simply brushed it aside.

The official timekeepers agreed with Hill and awarded him the race by 41.13 seconds from Clark. Granatelli backed down graciously, admitting that he had been as confused as everyone else. 'On the 47th lap we lapped Graham Hill,' he said. 'On the 50th it was announced that we had lapped all but the first five and that Hill was running ninth. But when Clark spun on the 62nd lap, Hill got by. We didn't see him do it and assumed Clark was still in front.'

In becoming the first rookie to win the 500 since George Souders in 1927, Hill averaged 144.32mph. So at the end of a race in which the first-corner carnage thereafter earned it the nickname of the 'Demolition Indy', the Americans were left licking their wounds for the second successive year. Hill mischievously suggested that in future they should award a trophy for the first American to finish. The reply was probably not printable.

CLASSICAL GAS

INDIANAPOLIS 500, 31 MAY 1967

Andy Granatelli had an eye for the main chance. Bouncing back from the previous year's disappointment at Indianapolis, he spotted a loophole in the United States Auto Club rules which enabled him to enter a gas-turbine powered car in the 500. Its appearance created a sensation, all the more so since it came within eight miles of victory, only to be cruelly denied by the failure of a part with an estimated value of $5.

Granatelli had noticed that Indy rules at the time imposed no limitations either on engine size or gas turbines. So he commissioned the construction of a Ferguson four-wheel drive chassis powered by a 540bhp Pratt and Whitney ST6 turbine built by United Aircraft in Canada. The rest of the car was secretly built in-house so as not to alert possible competition. The turbine offered major advantages over piston-driven engines, including excellent fuel economy and tremendous acceleration. The dayglo-red car was entered by STP-Paxton and financed by the STP fuel-additive company, whose president was Granatelli. Wide and bulbous, it was christened the 'whooshmobile' by the press on account of its stealth and practically silent engine. Journalists flocked to interview its driver, Parnelli Jones, already an Indy 500 winner in 1963 and the man who had stunned the racing world in 1962 by capturing pole at what was thought to be the ultimate Indy speed of 150.37mph. Some queried whether the 'whooshmobile' was legal; drivers complained about the heat haze it emitted. But Granatelli was having none of it.

Boosted by their recent successes in the event, a number of Formula One drivers took part in the 1967 Indy 500 – previous winners Jim Clark and Graham Hill (Lotus) being joined by Jackie Stewart (Lola), Denny Hulme (Eagle Ford) and Jochen Rindt (Brabham BT25). But race day on the 30th turned out to be a damp squib, torrential rain causing the race to be stopped after just 17 laps. It was restarted the following day, the first time the 500 had ever been run over two days.

Despite qualifying only sixth fastest, Jones announced his intentions with a breathtaking start. He passed four cars on the outside of Turn One and then took Mario Andretti after Turn Two to snatch the lead in dramatic style. Even seasoned Indy fans had never seen anything quite like it. He went on to dominate the race, taking the shortest route – the inside – and leading for 171 laps en route to what appeared certain to be a famous victory. Meanwhile the European challenge failed to live up to its promise. Hill retired on lap 31 with a burned out piston and Clark dropped out seven laps later. Rindt retired after 108 laps while Stewart, who had started 29th from 33, had worked his way up to third on lap 170 when the car developed engine trouble.

Out in front, Jones continued serenely on his way – well, as serenely as anyone can at 150mph plus. With just three and a half laps to go, he had a lead of 30 seconds over A.J. Foyt's Coyote-Ford when the turbine car suddenly began to billow smoke. A minor gearbox bearing had failed and the 'whooshmobile' coasted to a halt. So near but yet so far for the turbine trailblazer.

Foyt made the most of his good fortune despite a five-car pile-up in front of the stands on his final lap. One car burst into flames but Foyt managed to pick his way through the smoke and debris at 50mph to win his third 500 at a record average speed of 151.207mph. Al Unser was second, Joe Leonard third and New Zealander Hulme a brave fourth. Jones was officially placed sixth.

Afterwards, Jones commented ruefully: 'You've got to have luck to win the 500. Foyt had some.'

Jones announced his retirement after the race but Granatelli tried again the following year with a modified version of the 'whooshmobile' driven by Joe Leonard for Lotus. Once again, the fates conspired to rob Granatelli of victory. Leonard was five seconds ahead of Bobby Unser's Eagle with just seven laps left when the shaft broke in the fuel pump of the gas turbine. Leonard rolled to a halt and Unser went on to win. That was to be the turbine's last stand, as new rules were introduced outlawing them at Indianapolis. As someone once said of Prohibition, it had been a noble experiment.

A HARE'S BREADTH

ITALIAN GRAND PRIX, 7 SEPTEMBER 1969

Jackie Stewart's Matra had dominated the 1969 season. With victories in South Africa, Spain, Holland, France and Britain to his name, he had turned the Formula One World Drivers' Championship into a one-horse race. The only question to be answered was precisely when he would clinch the title. Following a rare display of fallibility when he retired at the German Grand Prix, Stewart and the circus moved to Monza. Even if he failed in Italy, there were still three more races to come but he had no intention of letting matters drag on unnecessarily. The Italian Grand Prix had a recent history of close finishes. Two years earlier John Surtees had pipped Jack Brabham by 0.2 seconds. This one would prove even tighter, with no fewer than four drivers harbouring hopes of victory going into the last corner of the last of the 68 laps.

Qualifying put Austrian Jochen Rindt on pole in a Lotus alongside the 1967 world champion Denny Hulme in a McLaren, while Stewart shared the second row with the Brabham of Briton Piers Courage. Rindt was first away, followed by Stewart, but the positions were reversed after the Lesmo Curves. With a clear road ahead of him on the second lap, Stewart spotted a tiny movement in the distance. It was a hare. Suddenly the animal darted towards the Matra. There was no chance – or indeed desire on a crowded race track – to take avoiding action and the hare smacked into one of the car's front tyres. Stewart's immediate concern was that a bone from

179

the hare might cause a puncture. From then on, he closely monitored the shape of the tyre, looking for any sign of abnormality.

Before the inevitable chicane came to town, the high-speed Monza circuit was ideally tailored for slipstreaming and as the race unfolded, a gaggle of eight cars jostled for the lead – Stewart, Rindt, Hulme, Jean-Pierre Beltoise (Matra), Jo Siffert (Lotus), Bruce McLaren, Courage and Graham Hill (Lotus). Positions among this leading group chopped and changed on a regular basis but, one by one, Hulme, Siffert and Hill all fell away with mechanical trouble. Courage also slipped back, leaving the remaining quartet to fight it out. At the start of the last lap, the order was Stewart, Rindt, Beltoise, McLaren, with under half a second covering the four. Rindt snatched the lead at the sweeping right-hander, the Curva Grande, and held on through the Lesmo Curves but going into the long, final bend, the Curva Parabolica, both Stewart and Beltoise made their moves. Utilising Stewart's slipstream, Beltoise edged out and then dived inside, seizing the lead momentarily. But he had shown his hand too soon. The Frenchman's impetus carried him wider than he would have wished and Stewart was able to sneak up the inside with Rindt in his slipstream. Having prepared his car with a fourth-gear ratio specifically for such an eventuality, Stewart saw his decision bear fruit as he just managed to hold off Rindt on the 250-yard dash to the flag. They flashed across the line virtually side by side but Stewart had his nose in front by approximately half a length of racing car. The official distance was 0.08 seconds, at the time the closest-ever winning margin in a championship race. Beltoise was 0.09 seconds further back in third with McLaren a mere 0.02 seconds behind him. Thus the first four were covered by 0.19 seconds. It was that close.

So Stewart claimed his crown and the Italian crowd saw a tremendously exciting race. In fact the only real loser on the day was the hare.

THE FALL GUY

TAP PORTUGAL RALLY, OCTOBER 1969

By 1969 the Autumn in Portugal Rally, sponsored by the country's national airline, TAP, was in its third year. It had proved a popular addition to the rallying calendar, not least in Britain for whom Tony Fall had won the 1968 event in a Lancia. Fall was back the following year to defend his title, but this time the ending was shrouded in controversy when he was disqualified for giving his wife a lift!

There were 126 entrants, representing 11 different countries, among them 19 British cars, 11 of which started from London. The five-day event had a multi-start from various European cities progressing to a converging point at San Sebastian in northern Spain. Ten special stages took their toll, as did the wet cobblestones which were a feature of many Portuguese village squares. Other competitors got lost, broke down or were simply not quick enough, as a result of which only four cars completed the route within the time allowance. Leading was Fall in a 1,300cc Lancia, who had made such good time that he arrived at the final control a few minutes early. Stopping some ten yards short of the actual control zone, he became concerned when the car was mobbed by well-wishers, eager to greet the likely winner. Such was the commotion that Fall's wife, who was waiting to meet him, was in danger of being crushed against the side of the Lancia, so he allowed her to hop in and take refuge. She was still in the car when Fall's time card was stamped a few yards along the road and consequently he was disqualified for carrying an 'unauthorised passenger'.

Although Fall carried his 'passenger' for only a short distance and in mitigating circumstances, it was technically a breach of the rules. However, those who considered his treatment harsh point to the fact that a Portuguese driver, F. Romaozinho, was subsequently declared the winner...

ON TOW AROUND MONZA

CARAVAN SPEED TRIAL, MONZA, OCTOBER 1969

When Caravans International announced that it was staging a speed trial in which two cars would tow caravans around Monza for 5,000 miles over a period of three and a half days, the first question on everyone's lips was: why? Perhaps the idea was in response to Jackie Stewart's concerns about Formula One safety – after all, giving a Ferrari or a Lotus a caravan to tow would certainly have had the desired effect of reducing speeds on Grand Prix circuits... all the more so if the likes of Clay Regazzoni and Jacky Ickx had to stop every couple of laps to shut the caravan door! Instead it seems that the exercise was simply an attempt to demonstrate the reliability and durability of the humble caravan.

The two vehicles taking part were a Ford Cortina 1600 (towing a four-berth, 10-foot caravan) and a more powerful Ford Corsair 2000E (towing a bigger and therefore heavier four-berth caravan, 12ft 6in long). A team of nine drivers (including two reserves) was assembled to work in three-hour shifts. To qualify beforehand, the drivers had to do two laps without stopping at 37.5mph, then two laps at 44.5mph, and finally two laps at 52mph. Obviously there was a little leeway either side of these figures.

One might think – and with some justification – that towing a caravan round and round a deserted race track for over three days and nights at a steady speed of 60mph would achieve a level of mind-blowing tedium normally reserved for Channel

5 entertainment shows. As a spectator sport, it would be considered on a par with tile-grouting or pro-celebrity ironing. Yet the event was far from incident-free, enlivened considerably by the hundreds of rabbits which come out to play when Monza is not invaded by the *tifosi*. Other things went bump in the night, notably a wolf-like animal which Alan Hayes hit at 2 a.m. on the back straight while doing 70mph. The Cortina suffered a little damage but was able to continue after a two-minute stop to straighten out the wing. The mystery beast was left at the side of the track. On another occasion Ian Mantle encountered two young motorcyclists trying to ride up and down the banking and was fortunate to be able to squeeze car and caravan through between them. And John Yoxall narrowly avoided a young woman who had tried climbing the banking on foot but was sliding down out of control . . .

An additional hazard was the fog which had a habit of descending on the circuit at night, making it not only difficult to spot the rabbits but also to maintain the speeds necessary to produce a healthy average rate. After two days the Corsair began to lose a little power and resorted to following in the Cortina's slipstream for long periods, but overall it was the bigger-engined car which came out on top. The Corsair (which made a total of 23 pit stops and lost 18 minutes for a generator change) covered the 5,000 miles in 81hr 22min at a speed of 61.44mph; the Cortina (with 27 pit stops) did the same distance in 82hr 47min at a speed of 60.42mph.

As for the caravans, they were towed impeccably throughout, any damage sustained being negligible. Happily, however, nobody present at Monza over those three days thought they had seen the future of motor racing.

PUNCH-UP AT THE PALACE
SHELL FORMULA THREE CHAMPIONSHIP, ROUND 11, 3 OCTOBER 1970

By 1970 James Hunt had only been racing for three years, but in that time he had already earned a reputation as someone whom trouble seemed to follow around. His proposed debut, at Snetterton in 1967, came to nought after he was refused permission to race because his Mini had no windows. Two years later he had worked his way up to Formula Ford but was prevented from taking part in a European Championship race at Vallelunga in Italy because he did not have the necessary medical certificate. His reaction was to sabotage the start of the race by deliberately parking his car at right angles across the front of the grid! As controversy continued to dog his every move, a fellow competitor's mother remarked that Hunt always carried £5 on him in those days so that he had enough money for a protest. He was never one to shrink away from confrontation.

By 1970 he had entered the ranks of Formula Three and was making people sit up and take notice for the right reasons. Competing in the Shell Formula Three Championship, he had scored points in five of the ten rounds, including a second at Oulton Park and a third at Cadwell Park. In between he had also posted his second major Formula Three win, in a non-championship race at Zolder in Belgium. So his star was definitely in the ascendant when he came to the compact Crystal Palace circuit in South London for round 11, the penultimate race in the series.

Driving a Lotus 59, Hunt finished second in his heat, thereby qualifying for the final. With BBC *Grandstand* cameras covering the event, there was huge anticipation that the drivers would put on a memorable show for the armchair audience. Hunt made sure the TV viewers got more than they bargained for.

Australian David Walker, lying second in the championship, took the race by the scruff of the neck and so the main interest centred on the six-car battle for second place, which included Hunt's Lotus and a March 703 driven by Dave Morgan. Approaching the last corner on the penultimate lap, the two cars were virtually abreast but Hunt appeared to have the better line. However Morgan refused to yield, with the result that the pair collided, the Lotus ending up in the middle of the track and the March embedded in the pit wall, both minus one wheel. Hunt exploded, leapt from his car, rushed over to Morgan and lunged at him, aiming a punch which, perhaps fortunately for both parties, missed by a country mile. Morgan recalled: 'The silly arse leapt out of his car and ran across the track, all these racing cars coming past him. I was amazed he wasn't run over. I was trying to undo my helmet and as he turned to punch me I lost my balance and fell so he missed. Then other people got hold of him and dragged him off.'

Autosport wrote that 'a justifiably enraged Hunt felled Morgan in the heat of the moment' but *Motor Sport* adopted a less partisan line, reporting: 'A stewards' enquiry was convened but by then Hunt had regrettably resorted to fisticuffs to settle his differences. This is very much against the spirit of camaraderie which exists in motor racing and was greatly deplored.'

Hunt was widely pilloried over his latest transgression by people who saw him as a hot-headed upstart who was bringing the sport into disrepute. Hunt protested his innocence and at the subsequent RAC tribunal, which both drivers were summoned to attend, he produced BBC footage of the incident. This clearly showed that his car had not hit Morgan's first. Furthermore three other drivers testified that, in their opinion, Morgan had overtaken in a dangerous manner. Consequently the outcome of the tribunal was that Hunt was exonerated and Morgan was banned for a year.

For Hunt at least, the punch-up at the Palace had a happy ending. But it would by no means be his last brush with authority.

MAD DOGS AND MEXICANS

MEXICAN GRAND PRIX, 25 OCTOBER 1970

The 1970 season was a sad one for Formula One, the death of Jochen Rindt at the Italian Grand Prix resulting in the first posthumous world champion. Somewhat appropriately, the year ended in turmoil with a chaotic Mexican Grand Prix which posed serious questions about the control of both humans and animals.

There were only 18 starters for the 65 laps of the Mexico City track as the organisers, on a limited budget, still adhered to the practice of paying starting money rather than allocating prize money according to finishing order. At 44, Jack Brabham had announced that this would be his final race but he showed no sign of easing up and made fourth fastest on the grid behind Clay Regazzoni (Ferrari), Jackie Stewart (Tyrrell), and Jacky Ickx in the second Ferrari. As expected, race day was warm and sunny, but what nobody had anticipated was that a crowd of around 200,000 would turn up to watch an essentially meaningless race. As the start time drew nearer, the spectators became increasingly unruly and began tearing down safety fences and barriers to obtain a trackside view. Soon rows and rows of them were standing, tightly packed, on the very edge of the circuit. When it was announced that the start would be delayed so that the crowd could be moved back, bottles were thrown on to the track in protest.

The race might well have been called off but for the very real fear that a cancellation would have provoked a full-scale riot,

188

so instead Stewart and Mexican driver Pedro Rodriguez toured the circuit, appealing to the crowd to move back a little behind the barriers. Even this extremely reasonable request had little effect, but, after the broken bottles had been swept up, the drivers came out for an inspection lap. Although some still harboured reservations, the situation was thought to be just about under control and the race was quickly started – well over an hour late.

Regazzoni led into the first turn but by the end of the second lap he had been overtaken by both Ickx and Stewart. On lap 14 Stewart's steering column worked loose, and the resultant pit stop cost him almost exactly one lap and relegated him to last but one place. Stewart rejoined the race right behind third-placed Brabham on the road and wasted no time in unlapping himself from both Brabham and Regazzoni. At half-distance Ickx was 15 seconds ahead of Regazzoni, who in turn led Brabham by another 12 seconds. Having worked his way up to tenth, Stewart then fell foul of a marauding Mexican dog which ran on to the track in front of the Tyrrell and bent the car's front suspension. A forlorn Stewart had no option but to retire.

Brabham kept plugging away in typical fashion until on lap 53 his engine blew up to deny him the farewell for which he had been hoping. The two Ferraris were now out on their own and Ickx came home the best part of a minute ahead of Regazzoni, with Denny Hulme's McLaren back in third.

Over the closing laps the crowd had once again pushed forward to the edge of the track, and no sooner had Ickx taken the chequered flag than they swarmed all over the circuit, forcing the remaining cars to slow right down in order to avoid any number of accidents.

The repercussions of the crowd behaviour were severe. The International Sporting Commission cancelled the 1971 Mexican Grand Prix when it was unable to obtain a guarantee from the organisers that there would be no repeat of the 1970 farce, and it turned out to be another 15 years before the event was finally restored to the motor-racing calendar.

THE RALLY WITH NO FINISHERS

BANDAMA RALLY, DECEMBER 1972

The organiser of the daunting Liège-Rome-Liège Rally once proclaimed that his ideal was to create an event with single-figure finishers. Well, the brains behind the 1972 Bandama Rally in West Africa went one better in 1972 by producing such a punishing schedule that there were no finishers at all!

This was only the second-ever Bandama Rally. When Bob Neyret won the 1971 event in a Peugeot 504, the result hardly warranted a mention, but the following year the rally achieved instant notoriety.

A total of 52 cars set out, but a schedule which most of the drivers described as 'ludicrous' quickly saw wholesale eliminations. When the teams protested that the time limits were virtually impossible to meet, the organisers simply shrugged their shoulders and flatly refused to modify the targets. Shekhar Mehta in a Datsun 240Z did manage to complete the route but was adjudged to be out of time, while Tony Fall in a Peugeot 504 actually finished within the time limits, only for the entire results to be scrapped following protests from the aggrieved Renault team.

In what was probably an attempt to distance itself from the 1972 fiasco, the event was subsequently renamed the Ivory Coast Rally.

THROUGH THE BARRICADES

MONTE CARLO RALLY, JANUARY 1973

A total of 278 starters set off from such diverse cities as Athens, Glasgow, Frankfurt, Oslo, Rome and Warsaw to take part in the 1973 Monte Carlo Rally. Yet only 51 made it through to the Mediterranean as mass disqualification led to barricades being manned by protesting drivers and patrolled by armed police in what became an additional – and unforeseen – hazard in the world's showpiece rally.

That year's Common Route – to be taken by all competitors – began at the French town of Alès and consisted of ten stages over a distance of 1,040 miles. The day before the Common Route was due to begin, however, three of the stages were blocked by snow, among them the third stage, the Burzet loop. This section had been blocked for several days prior to the rally and although no fresh snow had fallen in the meantime, the strong wind had prevented the road from being cleared. Competitors waiting for the Common Route to begin heard about the problem via advance ice-note crews who had been unable to get through, and so it was generally assumed that the rally would be rerouted. And when there was no news of a reroute, they deduced – not unreasonably – that conditions on the Burzet stage must have improved. In fact a snow plough had been sent out to try and create a way through, but as soon as it cleared a path, the wind blew the snow back on to the road.

Feelings were already running high over a proposal that studs should be banned on the special stage across the Col du

191

Corobin between Digne and Monte Carlo. Factory teams and tyre companies launched an immediate objection, and the proposal was scrapped. But it was an indication that all was not sweetness and light in the world of rallying that year.

In spite of the snow, the Burzet stage went ahead. Sixty-five cars managed to pick a way through before a Capri spun and wedged itself between two snow banks, rendering the road completely impassable. For some inexplicable reason, however, the marshals at the start of the stage kept sending competitors in, with the result that there was soon a nose-to-tail jam of rally cars with nowhere to go. To compound their blunder, the rally organisers ruled that no extra time allowance would be given. Consequently the 144 cars stuck behind the Capri were all disqualified, not only because they had failed to complete the stage but also because they were over the set time limits.

The excluded crews, many of whom had spent a fortune travelling across Europe in order to compete, were outraged at the organisers' intransigence and decided that if they were not going to be allowed to finish the rally, nobody else would be either. So they raced off to Digne and set up barricades across the road leading into the town, the idea being to delay the remaining competitors until they, too, were over the time limit. Learning of the proposed sabotage, the organisers alerted the French police who despatched vanloads of gendarmes with orders to stop all but the surviving crews from reaching the Digne road. But by the time the police arrived on the scene, the barricades were already in place. The protesters dug in for a pitched battle, if necessary, leaving those who intended completing the rally to find ingenious methods of circum-navigating the blockade. Timo Makinen got through by driving his Escort directly at the barricade before veering up a steep bank at the last minute and flying past the frustrated pickets. Rauno Aaltonen opted for a more extreme detour. Revving the engine of his Datsun, he mounted a bank, burst through a hedge, drove across a field, jumped a ditch, and emerged through the hedge on the other side, having neatly sidestepped the protesters.

Sometimes the mood turned ugly. Two women competitors, furious at the bar to their progress, were further enraged when a pair of pistol-waving gendarmes insisted that the barricade be lifted to allow a local shopper through in her 2CV. The driver of the rally car promptly stood in front of the 2CV and refused to let it move until she was allowed to follow. The police threatened retribution, but were eventually forced to back down and let both cars through.

As the remnants of the rally soldiered on towards Monte Carlo, Makinen's hopes were hit when he lost a front wheel... and five minutes while a spare was being fitted. The snowy conditions favoured the Alpine-Renaults, who were able to make considerable ground on the Common Route and ended up filling five of the first six places in the final classification. Makinen's delay handed victory to the Alpine of Jean-Claude Andruet and co-driver Michele Petit (who used the pseudonym 'Biche'). They finished 26 seconds ahead of Ove Andersson's Alpine.

The end of the rally did not bring about an end to hostilities and the winter of discontent rumbled on. As a peace gesture, the organisers offered the disqualified crews free entries for the 1974 Monte. But the energy crisis meant that the rally never took place. Some disputes are simply not meant to be resolved amicably.

SAFETY FIRST

CANADIAN GRAND PRIX, 23 SEPTEMBER 1973

The penultimate race in the 1973 Formula One World Championship season at the Mosport Park circuit near Toronto marked the first occasion on which a safety car was used in a Grand Prix. It was not exactly an auspicious beginning, the car's introduction creating wholesale confusion which lasted until long after the chequered flag had been shown.

With Jackie Stewart having already clinched his third drivers' title, the outcome of the Canadian Grand Prix was academic apart from whether Tyrrell or Lotus would take the constructors' title. In misty, damp conditions Ronnie Peterson put his JPS Lotus on pole, ahead of the McLarens of Peter Revson and Jody Scheckter. Race morning produced heavy rain, turning the untimed practice session into a lottery as a succession of cars spun off. The conditions were so appalling that the organisers allowed three exploratory laps before the race finally got under way 40 minutes late.

Peterson was first away in a plume of spray but the Swede was on Goodyear tyres, and judging by the way that Niki Lauda on Firestones had come through from the fourth row on the grid to be third at the end of the opening lap, it was quickly clear that these were better suited to the wet track. On lap three Lauda's BRM calmly went past Scheckter and Peterson to take the lead and proceeded to draw away at the extraordinary rate of four seconds per lap. With cars spinning at regular intervals, Peterson lurched into a guard rail on lap

17 because of a deflating tyre, but as the track began to dry out, Lauda dived into the pits three laps later to change to intermediate tyres. When the Austrian rejoined the race, he had dropped to eighth behind Emerson Fittipaldi (JPS Lotus), Jackie Oliver (Shadow), François Cevert (Tyrrell), Scheckter, Stewart (Tyrrell), Howden Ganley (Williams) and Carlos Reutemann (Brabham).

The pits were now full of drivers changing from wets to intermediates, with the result that it became difficult to know who was actually leading the race. When the leaders came in, Jean-Pierre Beltoise's BRM took over briefly until he, too, pitted. In this state of confusion when some of the front-runners had come in and others hadn't, Scheckter and Cevert collided going into Turn Two on lap 33 while battling for fourth place. Although neither driver was badly injured, their damaged cars partially blocked the track, bringing the safety car into play for the first time. The driver of the safety vehicle waved a number of cars past until, to the surprise of just about everyone, it took up station immediately ahead of Ganley. The New Zealander had started three rows from the back of the grid and was not leading by anyone's calculations... except, apparently, those of the safety driver. Stewart and Fittipaldi were tucked in behind Ganley and an orderly queue duly formed. Those who capitalised most from the situation were Revson and Oliver who, being just ahead of Ganley, were able to continue at normal race speed until they fell in at the back of the 21-car queue. Meanwhile argument was raging in the pits as to who was leading. Was it Fittipaldi? Or Oliver? Or Revson? The only thing the teams seemed to agree upon was that it definitely wasn't Howden Ganley.

When the safety car eventually turned off, Ganley proceeded to drive an inspired race, holding Stewart and Fittipaldi at bay for eight laps. By now the general consensus of opinion was that the real race leader was Oliver, with Fittipaldi second nearly a lap behind, but nobody could be sure. Fittipaldi soon passed Stewart and began to rein in Oliver, who lost precious seconds on lap 47 when the Shadow developed sticking throttle slides. By lap 76 – with just four to go – excitement was high as Fittipaldi and Oliver ran nose to tail. But what neither they nor any of the spectators knew was that they weren't battling for the lead at all – they were competing for second place.

On the penultimate lap Fittipaldi managed to pass Oliver and held on to what he thought was the finish. As the Brazilian crossed the line, Lotus team chief Colin Chapman threw his cap into the air in celebration... but there was no sign of the chequered flag. Half a lap later the flag was suddenly waved at a gaggle of cars comprising Ganley, Revson, James Hunt, Reutemann and Mike Hailwood. With Lotus still claiming a Fittipaldi win, it emerged that the flag was meant for Revson who had gained virtually a whole lap when the safety car picked up the wrong car! Fittipaldi had, in fact, been a lap behind when the safety car left the track.

Amid much discussion, interspersed with occasional acrimony, the winner's trophy was presented to Revson. Three hours later, when all the drivers' lap times had been examined and re-examined, the American was confirmed as the winner with Fittipaldi second and Oliver third. Having tasted his 15 minutes of fame, Ganley was officially placed sixth.

At the inquest into the confusion, it was generally accepted that the safety car principle was fine... but that it would help if in future it picked up the right car.

STUCK IN THE PIT LANE

BRITISH GRAND PRIX, 20 JULY 1974

The British Grand Prix at Brands Hatch was the tenth race of the 1974 Formula One World Championship. After a dismal 1973, Ferrari was on the way up again, thanks largely to the efforts of Niki Lauda whose victories in Spain and Holland had put him at the head of the contest for the drivers' title. In qualifying at the Kent circuit, Lauda met a formidable opponent in Sweden's Ronnie Peterson and the Ferrari and the Lotus ended up tying for pole position. The second row consisted of Jody Scheckter's Tyrrell and Carlos Reutemann's Brabham, while home eyes were focused on row three where James Hunt's Hesketh lined up alongside the Shadow of young Welshman Tom Pryce, who had already won the 100 bottles of champagne presented by the *Evening News* for the fastest lap during the Thursday morning practice session. Even as the cars left the pits before the start there was drama, Hunt's Hesketh hitting a Tyrrell mechanic and breaking both his legs. The crowded pit lane would be a foretaste of things to come.

At the end of the first of the 75 laps, Lauda held a two-second lead over Scheckter, ahead of Clay Regazzoni, who had shot up from the fourth row, and Peterson. Lauda and Scheckter pulled away steadily from the chasing pack, many of whom were being crippled by punctures. As early as lap 19 John Watson in a privately entered Brabham called into the pits with a puncture, caused by the proliferation of small flinty stones on the track, and over the next few laps five more drivers, including Regazzoni, Peterson and Graham Hill, were all forced to stop with deflated tyres. Out in front Lauda remained unruffled, his lead having stretched to a comfortable eight seconds, but then on lap 55 he, too, sustained a slow puncture. The previously smooth-running Ferrari began to handle erratically. His pit signalled that they had a new tyre ready and urged him to come in, but Lauda was desperate for championship points and knew that a stop at that stage would as good as hand the race to Scheckter. So he made a calculated decision to try and hold out to the finish.

It was not to be. Scheckter closed relentlessly and, five laps from the end, capitalised on Lauda's misfortune to sweep past into the lead. Lauda soldiered on gamely but two laps later Emerson Fittipaldi relegated him to third. Then on the penultimate lap the tyre finally burst. Bits of rubber were flying everywhere, leaving Lauda no option but to rumble into the pits on the flat. The Ferrari crew changed the tyre in 20 seconds but as Lauda accelerated away to rejoin the race, he found his way barred by crowds of people who had flooded the pit lane to watch Scheckter take the chequered flag. To make matters worse, an RAC official had backed his Ford Cortina across the exit in readiness for the winner's lap of honour. Fearing an accident, a marshal rushed out and showed Lauda the red flag, whereupon the Austrian climbed out of his car and stormed off.

The red flag signalling the immediate end of the race gave Lauda a finishing position of ninth (and therefore no championship points). Ferrari protested but the RAC stewards dismissed it, so Ferrari appealed to the sport's governing body, the FIA. They elevated Lauda to fifth (and two points) on the grounds that the red flag had been shown incorrectly. It was a chaotic end to a Grand Prix, and ultimately the two points which Lauda clawed back made no difference to the outcome of the championship as Fittipaldi took the title with something to spare.

HALF POINTS IN BARCELONA

SPANISH GRAND PRIX, 27 APRIL 1975

Set within picturesque parkland near Barcelona, the 2.35-mile Montjuich Park circuit first hosted the Spanish Grand Prix in 1969. On that occasion both Graham Hill and Jochen Rindt were involved in high-speed crashes when their Lotuses experienced identical wing failure over the same crest. For the next six years, it alternated with Jarama as the venue for Spain's premier motor race, but the events of 1975 brought its brief career as a Grand Prix circuit to an abrupt end.

Safety concerns were voiced during practice and on the eve of qualifying the Grand Prix Drivers' Association safety committee inspected the track. It found that bolts were missing from much of the Armco barrier, as a result of which the drivers announced that they would refuse to race until the bolts were inserted. When the organisers immediately threatened to seize the cars and equipment to cover their contractual losses, the team owners brought pressure on their drivers to take part. The drivers backed down . . . reluctantly. Reigning world champion Emerson Fittipaldi would complete just three slow laps – sufficient to guarantee McLaren its starting money – before sitting out the rest of the race in protest.

An accident occurred within seconds of the start. Braking into the first corner, Niki Lauda's Ferrari was rammed from behind by Mario Andretti's Parnelli as the American tried to force his way to the front. The Ferrari spun sideways and out of the race. In trying to take avoiding action, Lauda's team-mate,

Clay Regazzoni, sustained a damaged front wheel and nose cone and had to limp to the pits for repairs. He eventually rejoined the action four laps adrift. Hesketh driver James Hunt was the principal beneficiary of the first-corner smash, scrambling through a gap to lead at the end of the opening lap from Andretti, and John Watson in a Surtees.

Spilt oil on the track was now providing an extra hazard. On lap seven Hunt hit the oil slick, slammed into the barrier and retired. Watson proceeded to hit the barrier at almost the same point, but not quite as forcefully, and managed to hold on to second behind Andretti for four more laps until the car's handling deteriorated to such an extent that he was forced to call into the pits. By lap 17 Andretti had a 20-second lead over Rolf Stommelen's Hill-Ford, the Brabham of Carlos Pace and Ronnie Peterson in a JPS Lotus. But then it was Andretti's turn to smash into a guard rail and out of the race. On lap 24 Peterson retired, promoting Jochen Mass (McLaren) to third and Jacky Ickx (Lotus) to fourth.

Two laps later came the big accident that everyone had been dreading. Shortly after making a pit stop, Stommelen was travelling at 150mph when the wing of his Hill-Ford came loose. The car veered out of control and smashed into the safety barrier, killing four people who were standing behind it – a track marshal, two fire marshals and a photographer. Pace, close behind in second, braked hard and swerved but was struck by the half-airborne car as it came back across the road. The Brabham was sent sliding into the Armco but Pace was unhurt. Stommelen, however, sustained a broken leg. By a macabre coincidence, the car owned by Graham Hill had suffered the same accident as the one he was driving in 1969 . . . and over the same crest.

The yellow flags were brought out but in the confusion a number of drivers ignored them. Three laps later the organisers waved the cars down and stopped the race. At the time Mass was leading and so he was declared the winner from Ickx, Carlos Reutemann (Brabham), Jean-Pierre Jarier (Shadow) and Vittorio Brambilla (March). But as just 29 of

200

the scheduled 75 laps had been completed, the drivers were only awarded half the normal points.

There was one happy story to emerge from the shambles of Montjuich Park. Sixth place was filled by Lella Lombardi in a March, who thus became the first woman to score a Formula One World Championship point . . . or, more precisely, a World Championship half-point.

VICTORY IN SLOW MOTION

DAYTONA 500, 15 FEBRUARY 1976

The jewel in the crown in NASCAR's Winston Cup series of stock car races, the Daytona 500 is second only in status in the US to the Indianapolis 500. The high-speed Daytona showpiece is run in Florida on a similar 2.5-mile banked circuit to Indianapolis and was first staged in 1959. And it was a clash between two of the all-time great Winston Cup heroes, Richard Petty and David Pearson, which provided the most sensational finish in the history of the race.

Petty – justifiably known as 'King Richard' – had won the Daytona 500 on five occasions since 1964. In 1975 he won a record 13 NASCAR victories on the way to his sixth Winston Cup title. He was now seeking the 178th victory of his career. Pearson (the 'Silver Fox') had 88 career wins to his credit, including success in the opening race of the 1976 season – the Winston Western 500 at Riverside, California.

Qualifying at Daytona was eventful enough in itself. A.J. Foyt went fastest in a Chevrolet, closely followed by Darrell Waltrip (Chevrolet) and Dave Marcis (Dodge), before all three were disqualified for various technical irregularities. Foyt and Waltrip were kicked out for having illegal fuel pressure assist systems and Marcis for a radiator block that was unstable at high speed. These disqualifications left a surprise all-Chevrolet front row of Ramo Stott – the only pole of his career – and Terry Ryan, who was making his Winston Cup debut. Petty's STP Dodge was sixth on the grid and

202

Pearson's red and cream Wood brothers' Purolator Mercury was seventh.

There had already been 33 official leadership changes before Pearson overtook defending champion Benny Parsons on lap 177 of the 200. Eleven laps later Petty seized the initiative but as he started the final lap, Pearson was right on his tail. Exiting Turn Two, Pearson moved towards the inside and when Petty drifted high along the back stretch, the wily Silver Fox was able to forge a car's length ahead approaching Turn Three. But, all too aware of the threat from behind, Pearson entered the turn too quickly and drifted high, allowing Petty to shoot through on the inside. As the pair came out of the last of the race's 800 turns, Petty held a lead of around three feet. At that point, Petty's car nudged Pearson's. The Dodge touched the outside wall and lurched at a crazy angle for a few yards before Petty managed to straighten it out. Meanwhile the impact had sent the Mercury spinning into the outside wall and on the rebound, its nose caught the rear of Petty's car, sending the King spinning head-on into the wall. It looked for a moment as if he was going to spin all the way to the finish but instead he slid to a halt on the infield grass, just 75 yards short of victory. Pearson's car was equally crippled but he succeeded in steering it across the grass and rejoined the track less than ten yards from the finish, eventually crawling over the line at no more than 15mph for his only Daytona 500 success.

At the post-race inquest there was no hint of animosity between the two rivals. It was just one of those things. Pearson admitted that it was an unorthodox end to a race but added: 'If I'd backed across that finish line, it wouldn't have made any difference – as long as I was first!'

SIX WHEELS ON MY WAGON

SWEDISH GRAND PRIX, 13 JUNE 1976

One of the strangest sights ever seen in a Grand Prix was the six-wheeled Tyrrell Project 34, which competed in 1976 and 1977. Its four ten-inch front wheels were designed to reduce drag and give improved cornering and braking due to the larger tyre 'contact patch'. In the hands of Jody Scheckter and Patrick Depailler, this motoring oddity proved surprisingly effective in its first season, its finest hour being at the Swedish Grand Prix at Anderstorp.

The brainchild of Tyrrell designer Derek Gardner, the P34 was not definitely earmarked for a Formula One future until the prototype showed such promise in testing against the standard car that race versions were hurriedly built. The car made its debut at the 1976 Spanish Grand Prix, but it was in Sweden that it came of age.

Scheckter, a winner at Anderstorp in 1974, caused a sensation by putting the Tyrrell on pole, but hopes of a famous victory were dashed when Mario Andretti made a flying start. Andretti proceeded to gain half a second per lap on the South African and it looked as though the Tyrrell was destined to finish no higher than runner-up. By lap 28 Andretti was leading by a comfortable nine seconds, but then it was announced that he had received a one-minute penalty for jumping the start. The penalty pushed him back to 11th and although he fought his way up to sixth, he retired on lap 46 with an oil leak. Andretti's punishment left Scheckter in command and he drove a steady race ahead of his team-mate. Depailler was pressed for a while by Chris Amon until the New Zealander went off in front of the stands. From fifth on the grid, the Ferrari of reigning champion Niki Lauda was unable to make any impression on the two Tyrrells and had to settle for third place, 12 seconds behind Depailler and 31 seconds behind winner Scheckter. Jacques Lafitte was fourth in a Ligier with James Hunt fifth in a McLaren.

Following this magnificent one-two, the Tyrrells continued to perform admirably throughout the season, Scheckter and Depailler finishing third and fourth respectively in the World Championship. Tyrrell continued with the experiment in 1977, when Ronnie Peterson replaced Scheckter, but the car was no longer as competitive, partly because tyre development for the smaller wheels was not as advanced as for conventional wheels. Consequently the concept was abandoned. March and Williams later tested cars with tandem rear wheels but neither actually raced, although the March did take part in hill climbs. Anyway in 1982 regulations restricted Formula One cars to four wheels. The six-wheeled revolution was over.

HUNT'S FLAG DAY

BRITISH GRAND PRIX, 18 JULY 1976

Feelings were running high in the build-up to the 1976 British Grand Prix courtesy of a simmering feud between Ferrari and McLaren which was about to boil over. The bad blood had started at the Spanish Grand Prix earlier in the season, when James Hunt's apparently victorious McLaren had been disqualified two hours after the race for exceeding the maximum allowable car width by 18mm. The Ferrari number one, Niki Lauda, was awarded the race but two months later, on appeal, Hunt was reinstated as the winner. This controversial decision met with a frosty reception from Ferrari, not least because it cut Lauda's lead over Hunt in the World Drivers' Championship to 27 points – 52 to 25. The British Grand Prix at Brands Hatch was the next race on the calendar.

1976 was the long, hot summer when the British public basked in unexpectedly high temperatures and found a new sporting hero in 28-year-old Hunt, the dashing blond bombshell with the film star looks and the aristocratic accent. Hunt had acquitted himself creditably with the Hesketh team over the previous three seasons but this was the year which really catapulted him into the big time. Lauda was his friend and great rival, so it was fitting that the pair lined up alongside each other on the front row at Brands as the season reached its halfway point. The second rank was made up of Mario Andretti's Lotus and Clay Regazzoni's Ferrari. Having qualified on pole, Lauda chose to start from the left side of the track, thereby avoiding the steep camber of the opening right-hander, Paddock Hill Bend.

Lauda got away well but Hunt missed a beat, enabling Regazzoni to fly past from the second row and attack his team-mate at Paddock. It was a bold but misguided assault, one which saw the two Ferraris touch wheels. Regazzoni spun, Hunt veered left to avoid him but hit the sliding Ferrari. The McLaren rode over the Ferrari's wheels and was launched into the air, crashing down to earth in an upright position but with the right front steering arm broken. In the midst of the mayhem Jacques Laffite crashed his Ligier into the bank. Hunt motored on slowly up the hill to Druids with one front wheel at a crazy angle and drifted down the other side towards Bottom Straight. He thought he was out of the race until he saw red flags indicating that proceedings had been stopped, so he turned off the track on to a little back road that led to the pits. As a crowd gathered around, Hunt climbed out and asked the mechanics to push the McLaren to the pit.

Half an hour later it was announced that the race would restart as if the first lap had not occurred, but that no car would be allowed to take part in the rerun if it had failed to complete the first lap. Additionally, no spare cars would be permitted to start. When the crowd heard that Hunt and, to a lesser extent, Regazzoni and Laffite, would be excluded, there was uproar. The McLaren spare car was wheeled on to the grid and as Hunt climbed into it, the bulk of the 77,000 crowd started to boo and whistle at the stewards. The slow handclap started up and some frustrated spectators threw beer cans on to the track. Hunt later remarked: 'It soon became clear that the organisers were going to allow me to start because if they didn't, they would have a riot on their hands!' In a miraculous change of heart, the stewards did indeed suddenly rule that Hunt could start after all because his car had been mobile when the race had been stopped. And the issue of the spare car no longer applied since in the intervening period between the original crash and the restart, the McLaren mechanics had managed to repair the front suspension of Hunt's race car. So he got into that while Regazzoni and Laffite used their training cars.

In the restarted race Hunt sat behind Lauda for 45 of the 76 laps until he took the Austrian at Druids. With the Ferrari slowed by gear trouble, Hunt pulled away to win by a minute but even as he stood on the victory podium, moves were afoot to snatch away his moment of glory. Ferrari, Tyrrell and Copersucar all objected to Hunt's win on the grounds that his car hadn't technically been running when the original race was halted. Tyrrell and Copersucar subsequently withdrew their objections but Ferrari held firm.

Ferrari's appeal against the result was heard two months later. The McLaren hierarchy knew they were on to a loser when Lauda, having climbed out of his deathbed following his dreadful crash at the Nürburgring, was wheeled in by Ferrari swathed in bandages. Ferrari claimed that Hunt had abandoned his car, that the mechanics had pushed it with the race still in progress and that the McLaren would have been incapable of completing that first lap anyway. McLaren countered that Hunt had only stopped on seeing the red flag. Even though video evidence was produced to show that Hunt was still driving at the time, the FIA ruled that he hadn't actually been taking part in the race when it was stopped, and disqualified him. Lauda had won the sympathy vote, the general feeling being that Hunt's disqualification was to appease Ferrari following his reinstatement in Spain. It was a severe blow to Hunt's title aspirations. But the season was by no means over yet.

LAUDA SURRENDERS THE TITLE

JAPANESE GRAND PRIX, 24 OCTOBER 1976

Niki Lauda's horrific crash at the Nürburgring on 1 August had changed the complexion of the Formula One season. In an incredible display of courage he was back behind the wheel 33 days later to finish fourth in the Italian Grand Prix, a performance which captured even the imagination of people with little or no interest in the sport. The Austrian's burnt face and singed eyelids became one of the year's enduring images, a symbol of heroism. To the neutral observer, nobody was more deserving of the World Drivers' Championship than Lauda, although victories for arch rival James Hunt in Canada and the United States had sliced the once seemingly unassailable lead to just three points approaching the final Grand Prix of the season at Mount Fuji.

Mario Andretti had qualified on pole in his Lotus with Hunt's McLaren alongside and Lauda on the second row. Come race day and the weather was appalling. *Motor Sport* wrote that 'streaming rain and low cloud swirled round the circuit and completely concealed Mount Fuji', restricting visibility to around 100 yards. The track was frighteningly slippery for the untimed morning practice session. Just keeping the car on the road was a major achievement. Speed was very much a secondary consideration. The 73-lap race was due to start at 1.30 p.m. but the drivers appeared to have little appetite for driving nearly 200 miles in such conditions. John Watson was heard to remark: 'In the wet, with no visibility, you only want someone in the bunch to lose control and you might have a massacre.' Of the 25 drivers, only the fearless Vittorio Brambilla (March) and Lauda's Ferrari team-mate Clay Regazzoni declared a definite commitment to start, although a few others indicated that they would probably be prepared to race if push came to shove. Hunt was among them. Ideally he wanted the race postponed but, rain or no rain, mist or no mist, he was not going to miss out on the chance of winning the World Championship. He had come too far . . . and not only geographically. Lauda did not relish the prospect of racing at all. After Nürburgring he valued his life too much.

The inactivity around the pits made the 80,000 crowd restless and as it became apparent that no start was imminent, they started the slow handclap. The organisers shared the drivers' concerns but, in view of the crowd's reaction, feared that a cancellation might incite unrest and so they announced that the race would start at 3 p.m. A number of the drivers still thought that conditions were too dangerous but their protests fell on deaf ears. Race officials insisted that the rain had stopped and that the worst of the water had been cleared from the track, despite the fact that pools of standing water remained on the pit straight. In the absence of solidarity, the drivers decided to give it a go. By three o'clock it was raining again, but the race went ahead and after a tentative warm-up lap through plumes of spray, the cars were away. Hunt got a flyer, slithering around the first lap from Watson's Penske. Back in third, Lauda was already struggling. Understandably beset with apprehension, the last straw came when he felt the Ferrari aquaplaning on the pit straight at the conclusion of the opening lap. 'It was absolutely unbearable,' he said later, 'sitting there panic-stricken, seeing nothing, just hunched down in the cockpit waiting for somebody to run into you.' After two laps, Lauda came into the pits and told the mechanics he was retiring from the race. Trying to protect their man, Ferrari subsequently explained away the retirement as a technical problem, but Lauda was honest and admitted that he had been too scared to continue. 'It was like murder out there,' he added. 'Sometimes I could not tell which direction the car was going. For me it was the limit. There are more important things in life than the World Championship.'

With Lauda's exit, Hunt needed only to finish fourth to dethrone the reigning champion and claim the crown for himself. All of the cars were on wet tyres but as the race progressed the rain began to ease off, with the result that the track slowly dried out. It was merely a matter of time before the drying surface began to destroy the wet tyres. Not that this appeared to concern Hunt who, approaching half-distance, held a comfortable lead over McLaren team-mate Jochen Mass. With Mass riding shotgun, Hunt's charge towards the title appeared unstoppable. Then on lap 36 Mass hit a wet patch and slid into the barrier, out of the race, thereby elevating the six-wheeled Tyrrell of Patrick Depailler to second. By now the sky overhead was blue. Mount Fuji was visible once again. The soft wet tyres were wearing away at an alarming rate. Hunt was in a dilemma. He could feel the left rear tyre deflating. Each time he flashed past the pits he looked for a sign telling him to come in for fresh tyres. Nothing. Depailler and Mario Andretti were starting to close. On lap 62 both overtook the ailing Englishman, but when Depailler pitted for new tyres, Hunt regained second spot.

His relief was short-lived. With six laps remaining his front left tyre disintegrated as he rounded the long loop to the start/finish straight. His only consolation was that the tyre had blown near to the pits, for it would not have lasted an entire lap. Hunt's pit stop lasted 27 seconds and dropped him back to fifth behind Andretti, Clay Regazzoni, Alan Jones and Depailler. He rejoined the race in a blinding rage, convinced that his team's refusal to call him in earlier had cost him the championship. As he completed lap 69, a pit board mistakenly told him he was sixth. On lap 70 Hunt's fresh tyres enabled him to surge past Jones and Regazzoni, neither of whom had stopped. He was now third behind Andretti and Depailler, although he didn't know it at the time. Over the final two laps he desperately tried to catch Depailler but the

Frenchman was still some 30 yards ahead at the chequered flag.

As he rose from his car, Hunt was in a black mood and began ranting at McLaren team boss Teddy Mayer for costing him the title. Having sorted out his calculations, Mayer tried to explain to his driver that he had finished third and was world champion, but Hunt couldn't hear a word through his helmet and carried on screaming abuse. Even when he removed his helmet, he still refused to accept the fact that he was champion until he had seen it in writing. There had been too many false dawns already in that memorable 1976 season.

FAN WORSHIP

SWEDISH GRAND PRIX, 17 JUNE 1978

Just as the 1976 Swedish Grand Prix had witnessed the sole triumph of the six-wheeled Tyrrell, so the same race two years later saw the only win of the infamous Brabham fan car. Indeed it was to be the car's solitary Grand Prix appearance, since fans were outlawed a few days after the race. But despite the controversy surrounding the innovation, Niki Lauda's victory at Anderstorp was allowed to stand and lives on today in the record books.

What was described as the most famous fan since Lady Windermere's was the creation of the Brabham team's South African designer, Gordon Murray. At the time, the 'ground effect' phenomenon was all the rage in motor-racing, ever since Colin Chapman had managed to harness under-car air pressure in his 1977 Lotus 78. Murray's response was to move the water radiator on the Brabham Alfa BT46 to a horizontal position above the engine and then to add a large tail-mounted fan at the rear of the car, the fan being driven by a shaft running from the gearbox. Murray also designed special skirts on the underside of the car so that the fan was able to suck air from beneath the car, like a vacuum cleaner. The result generated tremendous downforce, sucking the car closer to the ground.

The car tested successfully at Silverstone and Brands Hatch before being unleashed in Sweden. 'Movable aerodynamic devices' had been banned since 1969 so the fan's appearance stirred up considerable argument, and during practice both Emerson Fittipaldi and Mario Andretti complained bitterly that their visors were covered in dirt after following the Brabham. They maintained that any cars following the Brabham on the track would suffer as the stones and dirt sucked under it by the fan were thrown out behind. Nevertheless the fan was found to be within the rules, and Niki Lauda and John Watson responded by putting the BT46s second and third on the grid behind Andretti's all-conquering Lotus 79.

Watson made a poor start, but Lauda set off in pursuit of Andretti. After a couple of laps Watson was passed by the Arrows of Riccardo Patrese and then the second Lotus of Ronnie Peterson, which had been fourth on the grid, came in early for a tyre change and rejoined the race in 11th. Seeking his first win of the season, Lauda swooped on the black and gold Lotus at half-distance and proceeded to pull away from Andretti with consummate ease. In a desperate attempt to claw back the ground, the Lotus eventually broke down. Behind, Alan Jones in a Williams was about to devour Patrese and move up to second when their wheels touched and Jones went off. Lauda went on to win much as he pleased by a commanding 34 seconds from Patrese, who held off Peterson by half a length at the finish. The fan car had given Brabham its first Formula One win for three years and Alfa Romeo engines their first victory since 1951.

Its success immediately prompted rival teams to attempt to develop their own system but before they had a chance to do so, the fans were declared illegal by the sport's governing body. However Lauda's victory was not taken away as, at the time of the race, the car had been perfectly legal.

Andretti and Lotus had the last word, going on to win the title, but they had been no match for the Brabham fan car on its one and only outing.

AN UNEXPECTED OBSTRUCTION

MONTE CARLO RALLY, JANUARY 1979

Since the very beginning of motor sport, French fans have earned an unwanted reputation for partisanship which occasionally borders on outright sabotage. Early motorcyclists from overseas found their chances of winning on French soil diminished greatly by the sudden appearance of tacks scattered across the road. The Monte Carlo Rally has long been a hotbed of dissent. Accusations of official bias against the British Minis were rife in the 1960s, but in 1979 it was the French spectators who were seemingly up to their old tricks, putting obstacles in the path of a Scandinavian victory and at the same time paving the way for a home triumph.

A total of 233 cars set off from nine European cities, the Common Route starting from Val le Bains. On arrival at Monte Carlo Hannu Mikkola in a works Ford Escort led Bjorn Waldegard's Escort RS by seven seconds with Walter Rohrl and Markku Alen, both in Fiats, a further 20 seconds adrift. France's Bernard Darniche, driving a Lancia Stratos, was back in sixth – 3min 7sec behind the leader. Divine intervention appeared to be his only hope of success.

Fifteen special stages followed, during which the Escorts pulled further away until Mikkola was handed a controversial five-minute penalty by the organisers for 'dangerous passing' on a public road near Digne. This action prompted dark mutterings of French bias. Waldegard was now 4min 7sec ahead of Alen and 6min 27sec ahead of Darniche. With the

215

best 100 cars tackling the Mountain Circuit, Darniche set about clawing back the deficit, but his chances of overhauling the Swede still appeared remote.

On the final night there were ten stages, covering a total of 109 miles. The first stage saw Darniche reduce the deficit by 22 seconds and on the first pass of the Col de Turini – where enthusiastic spectators tried to liven things up by shovelling snow off the banks on to the road – he pulled back another 42 seconds. With two stages remaining Darniche trailed by 1min 31sec, but then on that penultimate Villars stage, Waldegard, running first on the road, suddenly found his route blocked by two large boulders. He gamely tried to drive over them, but to no avail, whereupon his navigator, Hans Thorszelius, jumped out of the car, ran round to the front and levered them away. The delay cost Waldegard 25 seconds... and the rally. For on the final stage Darniche was 21 seconds quicker than his rival to win by just six seconds overall. The French had lifted the Monte!

After five days and 2,500 miles of motoring, the rallying year's most prestigious event had been decided by a pair of judiciously placed rocks. Waldegard diplomatically preferred to attribute his defeat to the wrong choice of tyres over the closing stages, but others pointed the finger of suspicion firmly at French spectators whom they accused of positioning the boulders deliberately to scupper the Swede and engineer a home victory. The unsavoury incident left a nasty whiff hanging over the sport for several months.

THE RACE THAT NEVER WAS

SPANISH GRAND PRIX, 1 JUNE 1980

The early eighties were marked by an unseemly power struggle between motor racing's governing body, FISA (Fédération Internationale du Sport Automobile), and FOCA (Formula One Constructors' Association), which represented the interests of the British teams – which in 1980 meant everyone except Ferrari, Renault and Alfa Romeo. This latest row concerned the use of skirts on cars. These greatly increased downforce but could also be dangerous. If a skirt suddenly stopped functioning, which was liable to happen in the event of it being damaged by the car running over a kerb, the resultant loss of downforce could send the car spinning out of control. FISA wanted a ban on car skirts, but FOCA was determined to stand firm.

Already that season there had been skirmishes in Belgium and Monaco when FOCA drivers supported the stand their teams were making by refusing to attend the compulsory pre-race drivers' briefings. FISA president Jean-Marie Balestre's reaction to this outbreak of rebellion was to fine each offending driver $2,000. When the 15 drivers in question refused to pay the fines, their licences were withdrawn. This ugly stand-off came to a head shortly before the Spanish Grand Prix. Ferrari, Renault and Alfa Romeo remained loyal to FISA but the remaining teams demanded that the drivers' suspensions be lifted. FISA refused to back down and, with no solution in sight, pulled the Spanish Grand Prix from the World Championship schedule.

217

The prospects of the Grand Prix going ahead appeared remote but RACE (Royal Automobile Club Espagne), who owned the Jarama circuit north of Madrid and who organised the event, decided to defy FISA and take over direct control of the race from the international body. FOCA gave its backing so the Spanish Grand Prix went ahead, albeit without championship status and minus Ferrari, Renault and Alfa Romeo. With only 22 entrants, nobody could fail to qualify, as a result of which both Shadows made the starting line-up for the first time that year. But pole went to Jacques Laffite in a Ligier.

From fourth on the grid, Carlos Reutemann shot through to lead on the first of the 80 laps, followed by Laffite. Passing places were at a premium at Jarama – the only realistic overtaking spot being at the end of the main straight – and consequently Laffite found himself stuck behind Reutemann for longer than he anticipated. Then on lap 35 the pair came to lap one of the tail-enders, local driver Emilio Villota in a Williams. In attempting the manoeuvre, Reutemann and Laffite collided, putting both of them out of the race.

Nelson Piquet, who had been running third, now took the lead in his Brabham, only to retire on lap 47 with gearbox failure, thereby allowing Didier Pironi's Ligier into first place, pursued by Alan Jones in a Williams. With 14 laps to go Pironi lost a front wheel and Jones inherited a comfortable lead which he kept to the finish. Jochen Mass (Arrows) was second, ahead of Elio de Angelis (Lotus) and Jean-Pierre Jarier's Tyrrell.

Of course, Jones's victory counted for nothing and is excluded from the record books. To all intents and purposes, the 1980 Spanish Grand Prix never took place.

The next Grand Prix, the French, was due to be run on 29 June. That race – and indeed the remainder of the Formula One season – was in jeopardy until five days beforehand when representatives of all the teams met in a London hotel and thrashed out an agreement. The skirts stayed – at least for the time being.

As for Jones, 'the race that never was' did no lasting damage to his title aspirations since he went on to win the championship anyway. Apart from the sport's reputation, the real loser was Patrick Gaillard who had finished sixth – and last – at Jarama in an Ensign. Denied a World Championship point, he never won another.

MANSELL: A PAINFUL BEGINNING

AUSTRIAN GRAND PRIX, 17 AUGUST 1980

Forthright, demanding, paranoid and sometimes downright stubborn, Nigel Mansell has been described as a pain in the backside on more than one occasion. Whether or not he deserved that label, it was certainly applicable in a literal sense to his Formula One debut at the Österreichring in 1980.

Mansell came from the school of hard knocks. His was no overnight success story. He had served his apprenticeship in Formula Ford and Formula Three and was so determined to make it to the top that he accepted a Formula One test drive for Lotus even though he had a broken back at the time! Defying the pain, he showed enough speed on that test to persuade Colin Chapman to give him a chance. And so it was that Mansell came to line up in the 1980 Austrian Grand Prix.

Going into the race, Australian Alan Jones had a clear lead in the championship race courtesy of wins in Argentina, France and Britain. The Österreichring was the fastest circuit of the year (Spa being out of favour between 1970 and 1982) and in practice six drivers were fined a total of 30,000 Austrian schillings (about £11,000) for ignoring a red flag when Jochen Mass spun. René Arnoux put the turbo-engined Renault on pole, breaking his own lap record by a colossal five seconds, from team-mate Jean-Pierre Jabouille and Jones's Williams. Twenty-fourth and last on the grid was N. Mansell at the wheel of the exceedingly moderate Lotus-Cosworth 81B.

If Mansell thought things could only get better, he was

mistaken...sorely mistaken. A few minutes before the start the Lotus mechanics put the final touches to his car, including topping up the fuel tanks. Almost immediately he began to feel 'an intense burning pain in my backside and down my legs'. He realised that fuel had been spilt over him, whereupon the mechanics asked him whether he wanted to get out and live to race another day. But Mansell had waited so long for this opportunity that nothing was going to deny him, and he insisted on racing. In an effort to dilute the petrol, the crew tipped a bucket of cold water down the back of his seat. This had the desired effect for a while but after ten or so laps Mansell could feel the return of the burning sensation. The pain grew progressively worse. He likened it to being slashed with a knife. His agony lasted until lap 40 out of 54 when the engine of the Lotus blew up in sympathy. For the only time in his career, Mansell was relieved to be out of a race.

'The decision to race was the right one,' he said later. 'It showed I wasn't a quitter. But the problems started when I got out of the car and discovered that my hamstrings had shrunk where they'd been immersed in petrol for so long. Afterwards I had to have them stretched.' Scarcely able to walk, once home he went straight to hospital in Birmingham for treatment on the red raw blisters which covered his backside.

The race provided more pleasant memories for 37-year-old Parisian Jean-Pierre Jabouille who, after failing to finish in his previous nine Grands Prix, picked up only his second ever championship victory (he had won in France in 1979). Although team-mate Arnoux was the more fancied of the two Renault drivers, he was delayed by making three pit stops to rectify tyre trouble. This allowed Jabouille to build up a healthy ten-second lead over Jones, only to experience mechanical difficulties over the closing laps. Jones reduced the gap dramatically and at the final corner was right up behind the Frenchman, Jabouille hanging on to win by less than a second. Carlos Reutemann came third in the other Williams, while the unlucky Arnoux could finish only ninth despite breaking the lap record again towards the end.

Second place put Jones 11 points ahead of Nelson Piquet with four races to go, although the outspoken Australian was less than happy with his pit crew, claiming that they failed to keep him properly informed of the narrowing gap between himself and Jabouille. Had he known, he said, he might have been able to put on an extra spurt and snatch victory at the death.

Similarly for Mansell, it was not a race he would forget in a hurry. In fact for weeks to come he would be reminded of it every time he sat down.

THE LONG WAIT

INDIANAPOLIS 500, 24 MAY 1981

When Bobby Unser crossed the finish line eight seconds ahead of Mario Andretti for his third Indy 500 victory, little did he know that far from being the end of the race, it was really just the beginning. Sensationally disqualified the following day, Unser was eventually reinstated as the winner five months later after the longest and most contentious sequel to an Indianapolis 500.

Having put his Penske PC9 – the Norton Spirit – on pole, Indy legend Unser quickly had the first inkling that this was going to be no ordinary race. 'After the announcement of "Gentlemen, start your engines", smoke came from under the dash of my car, which told me my radio literally had gone up in smoke.' Deprived of the more advanced technological means of communication, Unser and team manager Roger Penske had to resort to basic finger signs – one for pit, two for wing, three for tyres. Unser also survived a hairy pit stop fire, choosing to drive his way out of it 'because those invisible flames have a tough time surviving at 200mph!'

The race developed into a fierce contest between Unser and the Wildcat-Cosworths of Mario Andretti and Gordon Johncock. When Johncock dropped out, Unser and Andretti remained locked in battle but the Penske, having led for most laps, held on to the finish to record a winning time of 3hr 35min 41.8sec. at an average speed of 139.08mph. Unser was duly given the full Victory Lane treatment, bringing back memories of his two previous triumphs in 1968 and 1975.

Then came the sensation. Chief steward of the track Tom Binford stated that Unser had illegally passed ten cars while exiting the pit lane at a time when the yellow flags were out following a spate of accidents. The yellow flags created a 'hold station' period where overtaking was forbidden. Unser was penalised a lap for his misdemeanour. According to Binford, the second man home, Andretti, had only passed two cars in the same circumstances and so was promoted to first place. At the official victory banquet on the evening after the race, Andretti was declared the 'winner under protest'.

Unser launched an appeal and, after five months of investigation, he was reinstated as the winner of the 1981 Indianapolis 500. The appeal panel concluded that Binford's controversial penalty could only be imposed during a race. To illustrate their point, they used a basketball analogy where a game was concluded with a one-point margin of victory until the next day a foul was called, allowing the losing team to shoot uncontested free throws. These hypothetical throws were converted so that the losers became the winners. Obviously such a situation was no more acceptable in motor sport than it would be in basketball, and therefore Unser's appeal was upheld. The panel also determined that the rule in question had not been communicated clearly to any of the 33 drivers competing in the race.

Unser was fined $45,000, but the penalty was nothing compared to the rewards of winning a third Indy 500. And the verdict allowed Unser, one of the all-time great US drivers, to quit racing on a winning note before embarking on a new career as a TV commentator.

LOST IN THE DESERT

PARIS-DAKAR RALLY, JANUARY 1982

The annual rally from Paris to Dakar in Senegal on the west coast of Africa had always been one of the most gruelling on the calendar, necessitating as it did a journey across the barren wastes of the Sahara Desert. Open to all types of road vehicle – including cars, trucks and motorcycles – it was described by Thierry Sabine of the Paris-based organisers, the Automobile Sporting Association, as 'the notion of an adventure which no longer exists'. Three people died in the course of the 1982 event, yet all the headlines were reserved for the Prime Minister's son, Mark Thatcher, who went missing for six days after becoming hopelessly lost in the desert. The nation – well, his family – held their breath.

At 28, Mark Thatcher was a keen motor sport competitor but this was his first desert rally. Indeed his finest hour to date was arguably a victory in a ten-lap charity contest at Brands Hatch in 1979 for a House of Commons team against the House of Lords. However, what he lacked in experience, he more than made up for in confidence and he was convinced that a drive at Le Mans made him perfectly equipped to tackle the worst that the Paris-Dakar event could throw at him. His naiveté was staggering.

Thatcher was at the wheel of a Peugeot 504, which he shared with his French co-driver Charlotte Verney and a mechanic whom he knew only as 'Jackie'. On 8 January he was crossing the southern Sahara on the sixth leg of the 6,200-mile race near the Algerian border with Mali. He had been travelling in convoy with two other Peugeots but was delayed when his car broke a front steering arm. It took 13 minutes to repair – sufficient time for Thatcher to become detached from his team-mates. He had to continue using compass bearings and map references and quickly became lost. To make matters worse, at dusk a rear axle casing shattered. The Peugeot was stuck fast. On the third day they made a botched repair of the axle, but it lasted no more than 600 yards before the car gave out again. By now the crew's water supplies were dwindling fast. As concern mounted back in Britain, Mrs Thatcher was asked whether she was worried. 'Of course,' she replied. 'Every mother would be.'

Agency reports on the 12th said that Thatcher had been found unharmed and rescued by helicopter, but these proved a false dawn. By the 13th he had been missing for five days and his mother – the Iron Lady – was in tears. Husband Denis flew out to Algeria to join in the search, which already numbered three military planes sent into the desert by the French government, another seven from Algeria, 20 cross-country vehicles and local units of the Algerian army. Finally at 11.30 on the morning of 14 January, a C130 Hercules of the Algerian army spotted the Prime Minister's son standing beside his car and waving to attract attention. He had drifted some 30 miles off the rally route.

While Mark Thatcher merely expressed surprise that his disappearance had created so much interest, it was revealed that the bill for his search had amounted to £300,000. The Algerian government generously agreed to pay. Thierry Sabine expressed doubt as to whether Thatcher would be allowed to enter the following year's rally, adding caustically: 'At a pinch, we might accept him at the finish at Dakar . . . as a guest.'

A FALLING-OUT AMONGST FRIENDS

SAN MARINO GRAND PRIX, 25 APRIL 1982

The 1982 San Marino Grand Prix was shrouded in controversy even before the start. Most of the British FOCA teams boycotted the event in protest at the disqualification of Nelson Piquet's Brabham and Keke Rosberg's Williams from the top two places in the Brazilian Grand Prix for brake water-cooling irregularities. As a result only 14 cars stood on the grid at Imola – Ferrari, Renault, Alfa Romeo, Tyrrell (who were only competing because they were sponsored by an Italian washing machine company), ATS, Osella and Toleman. Despite the fanatical support of the home crowd, the Ferraris of Gilles Villeneuve and Didier Pironi were unable to compete with the Renaults driven by René Arnoux and Alain Prost. Arnoux took pole with Prost half a second slower. Villeneuve and Pironi were third and fourth on the grid, separated by 1.4 seconds, Pironi having survived a hairy high-speed accident during qualifying which saw him fly backwards into a barrier. There is no rule which says that team-mates have to get on – indeed most drivers regard their team-mate as their fiercest rival – but the Ferrari pair got on better than most. Both were highly talented drivers. Pironi was determined and resourceful while Villeneuve was fearless and flamboyant, a throwback to the likes of Nuvolari. Villeneuve was by nature a trusting guy, and he trusted Pironi. On the evening before the race the two men had dinner together with their wives. All was sweetness and light.

Come the off and Arnoux was first away, pursued by Prost, but the latter was passed by the two Ferraris before the end of the opening lap, and when Prost retired with piston failure on lap seven, the leading three were the only serious contenders. The trio were separated by less than a second when, on lap 44 out of 60, Arnoux was forced to retire, his car belching out smoke. This left the Ferraris to win as they pleased, the only threat, apart from some unforeseen mechanical problem, being fuel consumption, since Imola was the thirstiest circuit in Formula One. Villeneuve now assumed the mantle of leader. Eager to conserve fuel, he eased off for a few laps and did not worry when Pironi passed him. The French-Canadian soon regained first place. To the crowd, the pair were simply putting on a show to liven up what might otherwise have turned into a dreary procession.

However, the Ferrari pit, which was without team leader Mauro Forghieri (absent on family business), became concerned that this constant jousting was drinking up the fuel, of which there was only just enough to see them through to the finish even at normal levels of consumption. So they ordered Villeneuve to slow, and he immediately responded by easing off to the tune of two seconds per lap. Ferrari team orders were that the man ahead when the red cars became first and second (in this case Villeneuve) should be the man ahead at the finish. Villeneuve clearly understood that and, backing off as ordered, was not unduly perturbed when Pironi put on a sudden spurt to overtake him again seven laps from the finish. This time the lead was not so easy to retake. On lap 58, Villeneuve drew alongside his team-mate under braking at the right-hander known as Tosa, only to be unceremoniously cut off. But on the following lap, Pironi did let him past. As far as Villeneuve was concerned, that was that. Pironi's antics had been nothing more than showmanship and now the pair would cruise around for a stress-free one-two. Then as they headed down towards Tosa for the last time at a conservative 180mph, Pironi suddenly shot past on the approach to the corner, catching Villeneuve totally unawares. The two cars nearly touched.

Since that was the last overtaking point on the track, there was no opportunity for Villeneuve to retaliate, and it was Pironi who crossed the line the winner of the 1982 San Marino Grand Prix.

Pironi stood on the victory rostrum waving happily to the crowd but next to him Villeneuve had a face like thunder. He didn't want to be there at all and had to be persuaded by his wife to appear before the Imola fans. As soon as the ceremony was over, Villeneuve stormed away from the circuit without saying a word to Pironi. In Villeneuve's opinion, Pironi had stolen the race in an act of treachery. Pironi pleaded his innocence and expressed the hope that he hadn't upset his team-mate, but Villeneuve did not appear interested in platitudes. He told reporters: 'The first two or three times he came inside and passed, I thought, well, he wants to play a little bit, and I never defended myself. But him, he was just racing, and I was too stupid to realise it. I thought he was an honest guy...'

They never did make up. Villeneuve was killed while practising for the next Grand Prix at Zolder in Belgium. Some say his mind was still on Imola.

ALL CHANGE AT MONACO

MONACO GRAND PRIX, 23 MAY 1982

The 40th running of the Monaco Grand Prix provided arguably the most dramatic ending to a race since the inauguration of the World Drivers' Championship, as a combination of light rain and spilt oil turned the circuit into a skating rink over the closing laps.

Until then the race had been pretty much a procession with championship leader Alain Prost taking the lead on the 15th of the 76 laps after his Renault team-mate René Arnoux had dropped out with mechanical failure. Riccardo Patrese in an old Brabham-Ford was tagging along in second but Nelson Piquet in the new, but still unreliable, turbo Brabham BMW had been forced to retire after 50 laps. The main excitement had centred on the battle for fourth place where Keke Rosberg (Williams) pressed Andrea de Cesaris (Alfa Romeo), until the Finn called it a day on lap 64 with a damaged front suspension.

Then a race which had appeared to be drifting towards a quiet conclusion suddenly came alive when it started to rain with five laps remaining. The first casualty was Derek Daly's Williams, which slid into the barrier at Tabac when lying fifth. Despite losing a rear wing and damaging the gearbox, Daly managed to get going again and was far enough ahead of Elio de Angelis's Lotus to retain his place, but then the battered Williams seized up completely at Rascasse hairpin and Daly was out of the race. Up front, Prost still had a seven-second

230

lead over Patrese and seemed secure until on lap 74 the Renault slid sideways exiting the seafront chicane, hit the barriers and lost a wheel. This put Patrese into the lead but less than a minute later he, too, slid to a halt near Loews hairpin. Didier Pironi's Ferrari and de Cesaris both got through before Patrese was able to get moving once more.

Patrese began the final lap a distant third with seemingly no hope of victory, unaware that ahead of him both Pironi and de Cesaris were reduced to cruising because the punishing track had left them short of fuel. Pironi ground to a halt in the tunnel, out of fuel and with an electrical problem to boot. Seconds later, on the approach to the tunnel, de Cesaris ran out of fuel. Patrese could hardly believe his eyes as he passed the two stationary cars and proceeded to tiptoe to the finish for his first-ever Grand Prix win. Pironi and de Cesaris were credited with second and third places respectively a lap behind the winner, with Nigel Mansell a hard-earned fourth in the Lotus.

A FIT OF PIQUET

GERMAN GRAND PRIX, 8 AUGUST 1982

The 1982 German Grand Prix at Hockenheim is remembered for one thing – an amazing physical assault launched by Nelson Piquet on Chilean driver Eliseo Salazar. For many, Piquet's attempt to turn the race track into a boxing ring was horribly reminiscent of James Hunt's altercation with David Morgan at Crystal Palace 12 years earlier.

The reigning world champion, Piquet had a fragile temperament at the best of times and the turbocharged Brabham BMW's erratic performances in 1982 tested his patience to the full. For while the car was undeniably fast, it also had a tendency to break down when least expected. So when it did finally appear to be doing the business on the track, it was doubly frustrating for Piquet to be put out of the race by a back-marker. That, however, was no excuse for the bout of fisticuffs which followed.

Practice at Hockenheim was responsible for eliminating two of the top drivers. Ferrari team leader Didier Pironi was involved in a nasty smash which put him out for the rest of the season. His new team-mate, following the tragic death of Gilles Villeneuve, was Frenchman Patrick Tambay and now, in Pironi's absence, it was he who had the task of waving the flag for Ferrari. The other missing name was that of Niki Lauda, forced to withdraw after tearing wrist ligaments following a crash in his McLaren.

The race began badly for the Arrows team. Marc Surer

suffered engine problems on the warm-up lap and then Mauro Baldi's car refused to start on the grid. By the time Baldi eventually got away, he was a lap behind everyone else. At the sharp end of the grid, René Arnoux's Renault was first away but on lap two he was passed by Piquet. The Brazilian's plan was to make a mid-race fuel stop so he started with only half a fuel load and on softer tyres, aiming to build up a big lead. By lap 19 of 45, he had established a 26-second advantage over second-placed Tambay when he came to lap Salazar's ATS at the new East Curve chicane. Piquet expected Salazar to move over and let him through, but the Chilean didn't and as the two cars braked, the ATS caught the Brabham in the side, putting both cars out of the race. Piquet was incandescent with rage. He stormed over to Salazar and began kicking and punching him. It has to be said that the blows to the head were particularly misguided since Salazar was still wearing his helmet! When the red mist had finally evaporated, Piquet made dark mutterings about Salazar having also held him up at Zandvoort in the Dutch Grand Prix. They were clearly not bosom buddies.

By the time Piquet went off, a number of the leading contenders had already bitten the dust. His team-mate, Riccardo Patrese, had retired with engine trouble, Alain Prost's Renault dropped out after 11 laps with fuel injection problems when lying fourth, and John Watson was running third until he came to grief at a chicane. This left the way clear for Tambay, who proceeded to lap everyone bar Arnoux and came home the winner by 16 seconds. His first Grand Prix success gave the Ferrari team a timely boost. Third spot went to Keke Rosberg in the Williams, whose progress was impaired in the latter stages by gear selection difficulties. After an early stop for a replacement skirt for his Lotus, Nigel Mansell rallied to finish ninth.

But the next day's headlines belonged to Piquet.

A HINT OF NATIONAL BIAS?

SWISS GRAND PRIX, 29 AUGUST 1982

It could probably only happen in France. A French driver is leading with two laps remaining but is being rapidly caught by a Finn. So what does the man with the chequered flag do? He tries to wave it two laps early to secure a home victory.

Such a scenario might sound far-fetched, but few neutrals who were present at Dijon in August 1982 could come up with any other explanation for the curious antics at the end of the Swiss Grand Prix.

It was an odd race from the outset. But then again, it was an odd year all round in Formula One. For the answer to the riddle, 'When is a Swiss Grand Prix not a Swiss Grand Prix?' is simply, 'When it was in 1982.' Already that season the Spanish Grand Prix had not taken place, a race had suddenly appeared around the streets of Detroit, the Dutch Grand Prix had happened when everyone thought it would be off, there were four Grands Prix in five weeks when it had been universally agreed to allow two weeks between races, and, to cap it all, there were now two Grands Prix in France. The official French Grand Prix had taken place earlier in the season at Paul Ricard, but now a second event – calling itself the Swiss Grand Prix even though it was being staged on French soil – cropped up at Dijon. It was all highly confusing.

Alain Prost put his Renault on pole from team-mate René Arnoux and Riccardo Patrese in a Brabham-BMW. But there was little jubilation in the Renault camp as Arnoux had just announced that he was joining Ferrari for the 1983 season. Renault had no intention of keeping him anyway – not after he had disobeyed team orders to snatch the prize from Prost at the official French Grand Prix – but the atmosphere in the pit was one of stony silence whenever Arnoux was around, not least because Renault were anxious to prevent him giving away precious team secrets to the opposition.

Patrick Tambay withdrew on the morning of the race with back trouble, leaving 25 starters. Arnoux got away fastest and led them around for the first time but then Prost took control. Nelson Piquet's Brabham-BMW went second, only to surrender the position to Arnoux when stopping for fuel and tyres at mid-distance. In fact Piquet's pit stop proved a disaster for the Brazilian as his replacement tyres were out of balance. He was lapped soon after rejoining the race and never again threatened the leaders.

Piquet's decline allowed Keke Rosberg to inherit third place in his Williams but a delay in lapping Andrea de Cesaris, who refused to let him by, meant that his chances of catching the two Renaults appeared remote. Then with ten of the 80 laps remaining, Arnoux retired, the car's fuel injection system having failed. And suddenly Prost was slowing too. He had lost fourth gear. As Rosberg pegged him back, the French crowd grew increasingly uneasy. With just over two laps remaining, it seemed only a matter of time before Rosberg caught and passed the Renault. At that point Williams team manager Peter Collins noticed that the official with the chequered flag was about to hang it out...two laps early. Collins quickly pointed out the 'error' and the flag was put away. Sure enough on lap 79, to the accompaniment of groans from the crowd, Rosberg caught and passed Prost at the downhill left-hander. The Frenchman had no answer.

After seconds that year in Brazil, the United States, Belgium and Austria, Rosberg approached the finish line for the 80th time and prepared to celebrate his first ever World Championship Grand Prix win – at the 49th attempt. Yet bizarrely, having tried to end the race two laps prematurely, the man with the chequered flag now compounded his blunder by failing to spot Rosberg as he roared by. So the bemused Finn did an extra circuit and finally received the flag at the end of lap 81! In mitigation, it was pointed out that the Swiss had not staged a Grand Prix since 1954...

Niki Lauda came third for McLaren while Nigel Mansell, having started from last on the grid, fought his way up to finish eighth of the 16 survivors. Rosberg's sole victory of the year turned out to be sufficient to clinch the title, but no thanks to the man with the chequered flag at Dijon... whether his actions were guided by sheer incompetence or something more sinister.

IT'S A WASHOUT

BIRMINGHAM SUPER PRIX, 25 AUGUST 1986

As far back as 1960, a group of motor sport enthusiasts proposed turning Birmingham into Britain's answer to Monte Carlo. Perhaps because Gas Street Basin did not quite possess the allure of the French Riviera, this attempt to stage Britain's first street race came to nothing. But the idea was revived from time to time, and in the late seventies and early eighties permission was granted for a series of parades of old racing cars to be held in the city. These proved such an attraction that the plan for a Birmingham street race reared its head once more, but this time with the backing of the local council. It was a period of high unemployment in the West Midlands and the city council was anxious to improve Birmingham's rather dour image, to make it more attractive to investors and tourists. After a local referendum offered overwhelming support for the idea of staging a Grand Prix on the dual carriageways in the city centre, an Act of Parliament gave the official go-ahead. Public roads were to be closed over a two-day period around the 1986 August Bank Holiday. The Birmingham Super Prix was up and running.

A 2.5-mile, L-shaped circuit was mapped out around the inner ring road and adjoining thoroughfares, making it the fastest street circuit in the world. Sir Jack Brabham, who had business interests in the Midlands, voiced his approval of the event and the city council forked out £1.5 million in anticipation of attracting 100,000 spectators over the two days.

237

Temporary grandstands were built and eight miles of crash barriers and wire fences were erected to protect people and houses. The main race was announced as the 52-lap Halfords Super Prix – a round of the European Formula 3000 Championship, just one step below Formula One. Its inclusion was significant. For the ultimate goal was to bring the British Grand Prix itself to Birmingham.

Inevitably, not everyone in Birmingham welcomed motor racing to the city streets. Local church leaders decided to cancel some Sunday services because they thought the noise would make worship impossible and residents close to the circuit were made virtual prisoners in their own homes, a feeling intensified by the eight-foot-high wire fences which had suddenly appeared at the end of their small front gardens. Some were horrified at the prospect of trying to eat Sunday lunch while racing cars sped by at 150mph barely ten yards from their dining-room windows.

Despite a delay to the start of practice after vandals had removed bolts from crash barriers, Sunday passed off smoothly. The spectator numbers were high – their behaviour guaranteed by the presence of around 1,000 police officers – and the standard of racing was first rate. Monday's big race, the Super Prix, was therefore eagerly anticipated.

But the British summer rarely fails to disappoint. No matter that thousands of would-be spectators had pre-booked, that the event was being televised in 35 countries, or that a city's sporting reputation was at stake: the heavens opened. And the more it rained, the more people stayed away, the police estimating that only 20,000 braved the elements on that Bank Holiday Monday. The prolonged and torrential downpour reduced the streets of hope to a river of broken dreams. The signs were ominous when driver Robin Smith was taken to hospital in a Thundersports race after his Ford-Cosworth had hit crash barriers at over 100mph and burst into flames, but the organisers were determined that the main course on the sumptuous menu should proceed. Thus the Super Prix began, only to disintegrate into a series of high-speed crashes on the

238

slippery circuit. Finally with two cars strewn across the road after 25 highly eventful laps, the decision was taken to abandon the race. Victory – of sorts – went to Luis Sala in an F3000 Ralt-Cosworth, but many drivers were critical of the organisers for not stopping the race earlier.

Although faced with a loss of £400,000 on the event, John Charlton, chairman of Birmingham City Council's Road Race Committee, remained upbeat: 'I am amazed we have been able to pull it off when everybody said that we could not. We have produced one of the best road race circuits in the world and we are guaranteed to hold it until 1990. We don't do things by halves in Birmingham. We have bid for the Olympics in 1992 and we can bid for the Grand Prix. We want to make Birmingham the sporting capital of Britain.'

The world awaits.

A FAMILY AFFAIR

DAYTONA 500, 14 FEBRUARY 1988

The 30th anniversary Daytona 500 provided an appropriate story when father and son Bobby and Davey Allison finished first and second for a unique Valentine's Day family double.

At 50, Bobby Allison was a seasoned campaigner at Daytona with two previous wins there to his name, the first back in 1978. Davey was 26 and had already earned a reputation as a very fast racer. That is precisely the attribute needed for Daytona where, in 1988, Ken Schrader put a Chevrolet Monte Carlo on pole at a speed of 193.8mph – and even that was 15mph down on the previous year following the introduction of new regulations which reduced the cars' power by 150bhp. Schrader's Chevrolet team-mate, Darrell Waltrip (his car painted in the livery of Tide washing powder), started fourth on the grid of 42 but led the field for the first ten laps. He was followed by Rusty Wallace in a Pontiac, Bobby Allison in a Buick Regal and Davey Allison in a Ford Thunderbird. On lap 11 Bobby Allison moved into the lead, using the slipstream of the car ahead, but two laps later Waltrip pulled off a similar manoeuvre to retake first place and was followed through by Davey Allison.

On lap 32 Mark Martin's Ford blew its engine, bringing out the yellow flags. The drivers headed for the pits and when racing resumed Wallace found himself in the lead. Then on lap 53 Bobby Allison seized the initiative once more and this time began to pull away from the chasing pack, before Waltrip, despite being handicapped by extra-curricular pit stops, fought his way back into contention. A major incident occurred on lap 103 when Richard Petty lost control of his Pontiac coming out of a turn and was shunted by Phil Barkdoll's Ford Thunderbird into the path of A.J. Foyt's Oldsmobile Delta. Petty's car somersaulted through the air in spectacular fashion and smashed against the safety fence, sending pieces of debris flying in all directions. What remained of the car finished up in the middle of the track, necessitating another session of racing under yellow flags. Remarkably Petty escaped with nothing more serious than an ankle injury.

By lap 153 Waltrip had forced his way back into the lead from Davey Allison with father Bobby in third, but another crash led to more yellow flags and a further change in the order. After that final round of pit stops, Davey Allison led away from Waltrip and Bobby Allison, only for Waltrip's challenge to fade thanks to a blown cylinder. This left father and son to battle it out to the death, and Bobby's experience prevailed when he overtook the Ford to come home the winner by just two car lengths. His time was 3hr 38min and his average speed for the race a cool 137.5mph.

Afterwards the oldest-ever winner of the Daytona 500 was congratulated by his wife Judy, who joked: 'He'll probably be here till he's 95!' Bobby gushed: 'It's just a special feeling. I saw the nose of his car coming out of the corner of my eye, and I thought I had the suds to beat him. He is a tremendous competitor. It's a great feeling to see somebody you think is the best coming up in the sport and know it's your son.' Davey was equally complimentary. 'I've had dreams for a long time about battling down to the wire with my dad. The only difference was that I never had dreams of finishing second. The whole race I was trying to put myself in a position where I was going to win the race and, hopefully, Dad would finish second. My whole concentration was on winning. If my car could have beaten him, it would have. I didn't think of him as my dad until the chequered flag fell. But really, it's better than if I had won myself – he's always been my hero.'

However, it was not all happy families. In June that year Bobby Allison was involved in a horrific smash at Pocono, Pennsylvania, which put him in hospital for three months with fractured bones and serious internal injuries. He never raced again. As a result of the smash, he suffered memory loss and had no recollection of his third Daytona victory. Luckily his son was on hand to tell him all about it.

Three years later the Andretti family – Mario, his sons Michael and Jeff, and his nephew John – became the first four family members to start the Indianapolis 500. Michael finished second, John fifth, Mario seventh and Jeff 15th. Also in 1991 the Andrettis filled the first three places at the Milwaukee Mile, Michael winning from John and Mario. Jeff let the side down by only finishing 11th.

THE BATTLE OF SUZUKA

JAPANESE GRAND PRIX, 21 OCTOBER 1990

To say that there was no love lost between Ayrton Senna and Alain Prost is like saying that Britain and Germany didn't get along terribly well between 1939 and 1945. Although they were McLaren team-mates for a while, they were poles apart. Senna was the wild, hot-headed Brazilian, capable of moments of genius and moments of madness. Prost was the analytical – sometimes aloof – Frenchman, nicknamed 'the Professor'. Both were great drivers, but both thought they were king of the road.

The presence of two such strong personalities in the same team may have looked good on paper but in practice it was little short of a nightmare. It was similar to having an orchestra with two conductors, and neither was happy to play second fiddle. The tension between the pair first surfaced at the 1988 Portuguese Grand Prix when Senna ruthlessly chopped Prost at 190mph as the Frenchman tried to pass. Senna took the title that year, but in 1989 Prost was ahead on points as the season entered its penultimate round in Japan. Prost needed only to finish in front of Senna to become champion for the third time. Ominously, he issued an advance warning that he was not prepared to tolerate any of the Brazilian's rough-house tactics on this occasion. He would fight fire with fire. Prost led from the start but Senna, in a typically determined drive, gradually pegged back the advantage. With ten laps remaining the cars were running nose to tail, Senna desperately searching for a hint of an opening. Six laps from the finish he thought he had found one – up the inside at the chicane. He left the braking as late as he dared and dived for the gap. Prost simply turned in on him and took both cars out of the race. Prost was champion. Each blamed the other for the collision.

For the 1990 season Prost had joined Ferrari. Again the Japanese Grand Prix at Suzuka was the penultimate round but this time the positions were reversed. With only five wins to Senna's six, Prost had to score at least one more point than Senna to keep the title battle alive going into the final race at Adelaide. More significantly, as it transpired, if neither car finished at Suzuka, Senna would be champion. Senna put the McLaren on pole with Prost alongside him, just three-tenths of a second behind. It had all the makings of a charge into the first corner. Whoever got there first would have an outstanding chance of staying there. Senna knew that, and was furious at being ordered to start from the right-hand side of the track, which was much dustier than the left. Having gained pole, he thought he had earned the right to decide where he would prefer to start from. He protested, but FISA president Jean-Marie Balestre refused to reconsider. Senna simmered and sulked. In his eyes, Prost, although only second fastest, had been given the side of the track with the superior grip. Senna made a mental note of his race plan: 'If Prost gets the best start, then I'm warning him, he'd better not turn in on me because he isn't going to make it.' It was to prove a chillingly accurate prophecy.

Race day was warm and sunny, a deceptively tranquil backdrop to the drama that was about to unfold. On the front row of the grid, the two combatants sat in their cars a matter of yards apart, waiting anxiously for the green light. When it finally came, Prost, as Senna had feared, got the better start from the cleaner side of the track. Prost, with a slight advantage, inched towards the racing line which he would need to negotiate Turn One, the Ferrari's superior power giving him a lead of almost a car's length approaching the corner. Instead of coming across and blocking Senna completely, Prost edged back a fraction towards the outside. Senna sensed a gap, albeit a minimal one, and made for it. Prost eased off slightly to take the turn but Senna kept his foot hard down and smashed into the Ferrari, taking both cars out of the race. Mission accomplished. Senna was champion.

Prost was outraged. 'I am not prepared to fight against irresponsible people who are not afraid to die,' he stormed. Senna maintained the pretence of innocence...at least for another year. But in the meantime the shortest championship decider in history had gone his way. Sure, it was controversial, but in Senna's book the ends always justified the means.

THE 25-MINUTE GRAND PRIX

AUSTRALIAN GRAND PRIX, 3 NOVEMBER 1991

Ayrton Senna had already sealed the 1991 Formula One World Drivers' Championship by the time the cars headed for Adelaide for the last event of the season. It was to be one of the shortest races in living memory.

It was run in torrential rain with visibility down to the bare minimum. Many of the leading drivers, including rain-master Senna and Nigel Mansell, felt that the race should never have started, even though Mansell's Williams team still had a chance of lifting the constructors' championship at the expense of McLaren.

From the start, Mansell tucked in behind Senna's McLaren. Mansell said it was like groping in the pitch dark: 'I followed Ayrton round and gauged my driving by listening to his engine, to his gear changes. Then I would do the same, hoping I hadn't misheard his car. But as far as seeing is concerned, forget it.' Soon a number of cars went off on the hazardous back straight and while the marshals frantically waved yellow flags (to indicate no overtaking), the rescue services were busily lifting battered cars off the circuit. At one point Mansell poked out from behind Senna to have a look and found himself heading straight for a marshal's car!

Mansell was expecting to see the red flag signifying the end of the race after only four laps but the organisers kept the drivers out there for another ten circuits. Indeed the race was only finally stopped when Mansell spun off and crashed into a concrete wall, an accident which left him with a badly swollen ankle. As soon as Mansell went off, Senna started gesticulating angrily for the race to be stopped, and the stewards took the hint. Only 14 of the scheduled 81 laps had been completed but, despite the atrocious conditions, the clerk of the course was eager to give the rain a chance to ease off and kept everyone waiting for another 50 minutes before finally calling it a day. The placings were calculated on the last completed lap, which put Mansell second behind Senna despite his spin. Gerhard Berger was third in the other McLaren, a result which gave the team its fourth constructors' championship in a row. Since there had barely been 25 minutes' actual racing, half points were awarded to the first six drivers.

The curtailed race was unsatisfactory for all concerned, not least FISA vice-president Bernie Ecclestone who was highly critical of the marshalling and stewarding. He did not share the view that conditions were unraceable and thought that producing a white flag (to indicate there was a slow car on the circuit) together with yellow flags to stop any overtaking, would have given the rescue crews time to clear the debris. Senna, Mansell and co. were just happy to be back in the dry.

MANSELL AND THE SAFETY TRUCK

INDY CAR CHAMPIONSHIP ROUND 6,
13 JUNE 1993

Piqued by the signing of Alain Prost for the Williams team for 1993 and by the fact that Frank Williams was not willing to meet his pay demands, reigning Formula One world champion Nigel Mansell packed his bags and took his ample frame across the Atlantic to go Indy Car racing for Paul Newman's team. Many doubters thought he was taking one hell of a gamble simply to prove a point, but it turned out to be a gloriously successful year, with Mansell taking the United States by storm and powering his way to the Indy Car championship to become the first person ever to lift the two titles in successive years. Indeed for one week, before Alain Prost snatched the Formula One crown at Estoril, Mansell was in the unique position of being a dual champion, holding both titles simultaneously.

Inevitably the triumphal march was interrupted by the occasional hiccup. One was in Detroit.

The city had been synonymous with indifferent racing since 1982 when it first staged the United States Grand Prix, the potholed street circuit and uninspiring layout falling foul of the Formula One drivers. Alain Prost intimated that he would rather retire than have to race there every week and Keke Rosberg described it as dull. 'Most of the stuff,' said the Finn in 1985, 'is 90 degrees around the block, 50 yards and then another 90 degrees. I just can't get excited about it.' In 1989 the Detroit track became part of the Indy Car season. The following year's race was stopped when Mario Andretti smashed into one of the organisers' safety trucks, and then Mario's son, Michael, ploughed into his father. So it was by popular request that in 1992 the race switched to the city's tricky 2.1-mile Belle Isle Park circuit on the Detroit River. Here, too, there was to be no shortage of incident, especially when Mansell came to town in 1993.

After five weeks of racing on ovals, a twisting street course with 14 turns made a pleasant change for the Indy Car drivers, although it made little difference to the composition of the grid with Mansell, the clear championship leader, taking his familiar pole position in the Newman-Haas Lola-Ford ahead of the Penske Racing cars of Emerson Fittipaldi and 24-year-old Canadian Paul Tracy. Already that season Mansell had shown a tendency to throw away his hard-earned pole with sluggish starts and this looked to be no exception when, at the fall of the green flag, he was seen shaking his fist in frustration as Fittipaldi surged past him on the run to Turn One on the first of the 77 laps.

Mansell was clearly unhappy with the Brazilian's lightning getaway and 13 laps later Championship Auto Racing Team (CART) officials decided to give a stop-go penalty to Fittipaldi for jumping the start. This decision was met with disbelief in many circles, since the general rule was that once the green flag dropped, the race was on. If Fittipaldi had been moving forward at the start, it was up to the starter not to display the green flag. 'If there's something wrong with the start, they should throw the yellow,' said an irate Roger Penske. 'They threw the green and we went. What happened after that doesn't mean a thing.'

To add insult to injury, Fittipaldi crashed while trying to make up the lost ground and team-mate Tracy, who had been running second, was penalised for speeding on the pit road. But Mansell was not about to get off lightly either. First, he collided with Stefan Johansson while the pair were disputing third place and then – the ultimate ignominy – he crashed out of the race while swerving to avoid a safety truck!

Having started from tenth on the grid, 1988 Indy Car series winner Danny Sullivan now found himself narrowly in the lead from Galles Racing team-mate Al Unser Jr. Although Sullivan was slowed by a leaky turbo, Unser was unable to force his way past on the winding circuit. Increasingly frustrated, Unser made a desperate move with nine laps remaining but Sullivan refused to yield and forced his team-mate into the cones. Having penalised drivers in practice and qualifying for hitting the cones, CART steward Wally Dallenbach felt duty bound to be consistent and issued Unser with a stop-go penalty. Sullivan held on to win from Brazilian Raul Boesel, with Mario Andretti third. A disgusted Unser was back in sixth. His only consolation was that for once he had a better day at the races than Mansell.

THE RACE AGAINST THE TRAIN

ORIENT EXPRESS RACE, 9 SEPTEMBER 1993

Inspired by tales of derring-do from the 1920s when the famous Bentley Boys raced the Blue Train between London and the French Riviera, sipping champagne en route, the 96 Motoring Club organised a 1,000-mile race against the Orient Express from London to Milan.

So it was that 45 classic cars – among them a D-Type Jaguar, a Mercedes gullwing, a Daimler SP250 sports car, and a 1922 Vauxhall – lined up at London's Victoria Station one Thursday alongside the Orient Express. As the train pulled away from the station, Lord Montagu of Beaulieu waved off the cars on their journey across five countries, which included a crossing of the Swiss Alps. The rules of the race were simple: any car taking a short cut or exceeding that country's speed limit would be disqualified. Michael Scott of the 96 Motoring Club emphasised: 'Any car that arrives in Milan before 5 p.m. on Friday evening (the 10th) will obviously have speeded and will be disqualified.'

After racing around Brands Hatch and the Monthléry circuit outside Paris, the cars completed their first day with a lap of the Nürburgring, near Frankfurt. The second day, racing against the train resumed with a dawn start from Frankfurt. Although the drivers stopped off for the obligatory sip of champagne, the result was never in doubt, most of the cars arriving in Italy hours before the Orient Express. The first to reach Milan – eight hours in advance of the train – was Mark

Chauveau in a 1973 Maserati, but he admitted that he had cheated by missing out Germany in order to fulfil an important lunch date in the Italian city. 'It was such a complicated route,' he said, 'that I decided to go via Geneva in search of some entertainment. I don't think I can be classified as a winner, but I had great fun. In Italy I was mobbed at every traffic light as the Italians went crazy over the car.'

Ultimately Pentti Airikkala was declared the winner in a Mitsubishi 3000 GT. His scariest moment was arriving in Milan and not being able to find the railway station. He resorted to flagging down a young moped rider who led him to the station. As the organisers summed up: 'The train was thrashed.'

LET THE SUNSHINE IN

WORLD SOLAR CHALLENGE, 27 OCTOBER 1996

Held every three years and run over a 1,870-mile course from Darwin to Adelaide, the World Solar Challenge has earned a reputation as the world's biggest race for solar-powered transport. The 1996 event attracted no fewer than 57 cars and bicycles with the British hoping to improve on their dismal showing of previous years. Only one British competitor, Philip Farrand, an engineer with the Williams Grand Prix team, had ever even managed to complete the distance, coming second in the conventional lead-acid class in 1993. In that same year the only other British entrant, laboratory engineer Brian Hamilton, failed to make it off the start line.

But the British faced tough opposition from the Honda 'Dream' car which, with its covering of mono-crystal silicon cells, was capable of speeds in excess of 90mph and could cruise at 56mph. The energy from the solar panels was stored in a silver-oxide zinc battery powering a DC brushless motor. In the world of solar transport, it was a formidable machine.

The starters – scaled down from an original list of some 300 – set off from Darwin on 27 October for their long trek across the outback via Alice Springs to the south. The race was spread over four days, but there was rarely any doubt as to which car would be first to reach Adelaide. The Honda Dream car won in 33hr 32min at an average of 55.77mph, clipping over two hours off the previous record. A team of Swiss students were runners-up with their Schooler Spirit '96 car in a time of 35hr and Japan's Aisol III finished third in 37hr 18min. For the British, world solar supremacy remained a distant vision.

ROAD RAGE

EUROPEAN GRAND PRIX, 26 OCTOBER 1997

Ever since Michael Schumacher took Damon Hill out of the 1994 Australian Grand Prix to clinch the World Drivers' Championship, accusing fingers were pointed in the German's direction. Schumacher maintained that the Adelaide incident was simply a racing accident, but many – Hill included – suspected a more sinister motive. Schumacher's ability as a driver was not open to question, but few doubted his ruthlessness either. It seemed that, faced with the prospect of losing the title, he would not hesitate to remove his rival from the equation. He had done it once and got away with it, argued the cynics. If a similar situation arose in the future, would he be able to resist doing the same again? The answer came three years later in the European Grand Prix at Jerez in Spain. If you're a Schumacher fan, look away now.

This time Schumacher's chief rival was the young Canadian driver Jacques Villeneuve in a Williams. It had been a close-fought contest all season but after 13 rounds of the 17-race championship, Schumacher, now with Ferrari, held a ten-point lead. He was within sight of becoming the first Ferrari driver since Jody Scheckter in 1979 to win the world title, and he knew how much that meant to the Ferrari fans, the famous *tifosi*. But then Villeneuve retaliated with wins in the Austrian and Luxembourg Grands Prix before Schumacher countered with victory in Japan. Going into the final race at Jerez, Schumacher led by a solitary point. If neither car finished, he would be world champion.

Mindful of this, at the pre-race briefing Formula One supremo Bernie Ecclestone told all the drivers that he wanted a fair fight on the track. 'If one or other of the drivers takes the other out,' he warned, 'then the punishment will be draconian.'

The stage was set in qualifying when Villeneuve, Schumacher and Heinz-Harald Frentzen (Williams) all recorded identical times. Since Villeneuve was the first to set the time, it was he who started from pole, alongside Schumacher. The German was philosophical, pointing out that it was the start that mattered. And the next day it was Schumacher who made the dream start, roaring away from the two Williams to the delight of the 18,000 *tifosi* watching the race on a giant screen in the town square at Maranello. Villeneuve's slow getaway left him in third, but on lap eight Frentzen pulled over to let his team-mate pass and launch a full-scale attack on Schumacher.

For the time being, Schumacher, in the supposedly inferior car, was able to hold Villeneuve at bay and had extended his lead to 5.2 seconds when the first round of pit stops began. With new tyres, a frustrated Schumacher exited the pits, only to find himself stuck behind Frentzen and David Coulthard, enabling Villeneuve to close right up. When Frentzen and Coulthard pitted, Schumacher had a clear run and on lap 30 it was the Canadian's turn to suffer as he lost precious ground trying to lap Norberto Fontana's Sauber. By the time Villeneuve eventually got past, he was 3.2 seconds behind Schumacher. After the two leaders had made their second stops, Villeneuve was noticeably closer...close enough to attempt the bold passing manoeuvre which would ultimately decide the race and the championship.

Schumacher was leading Villeneuve along the back straight on lap 48 out of 69. Approaching the right-hander known as Curva Dry Sac, Villeneuve attacked Schumacher from a long way back, taking him completely by surprise. Diving through on the inside – into a gap which Schumacher had surprisingly left – Villeneuve braked extremely late and was able to draw level with the Ferrari. At the last minute, Schumacher suddenly jerked the steering wheel and drove into the side of the Williams. It was the same story as at Adelaide, but this time with a different ending. For while Schumacher finished up on the gravel and out of the race, Villeneuve's car, although damaged, was able to continue. The biter had been bitten.

Villeneuve nursed his car around the remaining 21 laps. At first he wasn't sure whether it would hold out but after two slow laps, he saw that the suspension was bearing up and felt confident enough to push on again. Then towards the finish, not needing a victory, he allowed the McLarens of Mika Hakkinen and Coulthard to pass, the Finn going on for his first Grand Prix win at the 96th attempt. The four points which Villeneuve secured for finishing third made him world champion.

At the post-race inquest into the drama on lap 48, Villeneuve was remarkably diplomatic. 'I was aware that Michael could take me out. In fact, I think the move only had a 50 per cent chance of success. But I had noticed that my car was definitely better after I fitted new tyres and I could not wait to attack. It would have been pointless to finish second and I preferred taking the risk of finishing in the gravel than to stay behind until the end.'

Schumacher once again protested his innocence. 'He tried a rather optimistic attack. It worked for him but not for me. I am human and, unfortunately, make mistakes. I do not make many, but this was a big one. I see no reason to apologise.'

His old adversary Damon Hill was predictably critical, maintaining: 'Michael showed his true colours and got what he deserved.' What Schumacher also got was the threatened 'draconian punishment' which saw him stripped of his second place in the World Championship. Few outside Germany or Maranello had much sympathy for him.

AFTER YOU, MIKA!

AUSTRALIAN GRAND PRIX, 8 MARCH 1998

Just over four months after Jacques Villeneuve had gifted him the European Grand Prix, Mika Hakkinen received another present – this time from his McLaren team-mate David Coulthard in the form of the 1998 season's opening race, the Australian Grand Prix. Whereas Villeneuve's gesture was motivated by self-preservation, plus the fact that the McLarens were going faster than him anyway, and consequently scarcely caused a ripple on the Formula One millpond, Coulthard's unprecedented act of generosity was a different matter altogether. At Albert Park, Melbourne, he handed over a winning position to a team-mate whom he clearly had the beating of on the day. Puzzled observers reckoned that it was a move the mild-mannered Scot would live to regret. How right they were.

The winter testing programme strongly suggested that McLaren would be the team to beat for 1998. Certainly the two drivers were full of confidence, to the extent that they made a pre-race pact whereby whichever of them was ahead entering the first corner would be allowed to stay there for the rest of the Grand Prix, barring mishaps. The idea behind the agreement was that it would stop the two team-mates from fighting – and possibly destroying – each other. Nevertheless it was a curious state of affairs for the cut and thrust of modern motor racing and one which led directly to the controversy which subsequently engulfed the 1998 Australian Grand Prix.

McLaren threw down the gauntlet in qualifying, Hakkinen and Coulthard posting the fastest times by over 0.7 seconds from Michael Schumacher's Ferrari and the Williams of reigning champion Jacques Villeneuve. That may not sound much in ordinary terms, but in the supercharged world of Formula One where technology is king, 0.7 seconds could seem like an eternity.

Coulthard later joked that when he agreed to the pact, he had naturally assumed that he would be leading into the first corner, but in fact the opposite was the case. With the cars held for a long time on the grid under the red lights, Coulthard's engine started to smoke. At the split second he glanced down, the lights went out. The momentary hesitation allowed Hakkinen to get away first and lead his team-mate through that all-important opening turn. Once safely in front, the McLarens set a blistering pace. Schumacher tried to hang on to Coulthard's coat tails but on lap six out of 58 he retired with engine trouble. Even at such an early stage, he was the sixth retirement, following in the wake of both Stewarts and his brother Ralf. Nor could Villeneuve stay with the McLarens and soon he was passed by Williams team-mate Heinz-Harald Frentzen, the Ferrari of Eddie Irvine and the Benetton of Giancarlo Fisichella.

With the McLarens apparently coasting to victory, a bizarre incident occurred on lap 36. Hakkinen was just about to lap Irvine when he heard indistinct noises over the radio. He thought he had to come in and refuel and since he was level with the pit lane entry, he dived in before checking on the radio. But when he reached the McLaren pit, there was nobody around, so he simply drove straight on and rejoined the race! However, the detour had dropped him back to second spot, some 13 seconds behind Coulthard.

Eight laps later the McLaren pit informed Coulthard over the radio that Hakkinen had lost the lead because of a misunderstanding. Remembering the pre-race pact, Coulthard thought long and hard about what to do. He said afterwards: 'It was a very difficult decision to take. But I was alone in front without any pressure, which allowed me to think about it calmly and to reach the decision that this was Mika's race by right.' Accordingly, he told the pit that he was going to let Hakkinen through. Thus, three laps from the end of what had otherwise been a keenly contested race, the Albert Park crowd and millions of television viewers across the world were treated to the strange – and somewhat unsatisfactory – sight of the leader slowing down and moving aside to allow his team-mate to pass.

Hakkinen went on to record a hollow victory from Coulthard, Frentzen, Irvine, Villeneuve, and the Sauber of Johnny Herbert. Of course when he crossed the finish line, only the McLaren team knew about the private agreement, but even when it became public knowledge there was widespread incredulity. How could Coulthard afford to give the man who was likely be his principal championship rival a four-point start? The answer was: he couldn't.

At the post-race press conference Hakkinen was asked whether he would do the same for Coulthard if the boot was on the other foot. There was a seemingly interminable pause before Hakkinen grinned: 'Yes, yes, of course.' Three years on, and Coulthard was still waiting.

SCHUMACHER WINS IN THE PITS

BRITISH GRAND PRIX, 12 JULY 1998

A rain-soaked British Grand Prix at Silverstone ended in mayhem with nobody seeming to know whether Michael Schumacher or Mika Hakkinen had won. It all centred on the interpretation, delivery and timing of a ten-second penalty to Schumacher but when the fuss had died down, it emerged that the German had earned the distinction of becoming the first driver ever to win a Grand Prix in the pit lane.

After a lightning start to the season when they looked destined to sweep all before them, the wheels had come off the McLaren wagon over the previous two Grands Prix. Comprehensive defeats in Canada and France – coupled with two Schumacher successes – had put a different complexion on the championship race. After eight rounds, Schumacher was within six points of Hakkinen with Coulthard – perhaps beginning to regret his largesse in Australia – languishing 14 points behind the German in third. Suddenly there was a real race on. Ferrari could sniff McLaren blood and their drivers, especially the outspoken Eddie Irvine, were making plenty of capital out of the Woking team's sudden vulnerability. But now McLaren were back on home soil. The British Grand Prix would be the perfect venue to answer their critics.

Hakkinen did his bit, qualifying on pole, but Coulthard was only fourth fastest – behind Schumacher and Jacques Villeneuve. Irvine and Heinz-Harald Frentzen made up row three. Hakkinen was cautiously optimistic but the weather forecast for Sunday's race was heavy rain, and Schumacher was the acknowledged rain-master.

Hakkinen and Schumacher both made good starts but Villeneuve was away slowly and found himself behind Coulthard and the Sauber of Jean Alesi, who gained four places from his grid position. Irvine also made a poor start and things looked grim for Ferrari when Coulthard eased past Schumacher at Abbey Curve. After a dozen laps light rain began to fall and when it became increasingly persistent, the cars started a mad scramble for the pits. Some didn't make it in time. To the dismay of the crowd, Damon Hill spun off on lap 14 and was followed two laps later by Frentzen. Only Hakkinen of the leading bunch moved on to wet tyres, the rest opting for intermediates. Coulthard made steady inroads into his team-mate's advantage until the rain suddenly started to get heavier around lap 26. Soon Johnny Herbert and Mika Salo (Arrows) went off and Esteban Tuero's Minardi was involved in a shunt with Ricardo Rosset's Tyrrell. Coulthard, in particular, was struggling in the wet conditions and spun three times in quick succession, finally exiting the race on lap 38. He later expressed his anger at being put on intermediates while Hakkinen had the benefit of wets.

The rain had now reached monsoon level, resulting in further casualties including Rubens Barrichello (Stewart), Olivier Panis (Prost) and Pedro Diniz (Arrows). Even Hakkinen went off on to the grass at Bridge Corner but managed to keep going. Conditions were so treacherous that the yellow flags were brought out, but while lapping the Benetton of Alexander Wurz, Schumacher failed to spot the flags and passed the Austrian. Moments later the safety car appeared. In an instant Hakkinen saw his 38-second lead over Schumacher reduced to nothing. To make matters worse, the McLaren had not emerged unscathed from its excursion on to the grass, although Hakkinen was unsure as to the extent of the damage. Six laps later the rain had eased sufficiently for the safety car to withdraw. Almost immediately Hakkinen went off at Becketts and Schumacher swept through into the lead.

But behind the scenes there was high drama. Schumacher had been awarded a ten-second penalty for passing Wurz under the yellow flags, but the Silverstone stewards took 31 minutes to notify Ferrari of the decision when the rules state that it should be delivered within 25 minutes of the offending incident. Moreover, the piece of paper handed to Ferrari sporting director Jean Todt was, at best, ambiguous and, at worst, illegible. Ferrari were unsure whether it was a stop-go penalty, which would necessitate Schumacher coming into the pits for ten seconds before rejoining the race, or if the ten seconds was simply to be added to his final time. In the absence of any clarification from the stewards, Ferrari let Schumacher continue on his way and then brought him in for the penalty at the end of the final lap, by which time he had a 20-second lead over Hakkinen. So at the end of the 60th and last lap, Schumacher came into the Ferrari pit, which was beyond the finish line, and served his ten-second penalty, this being added to his overall time. He thus won the British Grand Prix while stationary.

Not that any of the soaked crowd had any idea who had won at that point, for it was some time before it filtered through that Schumacher had officially been declared the winner. McLaren protested, arguing that as the yellow flag incident had occurred 12 laps before the finish the transgressor was supposed to sit out the ten seconds in the pit in a stop-go penalty rather than have them added to his time. However, the protest was rejected since the delay was deemed to be the fault of the stewards rather than Ferrari.

So Schumacher kept the race. Hakkinen's championship lead was down to two points. Game on.

CARNAGE AT LA SOURCE

BELGIAN GRAND PRIX, 30 AUGUST 1998

The 1998 Formula One season had already experienced more than its fair share of drama, but the Belgian Grand Prix was something else: a first corner pile-up involving 13 cars, an explosive confrontation between Michael Schumacher and David Coulthard and, at the end of it all, Jordan's first Grand Prix win at the 127th attempt. Who says motor racing is dull?

Since Silverstone, Mika Hakkinen had notched back-to-back wins in Austria and Germany and, although Schumacher rallied with victory in Hungary, the Finn held a seven-point lead coming to round 13 at Spa. After Jacques Villeneuve had emerged unharmed from a 186mph practice crash – 'the best accident I've had in Formula One so far', he joked – qualifying gave little hint of the excitement to come. Hakkinen and Coulthard put the super-fast McLarens on the front row of the grid for the third successive race and the ninth time in all that season. But the happiest man was Damon Hill who, following two fourth-place finishes in the last two races (his first points of the year), conjured up extra speed from the Jordan to go third fastest, ahead of Schumacher, Eddie Irvine and Villeneuve. Hill was ecstatic, declaring the qualifying perform-ance to be almost as good as a race win. 'At the start of the season our car was a disaster,' he said, 'and now we have completely turned the situation around.'

If qualifying had been a triumph for McLaren, the start of the actual race was anything but. Hakkinen got away best in the wet to lead into La Source hairpin from Villeneuve and Schumacher, but behind them Coulthard and Irvine touched, causing the McLaren to hit the wall of the old pits and rebound into the middle of the track. With visibility reduced considerably by the spray, the cars behind had no chance of taking evasive action. Car upon car crashed into one another, the track quickly becoming littered with red, white, silver and blue wreckage. As wheels bounced in slow motion down the hill towards Eau Rouge, the race was stopped. Fortunately the mass collision had occurred at the slowest point on the circuit, with the result that none of the drivers suffered anything more serious than bruising.

The cars were not so lucky. No fewer than 13 of the 22 starters were involved – Coulthard, Irvine, Johnny Herbert (Sauber), Alexander Wurz (Benetton), Shinji Nakano (Minardi), the Tyrrells of Ricardo Rosset and Tora Takagi, the Prosts of Olivier Panis and Jarno Trulli, the Arrows of Pedro Diniz and Mika Salo, and the Stewarts of Rubens Barrichello and Jos Verstappen. Since their teams only had one spare car, Panis, Barrichello, Salo and Rosset were unable to take part in the restart, leaving just 18 hoping for better luck next time around.

Following a 50-minute delay for the track to be cleared, they set off once more. Hill got a flier, leaving the McLarens and the Ferraris in his wake as they rounded La Source. This time it was Hakkinen's McLaren that didn't make it, clipping Schumacher on the exit from the hairpin and sliding along the track before being shunted by Herbert. Both Hakkinen and Herbert were out of the race. McLaren misery was compounded 30 seconds later when Coulthard had a coming-together with Wurz and dropped back to the rear of the field. The safety car came out for one lap while Hakkinen's broken car was towed away, and this enabled Coulthard to make up a little of the lost ground.

By lap five out of 44 the rain was getting heavier and Schumacher used his expertise in wet conditions to sweep past Hill into the lead. Elsewhere the slippery surface was taking its toll. Tagaki spun out of the race on lap 11, Villeneuve on lap 17 and Irvine from third place on lap 26. Schumacher now had a 37-second advantage over Hill. Victory – and with it, the lead in the championship – appeared a mere formality.

Then Schumacher came up to lap Coulthard, who slowed on the straight to allow the Ferrari to pass. But through the clouds of spray, Schumacher failed to detect Coulthard's reduction in speed and ploughed into the back of him. The front wheel of the Ferrari was ripped off and both cars limped back to the pits where Schumacher had no choice but to retire. In a blind fury, he headed straight for the McLaren garage where he had to be restrained by mechanics of both teams from hitting Coulthard, whom he blamed unreservedly for the accident. Schumacher even went so far as to suggest that it was deliberate. 'He slowed down at a point where we are normally flat out,' raged Schumacher. 'I was not expecting it at all. David has enough experience to know that in this rain there was no way I would realise he was slowing down and have enough time to react.' Coulthard, who accused Schumacher of behaving 'like an animal' when he stormed into the McLaren pit, argued: 'My engineer told me over the radio to let Michael through, so I stuck to the right-hand side of the track. All I know is he drove into me. What was I supposed to do? I cannot drive looking behind me all the time. It was not my responsibility to watch him. It was up to him to be careful.'

Meanwhile, in what was almost a carbon copy incident, Giancarlo Fisichella failed to spot Nakano's Minardi through the rain and spray and slammed into it. The safety car made another appearance while the remains of the Benetton were cleared from the track. When the safety car turned off, there were only 12 laps left and, with the field bunched up, Hill was just ahead of team-mate Ralf Schumacher and the Sauber of Jean Alesi. Ralf immediately tried to attack Hill at the next corner, only to be warned off by the Jordan team. The orders from the team were that Hill was to win the race. So for the remaining laps, Ralf sat frustrated in second place. It had not been a good day for the Schumacher family.

But for Damon Hill, Eddie Jordan and all those who watched this remarkable race unfold, it had been a day to remember.

THE SHED, THE BED AND THE BOOT

DONINGTON PARK WACKY RACES,
28 AUGUST 1999

In the summer of 1997 the *Sun* newspaper came up with the idea of staging an alternative British Grand Prix for bizarre customised vehicles. But what started out as a spoof has developed into a proper race, held annually at Donington Park's August Bank Holiday meeting.

The 1999 event was so popular that it had to be divided into two classes – road-going and non-road-going. The second category attracted no fewer than ten entries, including a motorised garden shed, a four-poster bed, a roller boot, a sofa, a giant orange, and a toilet and bath combination.

The shed was the brainchild of Derbyshire farmer George Shields, who originally built it in 1997 as a practical joke for a friend's wedding. 'I couldn't find the pony and trap he wanted,' said Shields, 'so I decided to make some transport of my own. My friend thought his stag party had finished the night before. Little did he know he was going to show up at the church in a garden shed!' The Shields machine, which held the distinction of being the only garden building ever to have completed the journey from John O'Groats to Land's End under its own steam, consisted of a quad bike engine underneath and a six-by-four garden shed on top, complete with five hanging baskets. It had a top speed of 55mph and did 50 miles to the gallon. 'Where to put the exhaust pipe was a bit of a problem,' he admitted, 'but I got it to go out of the door. The whole conversion is really comfortable, with a big cushion on the seat. It's very noisy and smelly to drive, but that's OK because there is a television and radio inside. And it doesn't like corners much – especially at 55mph.'

Race organiser Edd China had three entries – the sofa, the toilet and bath, and the four-poster bed. The bed, welded to a 1,600cc Volkswagen Beetle engine, was inspired by the 1960s TV series *The Monkees*. 'Their show would start with them pushing a bed around town,' said China. 'I just thought I wanted to live my life like that. It cost £5,000 and took two months to build, but it's a car that impresses the women.'

The toilet and bath combination was driven by 65-year-old Donington Park track marshal Frank Richardson. 'It is terrible to drive,' he confessed, 'although once you get it up to 40mph it tends to straighten itself out.' Richardson had a nasty moment during practice when clothes from the laundry basket on the front became entangled with one of the wheels.

At the wheel of the giant rollerskate, a promotional vehicle for Derby Rollerworld, was the firm's general manager Terry Wilcox. Other entrants included Mick Pike in a dodgem car, Geoff Quaife in the Outspan Orange, and Mike Hand driving a stuffed horse and covered wagon, in which the indicators were in the horse's eyes. Among those sadly missing for the 1999 event was a motorised skip.

It may not have been the full Grand Prix distance but a few laps of Donington Park still produced plenty of excitement. In the end victory went to the dodgem car from the Outspan Orange, which just pipped the bed. The shed broke down. The non-road-going class resulted in a win for a customised fire engine, beating an armchair and a gondola on wheels.

NO TYRES FOR IRVINE

EUROPEAN GRAND PRIX, 26 SEPTEMBER 1999

The 1999 World Championship season had been turned on its head following Michael Schumacher's broken leg at the British Grand Prix. The Silverstone race left Schumacher's Ferrari team-mate Eddie Irvine eight points behind championship leader Mika Hakkinen, but victories in the next two races – in Austria and Germany – had propelled the Ulsterman into pole position. Hakkinen fought back with a win in Hungary and a second in Belgium but missed out at Monza where Irvine, too, could only finish sixth. Going into the European Grand Prix at the Nürburgring, with just two more races to follow, the two chief protagonists were level on points. Irvine was relishing his new-found, albeit temporary, status as Ferrari number one while Hakkinen, judging from the way he broke down in tears at Monza after spinning off while comfortably in the lead, was definitely starting to feel the pressure. With Schumacher's legions of German fans rooting for Irvine, the Nürburgring appeared the ideal place to increase that pressure, yet in the heat of battle it was Ferrari that buckled.

The European Grand Prix was a race which had everything – tension, farce, joy, despair, drama, anger, and at one stage seemingly a new leader every lap. There was enough excitement for half a dozen Grands Prix.

As is so often the case in Formula One, the overriding factor was the weather. The morning rain had stopped before the end of the Saturday lunchtime qualifying session but the track

269

remained wet and the best times were set in the closing minutes, with Heinz-Harald Frentzen's Jordan snatching pole from David Coulthard and Hakkinen. Irvine could manage no better than ninth. He would be starting from a long way back.

The track was dry for start time but the overcast sky suggested that it was unlikely to remain so for the full 66 laps. An aborted start, after Minardi driver Marc Gene had signalled a problem on the grid, was an indication of the drama that was to follow almost from the moment the lights went out. As the field flowed into the first corner, Damon Hill's Jordan lost power and Alexander Wurz had to swerve to avoid it. In doing so, he clipped Pedro Diniz's Sauber which flipped over on to the grass. The safety car was called out while Diniz was extricated, happily with nothing more serious than a few bruises. When the safety car departed, Frentzen led from Hakkinen, Coulthard, Ralf Schumacher and Giancarlo Fisichella. By lap 17 Irvine had worked his way up to fifth. At that point it started to rain.

Three laps later Hakkinen, in second, pitted for wet tyres. This proved a grave misjudgement, as the shower soon passed and he found himself losing up to ten seconds per lap. But his move seemed to spread panic. On lap 21 the Ferrari pit were getting ready to bring Irvine in for new tyres when Mika Salo (Schumacher's replacement in the Ferrari team) came in unexpectedly, needing a new nose-cone and tyres. He was away again after a 30-second stop, but the unscheduled visit had caused his tyres to become mixed up with those of his team-mate. To complicate matters further, Irvine and Ferrari technical director Ross Brawn, seeing the rain easing off, hastily switched their choice of tyres from wet to dry, forcing the mechanics to shelve one set of tyres and find another four. Irvine wanted to stay out for an extra lap to give the mechanics time to prepare, but he didn't have sufficient fuel and so he had to come in just 23 seconds after Salo had left. As the Ferrari crew scrambled for Irvine's fresh set of tyres, they could find only three. The right rear tyre was still in the garage. This Keystone Cop performance cost Irvine a pit stop of 28.2

seconds – 20 seconds over the norm – and dropped him out of the points-scoring positions. It was an unmitigated disaster.

Irvine's only consolation was that Hakkinen had fallen back to tenth on the unsuitable wets, but on lap 24 the Finn tried again, this time calling in for dry tyres.

Eight laps later, the first and second-placed drivers, Frentzen and Coulthard, pitted together. Frentzen got away first but the Jordan ground to a halt with an electrical problem at the very next corner, handing Coulthard the lead. By lap 38 it had started to rain heavily again. Coulthard, on dry tyres, was slipping and sliding his way around the track but was hanging on to his ten-second lead over Ralf Schumacher until he pressed too hard and slithered into the gravel and out of the race.

This presented the younger Schumacher with a 20-second advantage over Fisichella, but Schumacher was on a two-stop strategy and when he pitted on lap 44, the Benetton driver became the new leader. But four laps later Fisichella, like Coulthard before him, failed to cope with the wet track and spun out of the race. Presented with the lead once more, Schumacher was prevented from taking advantage when, on the following lap, he suffered a right rear puncture and limped to the pits. With Schumacher down to fifth, Johnny Herbert, who had started a lowly 14th on the grid, suddenly found that it was his turn to lead.

Greatly assisted by a switch to wets on lap 35, Herbert kept his head while all around were losing theirs. Having previously finished just four races that season, the popular Englishman held on for his third Grand Prix win and, more importantly, the Stewart team's maiden victory. And with team-mate Rubens Barrichello finishing third behind Jarno Trulli's Prost, it was a highly emotional day for Jackie Stewart and his colleagues. There was joy, too, for Minardi. Luca Badoer seemed set to pick up the Italian team's first points for four years, only for his car to die on lap 54 when he was lying fourth. All was not lost, however, as team-mate Gene came through to finish sixth and earn Minardi a priceless point. But it was another hard luck story for former world champion Jacques Villeneuve, still seeking BAR's first point. He was poised for fifth place when his clutch failed.

Villeneuve's loss proved Hakkinen's gain. Having appeared to give up, Hakkinen found a new lease of life towards the end and, four laps from the finish, harassed Irvine into a costly mistake. Once past Irvine, Hakkinen profited from Villeneuve's late exit to finish fifth and pick up two vital points. Irvine ended up seventh to round off a hugely disappointing day for Ferrari.

Irvine was understandably angry at the prolonged pit stop. 'It is a problem when you have one team of mechanics serving two cars,' he said. 'We should have two teams doing it. We screwed it up.' Ferrari president Luca di Montezemolo was even more scathing. 'Ferrari's fans are rightfully very upset and we cannot tolerate it. We made a complete mess of it and it must never happen again.'

THE SIX-DAY WORLD CHAMPION

MALAYSIAN GRAND PRIX, 17 OCTOBER 1999

The penultimate round of the 1999 season, the inaugural Malaysian Grand Prix will long be remembered for Michael Schumacher's dramatic return from injury and for a Ferrari disqualification which saw Mika Hakkinen crowned world champion for six days.

Going into the race, Hakkinen was two points ahead of Eddie Irvine thanks to the Ferrari fiasco at the European Grand Prix. But now Irvine was able to welcome back team-mate Schumacher following a six-race absence. Schumacher himself had no chance of the title but Irvine and Ferrari were hoping that he would be able to protect the Irishman from the two McLarens. The question was, would Schumacher really be prepared to help Irvine win the title, thereby depriving himself of the glory of bringing that long-awaited World Championship to Ferrari? The cynics suggested that Schumacher would prefer to walk barefoot over burning coals than assist Irvine. They were to be proved wrong.

The pre-race noises were less than encouraging, however. A week before the showdown at Sepang, Schumacher was still expressing doubts about being ready to return to competitive driving, but a sudden change of heart (perhaps accompanied by a little arm-twisting from Ferrari) saw him make an emotional comeback. In qualifying he drove as if he had never been away, putting the car on pole, ahead of Irvine and the two McLarens. It was clearly going to be a race of tactics with each team trying to outmanoeuvre the other. For Ferrari, Ross Brawn committed Schumacher to one stop in order to allow Irvine to build up the gap he needed for two stops. The idea was for Schumacher to ride shotgun for Irvine, keeping the chasing McLarens at bay. It was a role he was to play to perfection. For their part, McLaren deployed Coulthard to hustle and harry Irvine in the early stages and accordingly the Scot began with a lighter fuel load than usual.

Schumacher made a perfect start and led away from Irvine, Coulthard and Hakkinen. As early as the fourth lap, Schumacher ushered Irvine through into the lead and then set about holding off the McLarens. But a lap later Coulthard caught Schumacher napping at the first chicane and dived into second place. For the next nine laps Coulthard pursued Irvine with a vengeance before the McLaren's fuel pressure fell and he was forced to retire.

Hakkinen now had to take on the Ferraris single-handed. Try as he might, he could not get past Schumacher, who used a variety of contentious blocking tactics to keep the Finn at bay while Irvine disappeared into the distance. When Irvine pitted for the second time, Schumacher, on his one-stop strategy, was in the lead but, obeying team orders, he duly waved his team-mate through once more. At the end of the 58 laps, it was Irvine who picked up the ten crucial points, with Schumacher second and Hakkinen, never able to break free from the red menace, picking up just four points for third place.

Hakkinen was not happy and accused Schumacher of repeatedly accelerating and braking to hold him back. McLaren team boss Ron Dennis moaned: 'Such tactics might be within the regulations, but it is not sporting. If that is the way you want to go about winning the championship, then fine. It's consistent with Ferrari's style.'

Then a few hours after the race had ended, while Ferrari celebrated and McLaren licked their wounds, the sensational news came through that both Ferraris had been disqualified by the stewards because the cars' air deflectors were found to be 10 mm under the regulation width. Hakkinen was promoted from third to first, making him the 1999 world champion.

Hakkinen was still unhappy – that wasn't how he wanted to win the title. Ferrari appealed, pointing out that the offending deflectors had been used at the European Grand Prix and on all three days in Malaysia. Nobody had queried them before. To lose the championship over such a tiny miscalculation seemed harsh in the extreme. The appeal was heard in Paris at the end of the week. Ferrari were reinstated. The 1999 season would go to the wire.

As it turned out, the Japanese Grand Prix was something of an anti-climax. Hakkinen won in a canter, Irvine unable to manage any better than third. Hakkinen was once again crowned world champion – and this time it was for longer than six days.

COULTHARD AND THE TRESPASSER

GERMAN GRAND PRIX, 30 JULY 2000

Most employees unhappy at the manner of their dismissal seek recourse through the law. Unfortunately a 47-year-old Frenchman chose to register his protest by wandering on to a race track in the middle of a Grand Prix. Miraculously his reckless behaviour did not result in an accident, but it did cause lasting damage to David Coulthard's hopes of becoming world champion.

With victories at Melbourne, Interlagos, Imola, the Nürburgring and Montreal, Michael Schumacher looked to have all but sewn up the championship by the middle of June. Then a retirement at Magny-Cours and a first-corner exit at the A1-Ring left the door open for McLaren, Schumacher's lead over Coulthard being cut to just six points prior to his home Grand Prix at Hockenheim.

In a wet qualifying session, Coulthard underlined his growing confidence by taking pole from Schumacher, Giancarlo Fisichella's Benetton and Mika Hakkinen. Schumacher's Ferrari team-mate, Rubens Barrichello, started back in 18th place from where it seemed that he would be unable to offer much help to the championship leader.

All year, the McLaren team had been unhappy with Schumacher's tactic of pulling across at the start. He had cut across Coulthard at both Imola and Magny-Cours, forcing the Scot to lift. Here, it was payback time. As the lights went out, Coulthard pulled across to the inside line to block

Schumacher, who reacted immediately by switching to the outside. In doing so, he drove straight into Fisichella's front wing and the pair slid off into the tyre wall – the second race in a row where these two had failed to make it around the first corner. The man to profit from this chaotic start was Hakkinen, who led at the end of the first lap from Coulthard and Jarno Trulli (Jordan), while further back Barrichello had shot up to eighth. The Brazilian soon forced his way up to third before a pit stop on lap 17 out of 45 made it clear that he was on a two-stop strategy, whereas the McLarens were intending to stop just once.

Hakkinen continued to lead Coulthard around until a bizarre incident took place on lap 24. A spectator burst through the fences, ran across the track near the Clark Kurve and began walking along the grass verge. It later transpired that he was protesting against his dismissal from Mercedes-Benz. While the race organisers waited for security guards to remove the man, the safety car was brought out. Coulthard had been due to pit on that lap but when he saw Hakkinen dart into the pits, he stayed out, unaware that the safety car was lying in wait. Stuck behind the safety car, poor Coulthard had to suffer a slow lap before he could get to the pits, eventually rejoining in sixth. The anti-Mercedes protester had cost a McLaren-Mercedes driver his chance of the race.

The safety car stayed out for three laps, during which time 14 cars pitted. Hakkinen retained his lead, from Trulli and Barrichello, but then on lap 29 the safety car was introduced again after the Sauber of Pedro Diniz slammed into the back of Jean Alesi, scattering wheels and bits of chassis from the Prost over the track. With 13 laps remaining, it started to rain heavily in the stadium section of the circuit, but not in the forest, placing the drivers in a dilemma. Eleven of the 15 cars still running pitted to go on wets, including leader Hakkinen, but Barrichello opted to stay out on drys. This propelled Barrichello into the lead and, driving with great skill on the slippery surface, he held on to win by seven seconds from the fast-closing Hakkinen, with Coulthard in third and Jenson

Button in fourth just missing out on his first podium.

For Barrichello and Ferrari, it was a moment to savour – his first Grand Prix win in his 124th start. For Coulthard and McLaren, it was the one that got away through no fault of their own. As McLaren's Ron Dennis caustically commented: 'We had flexibility in our strategy, but not sufficient to accommodate a deranged spectator who wandered on to the circuit costing us the race and endangering his and the lives of the drivers.'